Queer

Queer Objects to the Rescue

Intimacy and Citizenship in Kenya

GEORGE PAUL MEIU

The University of Chicago Press
Chicago and London

The University of Chicago Press, Chicago 60637
The University of Chicago Press, Ltd., London
© 2023 by The University of Chicago
All rights reserved. No part of this book may be used or reproduced in any manner whatsoever without written permission, except in the case of brief quotations in critical articles and reviews. For more information, contact the University of Chicago Press, 1427 E. 60th St., Chicago, IL 60637.
Published 2023
Printed and bound by CPI Group (UK) Ltd, Croydon, CR0 4YY

32 31 30 29 28 27 26 25 24 23   1 2 3 4 5

ISBN-13: 978-0-226-83056-8 (cloth)
ISBN-13: 978-0-226-83058-2 (paper)
ISBN-13: 978-0-226-83057-5 (e-book)
DOI: https://doi.org/10.7208/chicago/9780226830575.001.0001

Cover image credits:
Romuald Hazoumè, *Cocotamba*, 2017. Plastic and wood, 10 1/4 × 12 5/8 × 8 11/16 inches, 26 × 32 × 22 cm. © as provided by ProLitteris. Photo: Zarko Vijatovic. Courtesy Gagosian.

Romuald Hazoumè, *Algoma*, 2016. Plastic and raffia, 21 5/8 × 15 3/4 × 7 7/8 inches, 55 × 40 × 20 cm. © as provided by ProLitteris. Photo: Zarko Vijatovic. Courtesy Gagosian.

Romuald Hazoumè, *Wax Bandana*, 2009. © as provided by ProLitteris. Photo: Jonathan Greet.

Library of Congress Cataloging-in-Publication Data

Names: Meiu, George Paul, author.
Title: Queer objects to the rescue : intimacy and citizenship in Kenya / George Paul Meiu.
Other titles: Intimacy and citizenship in Kenya
Description: Chicago ; London : The University of Chicago Press, 2023. | Includes bibliographical references and index.
Identifiers: LCCN 2023015918 | ISBN 9780226830568 (cloth) | ISBN 9780226830582 (paperback) | ISBN 9780226830575 (e-book)
Subjects: LCSH: Homophobia—Kenya. | Homosexuality—Kenya. | Material culture—Social aspects—Kenya. | Masculinity—Kenya. | Sex—Political aspects—Kenya. | Citizenship—Kenya.
Classification: LCC HQ76.45.K46 M45 2023 | DDC 306.76/6—dc23/eng/20230417
LC record available at https://lccn.loc.gov/2023015918

♾ This paper meets the requirements of ANSI/NISO Z39.48-1992 (Permanence of Paper).

The object is "brought forth" as a thing that is "itself" only insofar as it is cut off from its own arrival. So it becomes that which we have presented to us, only if we forget how it arrived, as a history that involves multiple forms of contact between others. Objects appear by being cut off from such histories of arrival, as histories that involve multiple generations, and the "work" of bodies. . . .

SARA AHMED

What do we call a subject? Quite precisely, what, in the development of objectification, is outside the object.

JACQUES LACAN

There is a delicate empiricism which so intimately involves itself with the object that it becomes true theory.

JOHANN WOLFGANG VON GOETHE

No matter what object you study, if you study it correctly the entire society comes with it.

ANDRÉ-GEORGES HAUDRICOURT

Contents

1 Queer Objects: Introduction 1

2 Intimate Rescue: Grammars, Logics, Subjects, Scenes 37

3 "Male-Power": Virility, Vitality, and Phallic Rescue 59

4 Bead Necklaces: Encompassment and
the Geometrics of Citizenship 87

5 Plastics: Moral Pollution and the Matter of Belonging 117

6 Diapers: Intimate Exposures and
the Underlayers of Citizenship 142

7 The Homosexual Body: Gayism and
the Ambiguous Objects of Terror 163

Conclusion 191

*Acknowledgments 199
Notes 201
References 209
Index 225*

1

Queer Objects: Introduction

> Nowhere can a collective feeling become consciousness of itself without fixing upon a tangible object; but by that very fact, it participates in the very nature of that object...
> ÉMILE DURKHEIM

In February 2018, a member of the Kenyan Parliament posted on her Facebook page an image that startled her followers. It depicts a girl in her early teens standing in front of a small, traditional house of branches and clay in what looks like an arid savanna landscape. Shyly looking away from the camera, her face is barely visible. What stands out instead is her large bead necklace. Strings of red beads spiral up in concentric coils, covering her neck from her chest to her chin. From the front, the beads appear to form a flat-conic bundle resting heavily on her shoulders. Most Kenyans would recognize such necklaces as representative of ethnically Samburu women from the northern parts of their country. Young women wearing such necklaces feature widely in tourist ads and on the promotional materials of girl-empowerment organizations as representative of a traditional African culture. Samburu, however, associate such necklaces with women living in rural areas, who raise livestock or farm. Tokens of beauty and respectability, such necklaces display these women's attachment to local *lkereti*—a Maa (Samburu) language word that English-speaking Samburu translate as "culture" or "the normal way of doing things." To distinguish young stay-at-home rural women from "schoolgirls," Samburu call them "girls of the beads" (Maa [M]: *ntoyie ee saen*), their necklaces emblematic of a distinctly rural femininity.

When the MP visited villages to hold political rallies, she often photographed one or another "girl of the beads" whose schooling she had decided to sponsor. A Samburu herself and a well-known women's empowerment activist, she posted these pictures on her Facebook page to promote the education of rural girls and demonstrate her strong commitment to facilitating it. Her social media followers, mostly middle-class, educated, town-based Samburu, saw "girls of the beads" as legitimate beneficiaries of such humanitarian gestures. They would respond to the MP's posts with messages of gratitude, addressing her respectfully as "our mama" or "mother of Samburu." The image the MP uploaded on that day was similar to the ones she had posted in the past. But the text that accompanied it was different. "Some time ago," she wrote, "this boy took to wearing beads like a girl and elders cannot do much about it." "It is important," she said, "that he be rescued and sent to school to become a real man."

The MP's followers responded to her revelation by posting dozens of comments that expressed shock, pity, or disgust. Many saw the "boy with beads" (M: *layeni oo saen*) as proof of a recent global spread of homosexuality much debated in the national media. Some asserted vehemently—in English—that "homosexuality is un-African." They borrowed this phrase from political and religious leaders across the continent who, throughout the past decade, have used it often to depict same-sex intimacies as a threat to their nations and cultures. This threat, leaders implied, was foreign, coming from outside. The MP's other followers commented in Maa and the national Swahili language, calling homosexuality a "disease" (M: *moyan*) or "curse" (Swahili [S]: *laana*). "Homosexuality is an ungodly act that does not exist in our culture," one follower said. "Samburu people have known no such thing." "The world," said another, "is slowly turning to Sodom and Gomorrah." "The child is innocent," yet others countered, emphasizing a possible lack of "parental guidance" and urging the MP to help.

Why did the MP's post prompt anti-homosexual rhetoric among social media users from the region? What did it mean for the MP and her followers to want to "rescue" the child? And how did a bead necklace—otherwise emblematic of culture, rural femininity, and Samburu ethnicity—become entangled in denoting homosexuality? The MP posted this image at a time when, in northern Kenya, Samburu *laiyok* or "boys" aged twelve to twenty prepared for initiation, through ritual circumcision, into a new age set (M: *laji*)—that is, a named generational cohort of men. Such initiations take place once every thirteen to fifteen years. In February 2018, elders across the region were planning to commence these ceremonies within a few months. This was a time when locals expected novices to prove their strength and courage and convince elders they were ready "to become men." The girl the MP photographed was of the same age as these novices, but, once outed as a "boy," she generated unsettling ambiguity. For someone who was supposed to prepare for male circumcision to wear a girls' necklace and act shyly and modestly as girls of the beads typically did caused "gender trouble" (Butler 1990). For educated Samburu active on social media, these acts subverted cultural expectations of masculine assertiveness long associated with newly circumcised young men as "warriors" or *morans* (a Kenyan English and Swahili word derived from the Maa *ilmurran*, "warrior"). At a time when boys should have set themselves apart from girls to express their readiness to become morans, the MP's image and her statement affirmed and amplified concerns that binary gender roles were becoming blurry. This threatened the heteromasculinity that some now imagined as foundational to ethnic culture; men would no longer be *"real* men."

But it might be less clear what, if anything, this had to do with homosexuality. In fact, the MP did not identify the teen in her image as homosexual. Nor was there any explicit indication that this young person claimed a sexual orientation or had engaged in sex. Drawing on the language of global queer liberalism, one would have seen her as a transgender woman. But, unlike youths and LGBT activists in Nairobi or Mombasa—Kenya's largest cities—who commonly identified as such, a rural, Maa-speaking teen, without formal education, most likely did not. What is more, third-person pronouns in Maa (*niniye*, pl. *ninche*) and Swahili (*yeye*, pl. *wao*) are not gendered, thus making it easier to conceal gender ambiguity than English pronouns (hence, my use of gender pronouns here is more in tune with queer liberal politics and faces a certain challenge of translation). So, calling the pictured teen a "boy" and referring to her (or them?) as "he"—in English—asserted a biological interiority that was incongruent with her appearance. A new global surge of anti-homosexual rhetoric since the late 2000s certainly provided educated northerners with a discursive framework for apprehending the MP's revelation. Conservatives across the country deployed the English category of the "homosexual" as interchangeable with the derogatory Swahili *shoga*—"faggot" (also S: *fagoo*)—to refer to a wide spectrum of gender and sexual nonconformities pertaining primarily to people they saw as biologically male, including transgender women. The anti-homosexual rhetoric in response to the MP's post was certainly a reaction to gender nonconformity. But, as I will show, much more than gender was at stake.

In the Kenyan national public and on social media, the term "homosexual" often works to identify, name, and denounce persons said to embody cultural and sexual styles that are "foreign." Homosexuality's foreignness may pertain here to several fractal distinctions of culture and space. At one level, homosexuality figures as a Western affliction threatening the African nation from the outside. Conservatives across the world—from Brazil to Russia—have called this "the gay agenda" and described it as a white LGBT movement forced upon non-Western nations by Euro-American governments, lending agencies, and human rights activists (Gevisser 2020; Sperling 2015). At another level, within the nation, Kenyan elites have long attributed homosexuality to regions and ethnic groups that the state's Christian nationalism has marginalized, such as, for example, coastal Muslims (Porter 1995, 147). They have also associated homosexuality with tourist resorts or, more recently, public health NGOs, where foreign consumers and reformists appeared to use their capital to dictate how local intimacies should change.

As part of this nationalist spatialization of sexual immorality, schools and villages have played important roles. To Kenyan elites, schools have long represented both necessary avenues to development and progress *and* dangerous places that exposed African children to Western colonial values and sexual perversions. In recent years, the national media has repeatedly reported that boarding schools across the country faced "outbreaks" of *gayism* or *lesbianism*, terms referring less to immutable sexual identities than to contagiously expanding afflictions of desire. In contrast to schools, villages have figured in the national imagination as quintessential loci of cultural innocence, moral purity, and heteropatriarchal regeneration—safe havens from the "perversions" of modernity and globalization. Urban elites, for example, often sent their sons to the "home" village to undergo circumcisions and participate in initiation ceremonies, claiming that rural customs strengthen "soft town boys" and socialize them in the virtues of masculine endurance.[1] For elites, Keguro Macharia argues (2013, 283), villages are "intimate museums devoted to maintaining 'traditional' forms of intimacy." Thus, encountering homosexuality amidst rural "girls of the beads" surely came as a surprise to many. Moreover, the MP took this photograph in Samburu County's lowlands, a place that locals have seen as "isolated" and therefore more invested in "true" pastoralist culture (Holtzman 2004, 75). Her social media followers were outraged then that a "boy" from the lowlands—an "intimate museum" of their ethnic culture—wore a bead necklace and claimed femininity.

This outrage illustrates what Basile Ndjio (2016, 115) describes as an intensified "culturalization of sexuality" in late capitalism, that is, a set of "enduring efforts . . . to construct a more racialized and autochthonized form of sexuality . . . [as] a marker of racial and ethnic identity and an index of social categorization." Since colonialism, the definition of ethnicity in Kenya has revolved, in part, around intimacy (Macharia 2019, 119). Eager to reject racist colonial stereotypes that associated black bodies with sexual perversion, nationalist elites have often turned to ethnic customs in search of an enduring heteronormativity that would resonate with Christian notions of respectability. The culturalization of sexuality and the ethnicization of intimacy have, if anything, intensified with the political and economic transformations of late capitalism. Over the past few decades, Samburu, who have long been marginalized by Kenya's post-independence leaders (mostly Kikuyu from the central region of the country), have sought new avenues to power and resources through ethno-nationalist claims. Their ethno-nationalist politics—at times also involving other marginalized Maa-speaking groups such as Maasai and Chamus—revolved, among other things, around claiming sexual respectability and foreclosing colonial stereotypes of pastoralists' promiscuity. Colonial and post-independence leaders have long used such stereotypes as ideological alibis to marginalize Maa speakers economically and politically (Meiu 2017, 40–64). Culturalizing sexuality and disavowing homosexuality, local elites then sought to participate more fully in the Kenyan public sphere by redeploying its cultural grammars to their advantage. If ethnicity was to become a stable criterion of citizenship, respectable sexuality had to define Samburu relations of ethnic belonging.

A Twitter post from March 15, 2019, illustrates how sexuality became a central criterion of ethnic respectability in this context. Another Samburu politician, Naisula Lesuuda, shared an article entitled "Tribe Where Same-Sex Marriage Is Allowed in Kenya."[2] The article described a custom common at the Kenyan coast to the Indian Ocean, where a wealthy widow could marry—through bridewealth payment—a younger wife, thus continuing to grow her lineage even after her husband's death. The author, Eddy Mwanza, suggests that, under the country's Penal Code's criminalization of "carnal knowledge against the order of nature," such traditional arrangements should be persecuted. Initially published in *Kenyans*, a Nairobi-based newspaper, the article circulated on Twitter with a catchier image: a photograph of five Samburu women with colorful bead necklaces. The article shocked Lesuuda. "Are you serious?" she wrote. "Why use Samburu Women Picture in this story?" She reassured her followers that in her culture, "same-sex [relations] are outlawed." And her followers responded with an outpouring of anti-homosexual outrage. As bead necklaces made women identifiable as Samburu, associating them with homosexuality, educated and elite Samburu defended ethnicity by performing a culturalized aversion for same-sex relations.

To return to the MP's provocative Facebook post featuring what she saw as a "boy with beads," I suggest that the outrage it provoked should be understood as part of this wider political and historical context. This is a context in which many perceived gender and sexual nonconformity as symptomatic of globalization; anti-homosexual rhetoric as a central means for the culturalization of sexuality; and sexual respectability as key to the pursuit of ethno-national citizenship. To better understand the outrage the MP's post generated, it is productive to think here of the *homosexual body* imagined in ethno-nationalist politics as distinct from—though also constitutive of—the gender- and sexually nonconforming people whom it eventually comes to describe. Moral panics over homosexuality, scholars have shown, do not always require the homosexual to be anything other than an empty signifier, a specter that is initially independent of the concrete bodies upon which it is later inscribed (Bosia and Weiss 2013, 5; Murray 2012, 17–18; cf. Mayer and Sauer 2017). This signifier can generate fear and panics before any concrete bodies have been identified as its referents. At the same time, however, across the world, the homosexual is also an overdetermined signifier, predefined as involving foreign, devious forces that undermine local culture and heteropatriarchal reproduction. Meanwhile, the concrete bodies to which this signifier attaches itself at any time do not have to be *known* in order to be recognized as homosexual. The MP's Facebook followers did not know, for example, who the person behind the bead necklace was—her name; how she identified; or, following local modes of situating persons socially, to what clan and lineage she belonged. Looking away from the camera with her face barely visible, the protagonist was, if anything, an absence or an appearance hollowed of social identity. This empty appearance then gained an interiority and an identity suddenly when it encountered, on social media, the abstract homosexual body—an object foreign to itself. This encounter then produced the "boy with beads" as an "obvious" target of outrage and repudiation.

What mediated this encounter, among other things, was the bead necklace. Once the MP described the young person she photographed as a "boy," an incongruity emerged between this revelation and the large, visually imposing necklace that claimed, on behalf of its wearer, the identity of a "girl of the beads." But the necklace was more than simply a marker of rural femininity. In northern Kenya, this artifact has long generated social anxieties of its own. First, since the 1930s, colonials, missionaries, national leaders, and development workers have associated such necklaces with a custom known as "beading." In this custom, a moran offered a girl such bead necklaces and, if she accepted his gift, they commenced an intimate relationship which allowed them to have sex. British colonials and missionaries repeatedly tried to ban beading, seeing it as immoral. Since around 2010, the custom has gained new attention from child-rights and girl-empowerment NGO workers. Horrified that beading allowed "underaged children" to have sex, they called on rural Samburu to abandon both the custom and the beads (see chapter 4). Educated and elite Samburu, familiar with these humanitarian discourses, also saw bead necklaces as "sex objects"—proofs of unfolding sexual relationships. So, many might have perceived the bead necklace in the MP's photograph as evidence that the "boy" had sex with—or otherwise tried to seduce—morans. It is also important to mention that the idea of seduction has been significant to how the national media depicted *gayism* and *lesbianism* as contagions that "broke out" and—through seduction—"spread" among youths.

Second, if, throughout the second half of the twentieth century, colorful plastic beads became emblematic of Samburu ethnicity, the fact that they were made of plastic and industrially produced led many to question these objects' autochthony. In recent years, rural female prophets have called on women to abandon plastic-bead necklaces, arguing that wearing them leads to infertility (Straight 2007, 37ff). Meanwhile, state attempts to prevent environmental pollution through plastic waste have further solidified local ideas that plastic is a dangerous foreign substance that threatens local bodies, nature, and cultures. It is no coincidence then that plastic also has come to evoke the idea of foreignness more generally and to refer at times to migrants, refugees, and homosexuals (see chapter 5). On social media, for example, a Samburu man described homosexuality as a "polluting plastic import" that does not fit "the chemistry of Africans," and others warned that micro-plastics consumed in water are what is causing it. So, even as necklaces were emblems of ethnic culture and rural femininity, their plastic materiality underscored the growing impossibility of telling apart what is autochthonous from what is foreign: both plastic and homosexuality, it seemed, embedded themselves in culture and, to everyone's astonishment, could suddenly appear local.

In the MP's post, then, the bead necklaces sexualized the main protagonist and, through their material substance, further associated her with anxieties over foreign pollutions. The implicit argument went something like this: if a "girl of the beads" could be revealed to be a "boy," then foreign forces have already turned culture inside out, inhabiting it at its core. Or, if the threat of homosexuality was indeed coming from outside the nation, it now announced its presence from *within* rural ethnic culture. And so, wearing bead necklaces, the homosexual could easily be misrecognized as autochthonous. The bead necklace in the MP's image reminded elite and educated locals that neither culture nor nativist heterosexuality were the stable bases of ethno-nationalist attachments that they needed them to be. Children, the very promise of a collective future, were now at risk of early sexualization and *gayism*. This then explains, in part, the response: a rush to disavow loudly homosexuality as foreign, un-African, or against culture and to rescue the young from the intimate plights of globalization.

Over the past decade, anti-homosexuality campaigns across Africa, Eastern Europe, Russia, South and Southeast Asia, and the Caribbean, among other places, have made global headlines. Political leaders, hoping to occlude their complicity in market liberalization and legitimize the state as a source of moral protectionism, have named homosexuality a salient danger to the nation. In East Africa, Uganda's infamous "kill-the-gays bill" in 2009 also emboldened leaders in Kenya, Malawi, and Tanzania to call on police and citizens to purge their countries of homosexuality. (A similar bill was signed into law in Uganda in 2023.) However, in everyday life, this alleged homosexual threat—a signifier at once empty *and* overdetermined—was not easy to identify or pin down. To make the homosexual body a more stable target of outrage and violence, leaders, media, civil society groups, and citizens have therefore deployed a vast set of unlikely objects. Bead necklaces and plastics, as the northern Kenyan example shows, represent such objects that help constitute targets of anti-homosexual sentiment. Such objects may appear trivial to the violent politics of homophobia. But they are not. Their deployment in the political imagination constitutes the homosexual body in quite evocative ways, displacing and condensing anxieties over wider political and economic contexts and new conditions of social life.

*

Queer Objects to the Rescue explores a set of objects that have played an important, though not readily recognizable, role in state and popular attempts to rescue intimacy and citizenship in Kenya. These objects are central to understanding how the homosexual body is constituted as a target of outrage, repudiation, violence, and exclusion. But they are also important departure points for understanding emerging historical developments in the role of intimacy to citizenship, more generally. Offering a set of *ethnographic detours* through the meanings, logics, and political deployments of such objects, this book pursues what Lauren Berlant (1997, 12) calls "a counterpolitics of the silly object": "a mode of criticism and conceptualization that reads the waste materials of everyday communication in the national public sphere as pivotal documents in the construction, experience, and rhetoric of quotidian citizenship." Pursuing objects, I show how political imaginaries of intimacy and citizenship are not always tied to something readily recognizable as "sex" or "sexuality." Nor do they always pertain to common sexualized targets of state exclusion, such as the homosexual, the prostitute, the transgender person, the refugee, the immigrant, or the terrorist. Rather, sexuality-rescue projects, including anti-homosexuality campaigns, also work *through*—that is, disguise themselves in, build on, and borrow from—anxieties over and aspirations related to objects. To understand and critique the politics of homophobia, I suggest, it is important to take these objects seriously.

This book then is an exercise in ethnographic imagination as political critique. If the homosexual body is not a ready-made object against which violence is expressed, but rather is itself constituted through the imaginaries involved in such violence (Judge 2017), then it is important to ask: What do the objects *through* and *around* which people express fears and anxieties over homosexuality reveal about intimacy and citizenship in the late capitalist postcolony? In the past two decades, political homophobia, a tactic of power deployed by leaders, elites, and their supporters across the world, has "gone modular," Michael J. Bosia and Meredith L. Weiss (2013, 6) argue, "being imposed in a consistent way across diverse contexts." However, for political homophobia to do the work of power across these contexts, it must also resonate with local fears, anxieties, and aspirations. In other words, it has to (be made to) become meaningful. For this, the homosexual depends on a vast arsenal of objects that are central to the "cultural intimacy" (Herzfeld 1997) of any given national or ethno-regional public. And, like the homosexual, some of these objects (plastics, for example) are quite cosmopolitan in that they now do comparable political work across national boundaries. Pursuing such objects ethnographically offers a more complex picture of the social, political, and economic struggles that find expression in and shape intimate citizenship today.

Intimacy and Citizenship

Like elsewhere, in Kenya, debates over citizenship have intensified in the last four decades as the country has grown dependent on international loans and foreign investments and migration amplified both within and across its borders. With rapid urbanization, rampant unemployment, and a shrinking welfare state, 83 percent of Kenyans have turned to the informal sector—the so-called *jua kali*, "hot sun"—to make a living.[3] Competition over erratic income opportunities and decreasing access to land have sometimes exacerbated efforts to distinguish between ethnic groups, coastal and upcountry people, nationals and foreigners (Oucho 2002). A new imaginary of citizenship has featured labor migrants from Uganda and Tanzania, Chinese investors and laborers, and Euro-American tourists and humanitarians as problematic figures who shape local markets in ways that, at times, disadvantage Kenyans. It has also featured asylum seekers from Somalia and South Sudan as escalating security threats related to Al-Shabaab terrorism and the "radicalization" of Kenyan young men (Bachmann 2012; Kassa 2018). Private appropriation of public resources, fiscal inflation, and a rising gap between the rich and the poor have also rendered the inclusionary promises of citizenship suspicious (Blunt 2019; Smith 2008). Of late, speculation in the media that the government was selling citizenship—national ID cards and passports—to wealthy foreign nationals to pay off international debts has amplified such suspicions.[4] So too have, for example, the struggles of Makonde and Nuba ethnic groups to be recognized as citizens, after the government had denied them national ID cards ever since their forced relocation to Kenya during the time of British colonialism (Balaton-Chrimes 2016). And so, the very question of *what it means to be a Kenyan citizen* has been saliently debated.

Dorman, Hammett, and Nuget (2007, 8) argue that in Africa and beyond, global market reforms have threatened state-level national identity, making urgent "elite attempts to retain power through the molding of citizenship." "Citizens," they suggest, "are encouraged to rally around the state against external hordes" (8); they are urged "to exacerbate tensions and foster a strong sense of oppositional collective identity" (20). Redefinitions of citizenship have also sustained an urge to close off borders, secure autochthons, exclude foreigners, and anchor power closer to home, in various national, religious, or ethnic sovereignties (Geschiere 2009; Geschiere and Meyer 1998; Tonkens and Duyvendak 2016). As part of this effort, figuring out who truly belongs and who is an alien is a daunting task, albeit one pursued with much energy, urgency, and sometimes violence (Appadurai 1998; Nyamnjoh 2006). This quest has also intensified what Tonkens and Duyvendak (2016, 3) call the "culturalization of citizenship," "a process in which what it is to be a citizen is less defined in terms of civic, political or social rights, and more in terms of adherence to norms, values and cultural practices." The "culturalization of sexuality" (Ndjio 2016, 115) discussed above is an example of such a means for the culturalization of citizenship. The turn to autochthony has thus prompted calls to rehabilitate morality and exclude those who do not adhere to the values "of the land" (Tonkens and Duyvendak 2016, 6–8).

Debates over the meanings of citizenship have focused centrally on intimacy. As the hyphen between *nation* and *state* has come sharply into question (Comaroff and Comaroff 2001), political leaders claim to rescue and securitize normative intimate arrangements as bases of national identity, precisely to realign the nation with the state: to legitimize, that is, the state as the ultimate protector of national values. M. Jacqui Alexander (2005, 25–26) describes these late postcolonial transformations of intimacy and citizenship as "heteropatriarchal recolonization," a process through which "the state can produce a group of nonprocreative noncitizens who are objects of its surveillance and control . . . to veil the ruses of power"—to occlude leaders' own complicity in market liberalization. To legitimize state authority, leaders promise to protect their citizens from what they describe as the "perversions of globalization," to rescue traditional gender roles, nativist sexuality, and family values as seemingly durable foundations of citizenship. Through militarization, policing, and mass mediation, they deploy what Paul Amar (2013, 17) calls "tactics of hypervisibilization," "the spotlighting of certain identities and bodies as sources of radical insecurity and moral panic." Across the world, homosexuals, transgender people, prostitutes, and sexualized racial and ethnic

Others—whether "incestuous" indigenous people or "sexually aggressive" immigrants and refugees (Mack 2017; Partridge 2012)—constitute hegemonic targets of hypervisibilization and heteropatriarchal recolonization.

Beyond sexual types, in recent years, in Kenya, disputes have also intensified over sex education, abortion, female genital mutilation (FGM), forced marriage, teenage sexuality, customary widow inheritance or woman-to-woman marriage, and the "spread" of *gayism* and *lesbianism* (see, for example, Okech 2019; Van Klinken 2019; Wangila 2007). Questions over emerging forms of kinship, cohabitation, love, and consumption have intersected saliently with anxieties over sexuality—a key fetish of nationalisms, past and present (Mosse 1985). These have given rise to arduous debates on the street and on social media, in public panics and protests, but also in the regulatory practices of the government and NGOs preoccupied with surveying, medicalizing, or criminalizing intimacies. With the help of the media, leaders and reformists have spread the idea that rescuing nativist sexuality as a foundation of intimate life would grant people more easy access to resources, normative arrangements of gender, family, and reproduction, and, therewith, a respectable, prosperous future (cf. Cynn 2018). But this presupposes, first, securitizing intimacy from various moral threats. And these threats often appear ambiguous, fleeting, difficult to pin down—spectral forces yet to be revealed. David A. Murray (2012, 17) argues that part of these forces is a "spectral sexuality": "a threatening, perverted, and/or sick sexualized body or group of bodies [that] are continually incarnated in discourse but never fully instantiated in the flesh."

The process of imagining, identifying, objectifying, and repudiating such moral threats is constitutive of what I refer to as *intimate citizenship*. Ken Plummer (2011) defines the term as a set of practices and discourses concerned with private life as the basis of political recognition. Berlant (1997, 5) uses it to describe the late capitalist reorganization of citizenship away from the promise of a collective participation in the national public sphere toward a "constricted nation of simultaneously lived private worlds." It is "a condition of social membership produced by personal acts and values, especially acts originating in . . . the family sphere" (5). "The dominant idea," Berlant shows, "is of a core nation whose survival depends on . . . the intimate domains of the quotidian" (4). Once private worlds appear threatened by the globally recognizable sexualized threats mentioned above, the state pursues intimate noncitizens and offers them up to secure "native (hetero)sexuality" (Alexander 1994, 6). But how are intimate noncitizens imagined? And how are they made into threats that citizens are likely to recognize and from which they would then desire to be protected?

I suggest that to understand why citizens themselves often invest such sexualized threats with apocalyptic imaginaries, it is important to explore how they come to be assembled and deployed at any given time. Focusing on objects, I show how logics and sentiments associated with homophobia emerge not simply in relation to the reified category of *the* homosexual, but across a vast social terrain of struggles with bodies, work, reproduction, respectability, and futurity. Tracking objects ethnographically, I show how desires, fears, and anxieties shift across domains of social life to produce various targets of exclusion. Bead necklaces, to recall the example with which I opened this chapter, made anxieties over rural femininity, child sexualization, environmental pollution, and the very feasibility of ethnic autonomy central to the production of the homosexual in the moment I outlined. The meanings of such sexualized threats are at once overdetermined, that is, readily recognizable across the world, *and* underdetermined, open to the contingencies of their encounters with the myriad mundane objects that lurk around them in any given context.

Queer Objects: Decentering Sexuality

To understand why sexuality has become such a central criterion of intimate citizenship today, it is necessary to attend to its less visible, less recognizable objects; to show how these objects produce inclusion and exclusion, reorient desires, and shape particular kinds of subject-citizens; to understand how they subvert, transform, and reproduce state power or local, regional, and national attachments. I see these objects as *queer*, among other things, because they trouble presumptions of sexuality as a distinct domain of being and experience. And this even as they help produce and sustain the fantasy of a distinctly sexual domain. These objects, as I will show, may also challenge normative understandings of sexual citizenship as anchored in identity, rights, and legal recognition, offering unique insights into how such understandings emerge in the first place. Engaging ethnographically and historically with such objects, this book approaches sexuality politics through representations and practices located not only *inside* the conventional domain of the sexual but, more importantly, *outside* it. Objects thus decenter sexuality and show how its political salience rests on its myriad constitutive outsides.

Donald L. Donham (2018, 8) critiques "the attribution of an illusory power to the concept of sexuality: that is, that sexualities are consistent states of being, relatively stable forms of personhood, that stand behind and produce, cause, and organize erotic attachments." Refusing the idea of sexuality as an essence or identity, Donham argues, we would be better positioned to understand situational erotic attachments to myriad fetish-objects, including "race, color, wealth, language accent, lower-class style, smell, being dressed in a leather jacket or fur," and more (11). Here, Donham suggests, "the very process of eroticization may necessarily involve some 'objectification,'" but what is objectified is not reducible to gender as a determining factor of sexual orientation (15). Building on these insights, I explore how objects of a more broadly construed *erotic* investment—including the erotics of commodity consumption or collective mobilizations—both trouble sexuality *and* sustain its dominant role as a political fetish.

I use the term "queer objects" to de-essentialize sexuality and reflect on how its fetish-power depends on desires, fears, aspirations, and anxieties displaced from vast domains of social life. Sara Ahmed (2006) offers this term not to denote an essential class of things but to attend to how we position ourselves in relation to them. Bodies orient themselves in space and time, and are oriented by social pressures, with reference to particular objects. Objects, for example, direct us toward certain modes of living over others, toward pursuing some futures and not others. Some objects, Ahmed argues, must remain out of reach, relegated to the background, kept away from the normative alignments of family, reproduction, and genealogy. They become queer when our reflection brings them forward and, in focusing on them, generates unsettling effects. Foregrounding them gets things out of line and, in so doing, potentially reveals something new, unforeseeable. "Queer objects," Ahmed (2006, 169) suggests, "support proximity between those who are supposed to live on parallel lines, *as points that should not meet*. A queer object hence makes contact possible . . . creating other kinds of connections where unexpected things can happen." Yet, *pace* Ahmed, to me, queer objects do not always have to be "out of reach." Like the bead necklace or the plastics I described above, these may be artifacts widely used in everyday life. Hiding in plain sight, they can be—and often are—employed in the making of normative arrangements, without also being recognized as such. What makes such objects queer is their relational potential to reveal how normativities are produced and sustained, a potential that ethnography itself can activate.[5]

Foregrounding specific objects, then, can take us beyond a dominant domain of sexuality. Ethnography has already illustrated this possibility compellingly. In *Chisungu: A Girl's Initiation Ceremony among the Bemba of Northern Rhodesia*, Audrey Richards ([1956] 1982) shows how elderly women inculcate sexual values in the young novice by ritually aligning her body, at different times, with reference to different ceremonial clay figurines called *mbusa*. Mbusa, meaning "things handed down," include over forty types of pottery figurines with names such as "the water pot," "the hoe," "the garden," "the crocodile," "the porcupine,"

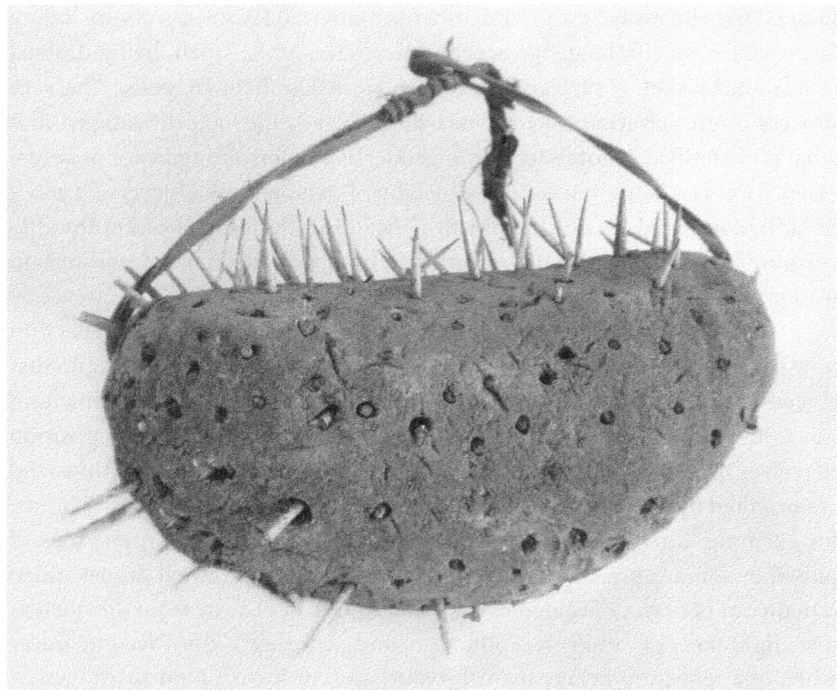

FIGURE 1. "The Porcupine," *mbusa* figurine used in Bemba girls' initiation rituals to represent a young man and the injuries sex with him may cause a girl. Moto Moto Museum, Mbala, Zambia. Photo by Mary Mbewe.

and "the man who is a fool" (59; 101–3). Each mbusa is accompanied by the performance of specific songs and gestures that reveal its secret meanings. "The figurines," Richards argues, "not only act as mnemonics for the songs but . . . they also come to represent moral attitudes and obligations . . . in a quotable form" (163). In other words, each mbusa involves and condenses meanings and sentiments associated with different domains of social life. Revisiting these objects, Henrietta L. Moore (1999, 13) argues that they "act as mnemonics not for the linguistic meaning embodied in verbal exegesis, but for the physical experiences which make up the lived world of sexuality, fertility and gaining a living, as well as for the long reflection on those activities which is the *chisungu* rite." In this rite, the novice learns basic moral norms through repetition "based on the body's orientations and movements" (1999, 15). Sexuality, then, whether as norm, practice, or pleasure, does not inhere in persons but in orientations of desire acquired and performed through one's positioning in relation to objects. I see queer objects as similar to the mbusa (and indeed, mbusa *as* queer objects) in that they condense meaning and orient bodies in space and time to produce legitimate kinds of persons and citizen-subjects.

To better explain the relation between objects and sexuality, it is important that I first clarify briefly what I mean by objects. Following a Marxian approach, I see objects not as "things-in-themselves," but as processes through which, at particular moments in time, certain surfaces or substances may come to appear as self-contained, thing-like entities. Here, the very separation between subject and object, as Theodor W. Adorno (1998) argues, is but an effect of ideology. Capitalism, for example, requires transcendental, rational subjects to remain distinct from the seemingly self-contained, stable objects they exchange and consume. In contrast to these "wishful projections," Adorno suggests, the "object becomes something at all only through being determined" (246, 250). And "in the determinations that seem merely to be affixed to it by the subject, the subject's own objectivity comes to the fore" (250). Following Adorno's dialectic of subject and object, I explore how people produce particular objects to externalize and displace intimate anxiety and how, in the process of objectification, particular citizen-subjects emerge.[6]

But, the reader might ask, am I not also actively participating in the objectification of the things that I describe here? Describing objects may certainly solidify the impression of their objectivity. After all, is ethnography not a way to represent worldly processes in an objectified form? In this case, I think ethnographic objectification is a necessary first step of my analysis—an excuse, if you will, to move away from the homosexual as a reified target of violence and show how various other objects constitute this target. In this sense, then, I embrace the critical potentialities of objectification, what Michael Taussig (1993, 1) calls its ability of "not awakening[,] but petrifying life," so that "living things . . . abruptly release their significance." I imagine my ethnographic pursuit to be similar to the *chisungu* ritual, where elderly women, the so-called *nacimbusa*, use clay figurines to objectify—indeed, "petrify"—otherwise abstract societal attributes they want the novice to experience. But like the *nacimbusa*, I am also only invested in my objectifications for this fleeting, momentary experience. At the end of the rite, the *nacimbusa* destroy these figurines. So too does my ethnography: as soon as my reader has perceived these objects, my analysis pursues their dialectical emergence and dissolution in context: how they produce and are produced by various subjects and social worlds. What interests me in any object, then, is less its objectivity. Rather, I explore the tensions between, on the one hand, its historical objectification, the centripetal process of its constitution, and, on the other, the centrifugal forces that entangle it in the making of intimate citizenship, its aspirations, anxieties, and subjectivities.

FIGURE 2. Turkana *ekidet* doll. Author's collection. Photo by George Paul Meiu.

It is precisely this process of alternating objectification and dissolution that often also grants things their transformative force in ritual. Consider the example of the *ekidet* fertility dolls from northern Kenya (fig. 2). Among Turkana engaged in fishing, these dolls were made of palm nuts, beads, fish bones, leather, and rope. Resembling a penis, the *ekidet* was an androgynous object that also represented a girl with long hair, an apron, and beads. A young girl received this doll from her mother and would play with and care for it as if it were her baby. The source of fertility that the doll embodies rests precisely in its capacity to objectify *the space between*—and thus also dissolve—mundane normative objectifications such as male and female, infancy and adulthood, the body and its parts. Fertility came from the subversion of such separations—and potentially from their enjoyment in the play with the penis-*cum*-girl-*cum*-baby.[7] For me, the *ekidet*'s ritual logic illustrates another important analytic strategy I wish to pursue through queer objects: an intentional and temporary objectification of the *in-between* things as a way to de-objectify and de-essentialize more normative objects of political mobilization, such as the (homo)sexual body.

Objects—their materiality, textures, and substance, but also the mimetic qualities involved in their objectification—can push our imagination to explore sexuality's various *elsewheres*. I see queer objects as points of access to what Sigmund Freud (1913) calls the subject's "other scene" (*der andere Schauplatz*), the social unconscious of the subject, that which is disavowed for the subject to emerge and against which the subject is to seek its coherence in perpetuity. Drawing on Freud, Jacques Lacan (1988, 194) puts it thus: "What . . . we call a subject [is] quite precisely, what, in the development of objectivation, is outside the object." In other words, objects may represent the subject's disavowed history, its "other scene": the thingification that needed to happen for the subject to gain some semblance of coherence.

For Lacan (1985), as for Freud (1905), sexuality is a central means for the subject's production. But rather than a stable aspect of the subject's identity, Lacan sees sexuality as a signifier, a domain of language (i.e., the Symbolic), through which we ascend to full subjecthood (i.e., Oedipal heteronormativity) (Dean 2000). In many contexts, this signifier helps sublimate erotic possibilities and pleasures other than reproductive heteronormativity. It turns desire away from what Freud (1905) calls the myriad "aim objects" or "erotogenic zones" of early childhood (mouth, anus, hands, feet, etc.) and condenses it on normative genitality, the only legitimate form of sexual expression. Or, as Lacan would see it, we come to desire those objects that most fully promise us "the desire of the Other"—something like social recognition.

Yet the affixion of desire to genital intercourse, that which is normatively recognized as the sexual, remains unstable. Thus, the very signifier "sex" is slippery. "Beyond all sexual content and practices," Alenka Zupančič (2017, 22) argues, "the sexual is not pure form, but refers instead to the absence of this form . . . an absence or negativity that has important consequences for the field structured around it." What is repressed, Zupančič claims, is not desire as such but the knowledge that "sex" lacks a concrete signified. In other words, what we should not know that we know, what should remain unconscious, is that "sex" is based on an absence or "ontological negativity." This ontological negativity, for Zupančič, drives insistent efforts to pin this signifier down through science, medicine, law, or commodity consumption. Hence, one might argue, sexuality itself is an unstable objectification, one that appears concrete only in its invocation in language and one that, not unlike the Marxian commodity, must continuously disavow the history of its production and erasures.

This is why it is important to analyze sexuality not from the domain it claims to denote (itself an ontological negativity or absence), but from its "other scene"—those zones in which, according to Freud (1905), only "perverts" linger. To the extent that queer objects relate to sexuality's various disavowed *elsewheres* and can help decenter the sexual and explain its historical centrality, an ethnographic imagination that dwells on them is itself "perverse," in the Freudian sense: it lingers where it must not, delaying arrival into normative subjecthood, thus raising unsettling questions about its importance.

Like slips of tongue that bring the unconscious into speech, queer objects connect scenes that explicitly invoke the sexual (e.g., anti-homosexual violence) to the *elsewhere*, scenes apparently unrelated to it: they slip background into foreground, aspirations and anxieties from one domain of social life into another, and thus often short-circuit their separation and reveal their co-constitutive entanglements. For example, saying, as the man I mentioned above did on social media, that gayism is "a polluting plastic import" can reveal the extent to which Kenya's "war on plastic" has shaped and has been shaped by the logics of anti-homosexuality rhetoric. Gayism thus becomes akin to the environmental pollution of Africa's "nature." Normative liberal separations between sexuality politics and environmental politics make this intersection hard to see. But plastics as queer objects lurking in between these domains subvert their taxonomic separation and reveal their co-constitutive entanglements. Operating on multiple scenes at once, objects such as plastics may also constitute instances of what Lacan (1977) calls the *objet petit a* (the object small-other)—the object-cause of desire—through or against which an ideal intimate order is to be pursued, rescued, and achieved, a promise of wholeness, happiness, and fulfillment ultimately realized. The repudiation of plastic can work at once to bring forth the fantasy of an unpolluted local nature *and* a "natural" sexual and gender order unpolluted by foreign "perversions."

To de-essentialize homophobia and understand its historical emergence, *Queer Objects to the Rescue* explores the production of its sentiments and logics beyond what is readily recognized as the (homo)sexual body. If a focus on same-sex politics has dominated research on intimate citizenship, this book troubles, methodologically and analytically, liberal categories of identity. It attends, as it were, to the "other scene" of sexuality, to objectifications that tell more complex stories about what is involved in the production of the sexual subject-citizen.

These objects, I show, constitute what Robert Lorway (2014, 9) calls "technologies of citizenship," that is, ways to commensurate particular forms of intimacy into national belonging, to channel desires into normative heteropatriarchal frameworks. By sustaining a shared popular concern with how to foreclose or optimize their presence, some of these objects constitute ways to generate "desire for desire of the state" (Butler 2002)—the fantasy that the state can securitize intimacy and the nation from corruption or pollution.

But, as we shall see, citizens often also turn such objects against the state, to imagine themselves as part of a moral nation that has been, if anything, betrayed by its political class, elites, and leaders.

Queer objects, to reiterate, can be used at once to securitize national sexual propriety *and*, as I shall do, to decenter hegemonic targets of sexualized exclusion. In this regard, I take "queerness" not as an essence of things (or people) but as a potentiality that emerges relationally, as a methodological "turning toward . . . certain objects, things, and persons" (Davidson and Rooney 2018, 3).[8] Echoes here of Walter Benjamin (1999, 459), who argues that such emancipatory potentialities can be activated in otherwise oppressive media "by a displacement of the angle of vision," so that "a positive element emerges . . . something different from that previously signified."

Before I outline how queer objects relate to the political economic contexts in which Kenyans craft futures and how the idea of "rescue," as an orientation toward objects, has become central to intimate citizenship, it is important to show how anti-homosexual sentiment has played out in Kenya. To do so, I move from Samburu County, in the north, where we encountered the controversy over the "boy with beads," to the coast to the Indian Ocean, my second major research site, where, in the past years, anti-homosexual demonstrations have made global headlines.

"Operation Gays Out"

On February 12, 2010, two to three hundred people, mainly young men but also women and children, approached the building of the Kenya Medical Research Institute (KEMRI) in the coastal town of Mtwapa. Some of them held up closed fists, sticks, and stones. Others crossed their arms in front of their faces as if to say "time was up." Young male motorbike cab operators, so-called *bodaboda*, stopped traffic along the road and led the procession. They honked loudly while protesters followed them jumping and chanting. "No to homosexuals," they cried. *Wachomwe kabisa*, "Let them be burned to death."[9]

When the demonstrators arrived at KEMRI's compound, they forced open its tall metal gate and pushed away the security guard. For many of them, this was the first time to catch a glimpse behind the high concrete walls that concealed the building from the street. Rumor had it that the organization worked safely hidden behind these walls to "promote homosexuality" or "lure young men with cash into gayism," as town residents told me a few months later. KEMRI had opened its Mtwapa office recently. Using funds from the Kenyan government and foreign donors, it responded to public health research findings which, in 2004, identified so-called MSM or "men who have sex with men" as a "key population" in the transmission of HIV in the country (Moyer and Igonya 2018). KEMRI health workers provided medical care to people they identified as MSM and carried out further research on their health. Town residents, however, saw the organization as supporting homosexuals with money and health benefits that others lacked. "There have always been *mashoga* in Mtwapa," a young man who had participated in the demonstrations told me in 2017, using the derogatory Swahili word. "But KEMRI brought them out and encouraged them. And many more came to Mtwapa because of KEMRI." Thus, to locals, the organization appeared to remunerate same-sex intimacies with welfare services and institutionalize homosexuality by offering it firmer social and spatial grounding in the township.

A few demonstrators entered KEMRI's offices and, some minutes later, reemerged in the street, dragging out two male health workers. The two men wore red T-shirts with the Swahili inscription *Komesha UKIMWI, tumia kondom*, "Prevent AIDS, use condoms." Political and religious leaders had already called the explicit language of sex education "pornographic" and warned that it could endanger children. In August 1995, for example, the Roman Catholic Archbishop of Nairobi and the imam of Jamia Mosque organized a major protest in Nairobi's Uhuru Park, where demonstrators burned sex education materials in a large bonfire to eradicate perversion—foreign NGOs' alleged attempts to sexualize children (Kiama 1999, 116). For the demonstrators in Mtwapa, the T-shirts confirmed that these KEMRI employees were involved in the "business of gayism," a business that, for them, meant accepting foreign aid in exchange for turning local young men gay through early sex education. The crowd beat the two health workers severely.

Around the same time, a twenty-three-year-old man, a security guard at KEMRI, approached the building to begin his shift. People in the crowd recognized him as an employee of the organization and accused him of being homosexual as well. They beat him along with the other two men. By the time the police arrived, demonstrators had already poured paraffin on all three, preparing to light them on fire. Police wrestled the three men out of the protesters' hands and drove them to the Mtwapa Police Station, where they were jailed along with two other suspected homosexual men. Earlier that day, police had accompanied a smaller crowd to the home of the latter two and arrested them because they found them wearing matching engagement rings, an indication that they had planned to marry each other. All five men were charged with "carnal knowledge against the order of nature," under Section 126 of the Penal Code. As I learned later, not all of them identified as gay. What made these men recognizable as homosexual in this context should become gradually evident throughout this book.

Town residents concluded their demonstration by gathering in front of the police station. There, local leaders took turns addressing them. "We thank God," said Bishop Lawrence Chai of the National Council of Churches of Kenya, "for saving this town from being turned to Sodom and Gomorrah . . . as we may have been on the verge of being doomed had these evil criminals managed to conduct this evil exercise within our neighborhood."[10] Sheik Ali Hussein of the Council of Imams and Preachers of Kenya said: "Even if blood needs to be spilled, it [gayism] won't happen. For something like that to happen, all the people of Mtwapa would have to be dead."[11] Finally, the Mtwapa police chief told journalists: "We are grateful to the public for alerting the police. They should continue co-operating with the police to arrest more. [Gayism] is an offense, an unnatural offense . . . repugnant to the morality of the people."[12] Construing the apparent institutionalization of gayism as a moral threat of catastrophic proportions, local leaders mobilized and reoriented collective desires toward securitizing, at all costs, the intimate lives of Mtwapa's residents.

Infamous for its vast sexual economies, including brothels, nightclubs, street sex work, an underground pornographic film production industry, and a large gay and lesbian community, Mtwapa has figured in the national media as the country's "sin city"—a place where national ideals of intimacy and respectability come undone. Over the past four decades, the location has grown from a small cluster of fisher villages of a few thousand residents at the time of the country's independence to an urban area of 51,000 in 2010. The town's spectacular growth is tied primarily to its various sex-for-money exchanges, involving Kenyans, wealthy foreign and domestic tourists, development workers, and expat retirees primarily from Switzerland, Germany, and Italy. Seasonal migrants and migrant settlers from all over Kenya—now, the largest percentage of Mtwapa's population—have been attracted to the town's unique money-making opportunities. Though central to state revenues (registering, for example, one of the highest real estate values in the country), Mtwapa is nevertheless peripheral to national sensibilities, a place that middle-class Kenyans regard with suspicion and shame. In 2010, residents demonstrated against KEMRI and gayism in part because they too thought that, in Mtwapa, things had gone too far.

The demonstration had been in the making for at least a month. In January that year, rumors began circulating that a "gay wedding" would soon take place in town. A local man told his barber—jokingly, by some accounts—that he would marry his male partner on February 12 in a nearby luxurious tourist resort. Shocked, the barber told his imam, and, in turn, during Friday prayers, the imam urged his congregation to be vigilant about the growing spread of gayism. Regional radio stations Radio Kaya, Baraka FM, and Radio Rahana also picked up the story, calling on their listeners to actively prevent gay weddings and chase homosexuals out of Mtwapa. In response to these rumors, Bishop Chai organized what he called "Operation Gays Out," a group of people committed to purifying the town of homosexuality. On February 11, he and Sheik Hussein held a joint press conference and, as the national newspaper *Daily Nation* reports, urged people to "investigate" KEMRI for "providing counseling services to these criminals" and to "take the law into their own hands."[13] They intended Operation Gays Out as a "rescue campaign" that brought together different town residents against a common threat. Young men, including the bodaboda, and women's groups, coastal people and up-country migrants, Christians and Muslims demonstrated together. Anti-homosexual protests in Senegal in 2008 and in Malawi in 2010 also targeted HIV clinics that catered to MSM and blamed them for "promoting homosexuality" (Biruk 2015; Coly 2019). These parallels illustrate how anti-homosexual imaginaries and their modes of expression travel transnationally via media and political discourse.

Operation Gays Out also coincided with—and was informed by—growing instances of anti-homosexual rhetoric across East Africa. In October 2009, in neighboring Uganda, Member of Parliament David Bahati introduced a bill that promised to strengthen anti-homosexual legislation by punishing same-sex acts with life imprisonment and, in some cases, death. Despite the bill's global condemnation, Uganda's president Yoweri Museveni eventually supported it, spurring numerous violent attacks against LGBT Ugandans (Kintu 2017). The same month, two Kenyan men, Charles Ngengi and Daniel Gichia, made national headlines in Kenya after marrying in London, where they lived at that time. Their wedding, Evan Mwangi (2014) shows, sparked furious debates among Kenyans, many calling on their state to strip these men of citizenship. Mwangi notes that, claiming they shamed the nation, "some advised the media against calling the couple 'Kenyan men,' suggesting that they simply be referred to as 'men,' with no mention of their nationality" (103). To be homosexual, in other words, was to be a noncitizen. In December 2009, just a bit over a month before the Mtwapa demonstrations took place, in Malawi, a gay couple was arrested for having performed a traditional engagement ceremony (Biruk 2015, 449). Kenyan and international media broadcast their trial, amplifying fears that gay weddings were suddenly on the rise across the region.

Importantly, this was also a time when Kenyans were debating drafts of a new Constitution. Citizens would vote on this draft in a referendum later that year. Along with abortion and Islamic courts, the possible decriminalization of homosexuality was a most contentious issue related to the new Constitution's nondiscrimination clauses (Parsitau 2021). If Western leaders, international lending agencies, and human rights groups called for the protection of sexual minorities, most Kenyan political leaders promised their voters that the new Constitution would secure them against the "perversions of globalizations." In response to the Mtwapa demonstrations, for example, Grace Kakai, district commissioner in Kilifi, the administrative division where Mtwapa is located, called on the government to follow Uganda's example and tighten anti-homosexuality laws "to suit society's concerns."[14]

This wider context is helpful for understanding how the homosexual came to be perceived as a cause of intimate trouble and a legitimate object of violence. But it does not explain how the concrete male bodies targeted by protesters in Mtwapa had been recognized as homosexual. This is a question I address throughout this book. But I shall begin to answer it here by turning, once more, to objects. Consider, for example, KEMRI's building. A large, elegant two-story villa-type house, painted in clean white, with blue door and window frames, and surrounded by high walls with barbed wire and metal gates, it resembled—and was built among—the homes of the wealthiest town residents. In Mtwapa, most of these residences have been built, within the last three decades, by young Africans married to or in long-term, long-distance relationships with elderly white men and women from Europe. These houses contrasted sharply with the homes of poorer residents, mostly mud and stone structures with thatched or iron-sheet roofs. Poor residents passed by such imposing compounds daily, speculating on the hidden flows of wealth that sustain them. KEMRI's building attested to such wealth. Furthermore, the fact that, in this building, many MSM received health services or payments for participating in research solidified locals' perception that foreign wealth now expanded gayism, indeed that gayism was a business. This phenomenon was not exceptional. Rather, it exacerbated locals' general sense that spectacular wealth was obtainable through illicit sex: non-normative sexual arrangements that included sex work, intergenerational intimacies, porn shoots, or same-sex intimacies. Trying to reveal what was hidden inside KEMRI's building, demonstrators expressed anxieties over how the commodification of illicit sex has become central to the production of wealth, all along undermining respectability.

This becomes even more evident when reflecting on another object: the engagement rings police and demonstrators used as evidence to arrest two gay men in their home. Rings are emblematic of the dream-wedding fantasies produced by a growing middle-class wedding industry (Muhonja 2017, 35–52). Dream weddings, however, remain out of reach for most Kenyans.

According to the Kenyan National Bureau of Statistics, in 2014, nearly 60 percent of Kilifi County residents and 63 percent of the national population had never married officially.[15] In this context, wedding rings are aspirational tokens of deferred respectability, elements of a "cruel optimism" (Berlant 2011), a continuous investment of hope in things that, amidst socio-economic precarity, can hardly come true. The very possibility of gay weddings thus became threatening precisely because heteronormative ideals of matrimony were difficult to achieve. Among the protesters, a woman shouted: "What will happen now that they [men] have turned to each other? Who will marry our daughters?"[16] For locals, the rings might have amplified a sense of stolen possibility: a concern that marriage, a key token of respectability, was being fundamentally redefined at the very same time that most people struggled to acquire the means for its realization. Emblematic of a more general predicament of uncertainty, the rings point to a displacement of desire and fear onto the homosexual body, a body to be pursued and excluded for a collective future to be rescued.

What would it mean, then, to foreground such objects—objects that lurk in the background of the essentialist categories of the homosexual body? And what can these objects tell us about the production of anti-homosexual desire and sentiment? Thinking with such objects demonstrates, for example, how the homosexual body as an objectification of sexuality politics is so salient today precisely because it comes to congeal myriad things beyond itself: struggles with inequality, work, and wealth; gender, marriage, and respectability; nature and pollution; the dissonance between the surfaces and essences of things; and much more. Each object analyzed in this book takes us across domains of social life where aspirations, anxieties, and fears are mobilized to produce not only the homosexual, but all kinds of "troublesome" bodies.

Toward a Political Economy of Homophobia

Euro-American liberal media depicted the events in Mtwapa as exemplary of rising homophobia across Africa. Images of the protesting crowds circulated widely, underscoring the violence and irrationality of an "African homophobia" and the importance of rescuing LGBT Africans from African homophobes. Articles with titles such as "Religion, Politics, and Africa's Homophobia" (BBC, 2010) or "Why Africa Is the Most Homophobic Continent" (*The Guardian*, 2014) and films such as *Africa's Last Taboo: Homosexuality* (BBC, 2010) have featured the Mtwapa demonstrations or similar incidents through the binary framework of a "pink line" (Gevisser 2020)—homosexual "victims" versus homophobic "perpetrators." While this reading can certainly be tempting when dealing with violence, it is nevertheless problematic. The language of global queer liberalism derived from Euro-American LGBT activism not only reifies the homosexual as an essential, universal category of subjecthood but also deploys homophobia to render black Africans nonmodern, irrational, violent Others (Awondo, Geschiere, and Reid 2012; Hoad 2007; Mack 2017; Puar 2007).

Images of violence, to be sure, have long played a central role in how Africa has been construed as lack, absence, or backwardness (Mbembe 2001; Mudimbe 1988). In January 2008, only two years prior to the Mtwapa events, Kenya made global headlines when, following its contested presidential election, violence erupted across the country. Then too, Euro-American media depicted violence as backward interethnic feuds or timeless tribalism. It is important, then, to explore further how forms of violence that, at a certain moment, become legible as homophobic—or, for that matter, ethnic—emerge at the intersection of regional, national, and global processes. Vigdis Broch-Due (2005) argues that if approached through the "thick" social relations in which it unfolds, violence is more than simply destructive. It is also generative: it is deployed to produce difference and identity, a sense of certainty in the face of ambiguity, or to render more tangible, more concrete, various utopias of "unpolluted" moral society. Understanding violence as part of its "thick" relations is not to relativize it. Rather, it is to attend to the complex logics and grammars that allow for its reproduction. It is doing so without, at the same time, reifying racist stereotypes of African political irrationality.

Homophobia is not a self-explanatory, universal category. Or, as Martin Manalansan (2009, 45) puts it, "there is no 'pure and simple' homophobia." Instead, sentiments, signs, logics, and grammars that become intelligible as homophobic at any moment require careful explanation. Murray (2009, 2) suggests that there is "a significant lacuna in understanding how and why certain sexuality and gender categories and practices come to be taboo, excluded, and/or repellant." "We must . . . focus on the other side of the coin," Murray argues, "that is, do research that focuses on understanding the causes, dynamics, forces, structures, and 'logics' which work to create, oppress, marginalize, and/or silence sexual alterity." Neither merely a product of a colonial exportation of sexual science or Christian morality, nor simply an outcome of the global proliferation of LGBT activism, anti-homosexual sentiment and violence involve complex articulations and contradictions between the discourses of leaders, institutions, popular culture, and civil society, among other things (6–8).

To understand the politics of homophobia in the African context requires first interrogating two persistent paradigms. First, as I have already intimated, the distinctness of an African homophobia. Rising violence against African gays and lesbians has lent urgency to scholarly engagements with sexuality on the continent. Scholar-activists have sought to make visible, through ethnographic and historical data, same-sex identities and practices that political and religious leaders now work to suppress or efface (Epprecht 2008; Nyeck 2019; Tamale 2011). With the rise of internationally funded LGBT activism on the continent, scholars have also studied emerging forms of queer activism and the social worlds to which they give rise (Currier 2012; Lorway 2014; Reid 2013; Rodriguez 2019). In these contexts, they show, homophobia has emerged not only through political leaders' strategic incitements to violence, but also through transnational religious networks, mass media, changing forms of consumerism and gender, and popular reactions against leaders or Western interventions in African affairs (Ireland 2013; M'Baye 2013; Msibi 2011; Ndjio 2012; Nyeck 2013; Thoreson 2014). Many scholars have also become wary of how homophobia in Africa is approached as distinct, exceptional. Essentialist logics, no doubt, are at stake in both conservative claims that homosexuality is "un-African" and liberalist portrayals of a "homophobic Africa" (Awondo, Geschiere, and Reid 2012; Hoad 2007; Gaudio 2009). Simple attributions of homophobia to various subjects or parts of the world—whether Middle Eastern or African people, states, or cultures—reproduce the "sexual ideologies of racism" (Hoad 2007; see also Puar 2007). It is important, then, to understand the deployment of anti-homosexual rhetoric as part of a wider global repertoire of governance (Bosia and Weiss 2013) and how particular states implement such global strategies of power (Currier 2018). Of course, local histories, categories, objects, and desire are central in rendering such global deployments of anti-homosexual rhetoric intelligible and meaningful. Indeed, there are also historically particular inflections in the politics of homophobia in African contexts. But attending to these historical particularities is very different from uncritically invoking an abstract "African homophobia" as an object-cause of violence.

Second, it is important to interrogate critically the seeming exceptionalism of the (homo)sexual in contemporary politics of intimate citizenship. Homophobia presupposes the homosexual subject as a target of its sentiment, violence, and possibility. Yet, homophobic discourse and violence is also productive of the homosexual as its object (Judge 2017). To de-essentialize homophobia, it is necessary to look at its production beyond the ready-made sexual subject; in the case of this book, to trace objects that, from the background, are constitutive of this target of repudiation. In this sense, merely carrying out ethnography of LGBT subjects is insufficient for understanding homophobia. It is also insufficient to stick closely to scenes, discourses, and practices that are immediately recognizable as homophobic, scenes such as those of the Mtwapa demonstrations. Following instead various objects that constitute the (homo)sexual body as an object of disavowal, hate, and violence, I show how anxieties and aspirations from across a wide array of social domains come to be displaced onto and thus constitute this body.

My approach involves strategies of contextualization and critique that I like to call, following Rahul Rao (2020), a "political economy of homophobia." This approach, Rao argues, entails "taking seriously the material and social anxieties to which the figure of the queer is indexed as an evidentiary scapegoat, as well as the extant evidentiary architecture within which such a move might appear plausible" (162). A political economy of homophobia can "account for social antipathy towards figures read as queer, without lapsing into orientalist accounts of a timeless and irredeemable 'African' homophobia" (162). Pursuing queer objects ethnographically allows me to explore precisely such material and social anxieties as well as the conditions of possibility that make the homosexual body a salient object of fear and hate.

At the time of the Mtwapa demonstrations, I had been doing fieldwork in Kenya for five years. In 2005, I began working primarily in Samburu County, but in 2008 I also joined northern migrants to Mtwapa, where they made a living in coastal tourism. In the weeks that followed the demonstrations, BBC journalists Robin Barnwell and Sorious Samura produced a documentary film called *Africa's Last Taboo: Homosexuality*. Steven, a Samburu migrant I knew quite well, figures prominently in the documentary. Video footage from the demonstrations shows him calling for homosexuals to be burned to death. Asked by Samura, later that year, if his views had changed, he promised to kill his own son or brother if he ever found out either was homosexual.

Steven lived in relative poverty at the coast. He came from a region and an ethnic group that—not unlike Kenya's gays, lesbians, and transgender people—had long been vilified and marginalized by the government for their difference, a difference also deemed sexual. Like many Samburu men, since the 1980s, he drew on colonial sexualized stereotypes of the erotic Samburu warrior to engage in transactional sex with women from Europe, a phenomenon I describe elsewhere (Meiu 2017). Throughout the decades he spent at the coast, however, Steven did not acquire savings. Although he was in his late forties—an "elder" by Samburu standards—he had no house or livestock in the north, and, at the coast, lived in so-called "come-we-stay" relationships, intimate relations with women that were, though common, much less reputable than marriage. I had trouble reconciling Steven's words on *Africa's Last Taboo* with his own non-normative life, what many of our common acquaintances saw as his own "unsuccessful" struggles to acquire respectability. Like Steven, many Mtwapa residents lived in poverty, deferring expectations of marriage and family to indeterminate futures. How then was demonstrating against homosexuals, gayism, or the KEMRI organization meaningful for them? What did they expect to achieve by imagining a town, a region, or a nation purified of homosexuality? And how can one begin to understand this violent demonstration without reifying queer liberalism's essentialist categories of race and sexuality?

As a gay man myself, I did not always find it easy or comfortable to think about anti-homosexual discourse at length or to listen with care to people, like Steven, with whose opinions and views I so radically disagreed. But researchers and activists at KEMRI and other Kenyan LGBT organizations inspired me to find patience and strength to do precisely that. Unlike some Euro-American liberals who simply demonize those they deem homophobes, my Kenyan colleagues did not have the luxury to do so. In a context in which same-sex relationships were criminalized and police often sided with anti-homosexual protesters, they had to tread carefully. In the years following the 2010 Mtwapa protests, KEMRI, for example, initiated a set of "sensitization" campaigns to understand how and why homophobic imaginaries emerged and to educate people to move past such imaginaries. It is ironic perhaps that by 2017, KEMRI featured Steven, of all people, as their "success story," someone its staff had managed to sensitize to same-sex struggles. This inspired me to listen carefully to those with whom I disagreed and imagine a political-economic approach that attends closely to the complexities of homophobia's reproduction.

This book began from a simple yearning to make sense of events such as the anti-homosexual demonstrations in Mtwapa and the social media outrage at the Samburu girl with a bead necklace. But as I found myself pursuing different objects, I learned that making sense of these events required decentering key paradigms of intimate citizenship and interrogating their production in a context in which the very idea of the future had become elusive, uncertain.

Elusive Futures, Diversions, Dis/Orientations

With late capitalism, there is a growing perception that futures, in general, are difficult to project. In 1980, Kenya's national newspaper, *Daily Nation*, published a cartoon entitled "Forecasters' Road Map of the 1980's: Alternative Prognostications, 1980–1989" (fig. 3). Designed by the World Future Society, "a Washington based association of people interested in what may happen during the years ahead," the map depicts futurity as confusingly rhizomatic. Rather than the straight line associated with the temporality of modernity,

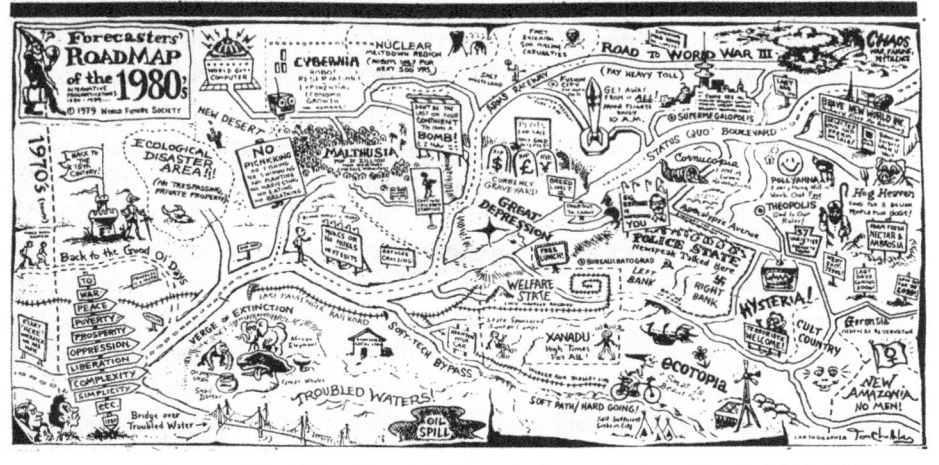

FIGURE 3. "Forecasters' Road Map of the 1980's: Alternative Prognostications, 1980–1989," *Friday Nation Magazine*, Kenya, August 1, 1980.

progress, and development (Koselleck 2004), the future figures here as a net of numerous intersecting and diverting roads, streets, and alleys peppered with imaginatively named stops, destinations, and signs: the "Status Quo Boulevard" leads through "Great Depression" and "Welfare State" to its final destination: "Chaos: War, Famine." Smaller paths are called "Refugee Crossing," "Back to the Good Ol' Days," or "Soft-Tech Bypass" and lead respectively to "Cybernia," "1970s," and "Ecotopia."

Evocative of a sense of temporal disorientation and uncertainty at the time, the map's strong resonance with the realities of Kenyan life must have informed the editors' decision to print it. Kenyans were certainly aware that their futures were rhizomatic (see, for example, Smith 2008), even if they did not necessarily celebrate such futures as ends in themselves. The straight linear time of modernity and progress continued to inform their quests for respectability. But straight time now worked in an ever-more-pronounced dissonance with the rhizomatic future of life-as-lived.

To find one's way across the disorienting terrain of future-making, people have engaged, in part, in myriad forms of speculation. In 2018, in a *Daily Nation* article suggestively entitled "The Making of a Casino Nation," Kamau Ngotho decries "just how deep gambling has dug into the Kenyan psyche."[17]

From gaming machines, lotteries, and online bets on football teams to more elaborate investments in pyramid schemes, Ngotho suggests, a "gambling culture" renders fluid Kenyans' otherwise most durable forms of wealth—houses and land, cars and cattle. "Forget about hard work," a former schoolmate told Ngotho. "In today's Kenya you either make it through gambling or tenderpreneurship." Indeed, anthropologists working across the world have described the widespread perception that, with the rise of neoliberal market ideologies and reforms, crafting futures has become akin to gambling, speculation, and entrepreneurship (Piot 2010; Weiss 2004). Speculation is here more than actual gambling. It is also a future-orientation: a perpetual effort to sustain an engagement with the world as a condition for making livelihoods and actualizing a tomorrow. And people are very much aware of this.

In 2018, across Kenya, in demonstrations that echoed the 1995 Nairobi burning of sex education materials and the 2010 Mtwapa attacks on homosexuals, police and citizens burned hundreds of gaming machines in public bonfires. This they saw as a general "clampdown" on the "culture of gambling."[18] According to Nairobi police officer Kang'ethe Thuku, who coordinated one such demonstration in Nairobi in October 2018, "young school-going children are not spared, hence the need to destroy the machines that encourage idleness and lack of productivity among youth."[19] In these demonstrations, gaming machines—queer objects of sorts—came to congeal an epochal ethos of speculation. The ritual burning of the machines, in turn, was a way to imagine, or incantate, a more secure, predictable future, a future where labor, value, and respectability could be restored to their normative, industrial ideals.

What then if we can recognize that, with the historical transformations of late capitalism, people have become more aware that much of their social life sustains non-normative articulations? That the making of futures often involves subversive means, circumstances, and outcomes? Or that future-making has been quite "queer" even when people have sought to disavow, displace, and repudiate—sometimes quite violently—the "queerness" of their own actions, desires, and livelihoods in order to reclaim (hetero)normative objects of desire? And how would this simple realization help us grasp emerging forms of nativist sexuality and ethno-nationalism in the present?

To understand this, it is important to distinguish between means and ends in relation to how the future is imagined and temporalized. Jane Guyer (2007) argues that the uncertainties of late capitalism have foregrounded anthropological concerns with an "enforced presentism" and a "fantasy future," at the expense of attention to the "near future"—the concrete ways people make a tomorrow. Calling for more "ethnographies of the near future," Guyer emphasizes the importance of attending to "a time that is punctuated rather than enduring: of fateful moments and turning points, the date as event rather than a position in a sequence or a cycle" (416; see also Goldstone and Obarrio 2017, 16; Piot 2010). As part of an intensely speculative economy, then, non-normative means to the near future may short-circuit long-term plans, the fantasy future, in ways that echo the diversions and disorientations of the map I discussed above.

Ethnographically, I am interested in the dispositions and desires such contradictions generate and the role different objects play—as the gaming machines illustrate—in people's efforts to realign themselves with particular visions of the future. Numerous value-making practices anthropologists have described in recent years evidence these contradictions.[20] In such contexts, as Jeremy Jones (2010) argues for Zimbabwe, "nothing is straight": a shadow economy of various "zig-zagging" survival practices operates in the "shadow" of the "normal." In my own work, I describe such moments of being out of synch with the temporal rhythms of the normative life course and respectability as "queer moments" (Meiu 2015). These, then, are examples of how the dissonance between the means, outcomes, and circumstances of future-making can indeed be read as queer.

If a general queerness can indeed be said to permeate conditions of everyday life today, then an objectified queerness—the homosexual body and the other objects I explore in this book—becomes, like the gaming machines, externalized representation of a generalized epochal condition. They represent objectified *causes* and *symptoms* of affliction: "It is *because* of homosexuals," so the logic goes, "that *our* futures are in jeopardy." In other words, one can argue that the subversive means of near futures are perhaps less troublesome to people than the desire for an explicitly non-normative far future, one that challenges the straight time of national utopia. And thus, the security state's legitimacy thrives off its promise to contain and eliminate bodies and things explicitly dedicated to—or promising to bring about—such a future and to reinstate the straight line of education, development, and progress. Can thinking of queer objects, including the body of the homosexual, as displacements of a general, shared sense of life as queer, out-of-line, exceptional, of futures as rhizomatic, begin to explain what occurred in the 2010 Mtwapa demonstrations?

As I began doing systematic research for this book, over twelve months, in 2015 and, again, between 2017 and 2019, I came to map rescue ideologies and practices of rehabilitation orchestrated between state institutions, humanitarian organizations, churches, and civil society groups. I learned that rescue became a common way to orient oneself toward the future, the nation, and other citizens. It presupposed the constant evaluation and realignment of people and objects to (re)instate ideal forms of intimacy. Rescue became a way to pursue the straight time of personal and collective "progress" and "development" (S: *maendeleo*) against the backdrop of myriad rhizomatic temporalities. The implicit logic went somewhat like this: *If I do not have the means to acquire respectability in the near future, my desire to rescue intimacy for the far future demonstrates my commitment to it. I am thus a good citizen.* Objects, as we shall see, can become straightening devices in such rescue projects.

Rescue as Moral Rehabilitation

Many of those involved in the violent demonstrations in Mtwapa saw their actions as ways of rescuing intimacy, and, therewith, their town and the nation. Demonstrators and religious leaders hoped to "save" people from "evil criminals," as Bishop Chai put it. So too did the *bodaboda* who saw themselves as more than motorbike cab drivers; they were also town vigilantes who, in their own words, "do the work of community rescue" (S: *tunafanya kazi ya community rescue*) (see chapter 3). For them, community rescue involved, among other things, catching thieves and, at times, homosexuals, the two categories growingly conflated as "evil criminals." The police also used "rescue," if in a more volatile, performative way. On the one hand, they arrested homosexuals, promising to support locals' efforts to rid the town and nation of "an unnatural offense . . . repugnant to the morality of the people."[21] On the other hand, faced with international human rights abuse accusations, in the following days, they claimed to have actually "rescued" these men from the "angry mob" ready to kill them. Similarly, in northern Kenya, let us recall, the MP's Facebook post prompted calls for her to "rescue" the "boy with beads"—to make "him" into a "real man." Interesting here is less the directionality of rescue (i.e., who rescues and who is to be rescued) and more the fact that intimacy now appeared under its sign: to be a good citizen is not necessarily to inhabit the right kind of intimacies. Rather, it is to desire to acquire such intimacies in the future, through constant rehabilitative efforts.

A key feature of the global humanitarian industry, the moral claim to rescue has come to permeate not only the language of governments and NGOs, but also the everyday life of citizens (Malkki 2015; Scherz 2014). Rather than understand rescue in the narrow terms of transnational humanitarianism or as merely a Euro-American import, I approach it as a historical idiom of "cultural intimacy"—that is, "the recognition of those aspects of an officially shared identity that . . . provide insiders with their assurance of common sociality" (Herzfeld 1997, 7). Seen thus, rescue reveals important things about sexuality and intimacy in the contemporary Kenyan national sphere. Most strikingly, it reveals how moral incitements to rescue have informed how some Kenyans imagine themselves as citizens, how they consume or mobilize politically, and how they navigate the slippery slopes of their daily lives.

But, far from being merely a Kenyan phenomenon, the deployment of rescue imaginaries is common across the world today. Inderpal Grewal (2017, 5) argues that saving, rescue, and surveillance constitute key modes of governance and subjecthood in "advanced neoliberalism," a time defined, among other things, by "the emergence and management of protests as well as the visibility of insecurities of imperial power." As Grewal notes for the United States, so too in Kenya and elsewhere, "private individuals who see themselves as normative citizens become empowered to take responsibility for maintaining the imperial security state. These individuals, produced as responsible and self-improving and thus products of neoliberal self-empowerment regimes, hope to repair the effects of imperial and neoliberal policies and thereby save the security state" (2). Here, "the will to rescue, to save, to become humanitarians" is a moral claim to "exceptional citizenship" (10) (see also Amar 2013).

In recent years, the language and logics of "rescue" have permeated engagements with intimate citizenship beyond homosexuality, strictly speaking. Kenyans' quests for respectability, social value, and national belonging have involved salient incitements to moral rescue, calls to save intimacy from the corrupting forces of contemporary life and to secure it as a condition for the nation's vitality and futurity. Political and religious leaders, the media, development workers, civil society groups, and other social actors have depicted, if in different ways, various non-normative intimacies as patently responsible for social and economic decay. In response, numerous drives have emerged to rescue citizens from the perils of dangerous intimacy. While very different in scale and magnitude, such interventions have drawn on the language of global humanitarianism and Christian evangelism but also on older, local forms of political protest and collective purification to imagine social and political order in new ways. Anti-homosexuality campaigns are certainly the best-known example of such rescue efforts, where opposing same-sex intimacies is, among other things, a way to secure nativist-*cum*-national heterosexuality as an ideal of autochthonous moral order and to do so for the future.

Ethnographic Detours, or, How to Read This Book

Echoing the life trajectories of many of its protagonists, *Queer Objects to the Rescue* proposes an ethnographic journey that is circuitous rather than linear:

it twists and turns, in ever wider concentric circles, around particular objects. To critique paradigms of sexuality without reifying them, I pursue a strategy of analysis and writing that I call *ethnographic detours*. That is, rather than tackle sexuality politics head-on, my ethnographic narrative moves *around* it, defers arrival, and—as in the Freudian notion of "perversion"—dwells where it must not, in the subject's "other scenes." "In language and life," Paul Stoller (1989, 142) argues, "human beings are meanderers; we continually take detours." Therefore, "*detours* are . . . paths that ethnographers clearly need to take to set themselves straight with the world as it is" (145). While "straight" is not necessarily how I would describe the end goal of my analysis (pun intended), detours help me delay my quest for concrete answers and, in so doing, produce richer, more nuanced findings. If indeed queer objects can be approached as the social unconscious of sexuality, then, as Lacan (2017, 22) puts it, "The unconscious . . . is only ever illuminated and only reveals itself when you look away a little . . . you look away and this makes it possible for you to see what is not there."

My ethnographic detours do not only pertain to objects relative to sexuality, but also to Kenya's geopolitics relative to its forms of intimate citizenship. I have carried out field research in Samburu County, northern Kenya, and in Kilifi County, at the coast. From the point of view of a national public, both places represent sexual and political *peripheries* of the nation. Samburu County figures in the national imagination as remote, underdeveloped, and backward, an image underscored by numerous media stories about the devious sexual lives of its indigenous pastoralist population. Meanwhile, the coast appears as a space of affluence, consumption, and cosmopolitanism, but also one of sexual perversion, sex tourism, prostitution, sex trafficking, and an excessive nightlife (Kibicho 2009). Christian nationalists have long associated the coast's Muslim Swahili with homosexuality to delegitimize their participation in state administration. These geopolitical ethnographic detours then help me approach intimate citizenship, not from within its core claims and discourses, but from its "other scenes," those subjects and spaces the nation disavows as a condition of its respectability. I supplemented research in these places with regular visits to the country's capital city of Nairobi. Shifting between different locales, scales, and actors, I trace and analyze the social poetics of objects related to moral rescue initiatives in Kenya.

Chapter 2 explores how Kenyans come to affirm that rescue is necessary and to desire that their intimate lives be redressed or securitized. Focusing on mundane moments of work and storytelling among sex workers and NGO workers in Mtwapa, the chapter traces the emergence of what can be loosely called the *subject of intimate rescue* as a template of intimate citizenship. If those who perform acts of rescue claim to occupy a moral high ground in relation to those they see as morally peripheral, rescue, I argue, is not a dyadic relationship. Rather, it is a "threesome": it also involves the perceived gaze of a national public for which rescue is a path to good citizenship.

Chapter 3 takes on the book's first object, the material substance of "male-power" (S: *nguvu za kiume*), a gendered bodily energy that subsumes virility and vitality—one's ability to have sex, sire children, work, and gain respectability. The chapter explores recent panics over the depletion of "male-power" in central Kenya, concerns over its excess accumulation among *bodaboda* (motorcycle cab operators), and various civil society attempts to rescue and reform men as a condition of good citizenship. Across these contexts, "male-power" turns out to be quite elusive, shifting and leaking unexpectedly, empowering women over men and poor youths over powerful big-men. Hence, preoccupation with its surveillance and containment becomes a key technology of intimate citizenship.

Chapter 4 takes as its queer object traditional Samburu bead necklaces. Echoing colonial discourses about morans giving beads to girls to engage in sex with them, girl-empowerment NGOs have recently sought to criminalize the custom and rescue girls from child sexualization. In this context, bead necklaces became emblematic of indigenous intimacies that remain unassimilable to the nation, customary incitements of child and teen erotic desires and pleasures. Analyzing ensuing conflicts between child-rights activists and rural Samburu, this chapter addresses the challenges of what I call *encompassment*: how different social actors seek to enfold or encircle bodies into polities and how, in the process, troublesome sexual intimacies offer new arguments for exclusion and the production of ethnic noncitizens.

Chapter 5 returns to the panics over plastics I briefly introduced above. Exploring a wide array of objectifications—"plastic rice," "plastic boys," "plastic in the womb" as an affliction of fertility, or "homosexuality as plastic import"—I show how plastic has become an evocative idiom of non-belonging and social toxicity in Kenya. Anxieties over health, well-being, social reproduction, and economic uncertainty have found powerful expression in discourses associating plastic pollution with the toxic permeation of bodies, boundaries, and belonging more generally. I argue that the historical objectification of plastics and efforts to define criteria of belonging and intimate citizenship have shaped one another dialectically.

Chapter 6 analyzes adult diapers as a new idiom for depicting the failures of intimate citizenship. Rumors about adults who end up in diapers because they engaged in anal sex, but also illicit forms of work or behavior not necessarily associated with sex, have become common in Kenya. They reflect a growing preoccupation with the hidden underlayers of social life, of which intimacy is an important part. Such preoccupation, I argue, informs a desire for *intimate exposures*: performative attempts to unmask signs of social failure hidden beneath appearances of normality or respectability, as a condition of good citizenship. As queer objects, diapers demonstrate how anxieties over the body's autonomy and labor capacity become displaced onto the homosexual body.

Chapter 7 returns to the homosexual body, this time by analytically turning it into its main queer object. Revisiting the 2010 demonstrations in Mtwapa and the 2018 panic over the "boy with beads" in Samburu County described in this introduction, this chapter offers some preliminary answers as to what has made the homosexual body such an efficient object of citizenship technologies. At once visible and invisible, concrete and abstract, promising categorical certainty (i.e., to hold an evil interiority) and remaining somewhat unknowable, mysterious, ambiguous, this body, I argue, efficiently resonated with salient social anxieties as well as with its other troublesome objects, including "male-power," bead necklaces, plastics, and diapers discussed in previous chapters.

Offering "ethnographic detours" as a method of thinking around objects, I demonstrate homophobia's complex entanglements in a wide range of uncertainties over intimacy, economy, and the state, in myriad efforts to "rescue" national social life from the effects of globalization. The title of this book plays on this idea. *Queer Objects to the Rescue* suggests that if indeed a rehabilitative language is widely appealing today, then an ethnographic focus on objects may repurpose it to "rescue" our political imagination from the dominant and obstructive fetishes of contemporary investments in intimate citizenship.

2

Intimate Rescue:
Grammars, Logics, Subjects, Scenes

> The problem of internalizing the master's tongue is the problem of the rescued . . . the rescued have the problem of debt. If the rescuer gives you back your life by taking you away from the dangers, the complications, the confusions of home, he may very well expect his debt to be paid in full. . . . Because the rescuer wants to hear his name, not mimicked but adored.
>
> TONI MORRISON

Mtwapa—January 20, 2017. It was only a few minutes past 9AM and KEMRI's reception launch was quiet. Patients had not yet begun arriving at the drop-in clinic and the staff was in a meeting. Several office workers had walked past me only a few minutes prior, laptops, files, and cups of hot coffee in tow. Then, silence. All that was left were the dim sounds of the street outside—car engines, motorbike horns, and the bells at the wheels of the water salesmen's pushcarts. The smell of coffee from the cup that the receptionist, Rose, had just brought me slightly tempered the sharp whiffs of disinfectant in the room. Waiting contentedly to meet with the organization's director, I looked around the reception area. An old, shabby couch with torn fabric upholstery and seven blue plastic chairs stood against the graying white walls by the entrance. Behind Rose's desk, a tall bookshelf with glass doors displayed dozens of red boxes with condoms of the Kenyan brand "Sure." A handful of vividly colored flyers printed on shiny paper were laid out on a coffee table. Their English and Swahili titles read: "Sexually Transmitted Infections: Symptoms and Tips for Prevention"; "Anal Sex and Rectal Health"; *"Kinga ni Bora"*; and "Heshima Rescue Center, Mtwapa." On the wall above the couch, a cork board held several posters with educational messages: "There are lots of things you want to share . . . and some you don't . . . Protect yourself. Protect others"; "HIV doesn't care if you have sex with men or women. Unprotected anal sex is the highest risk sex for HIV infection"; and "Stop homophobia. Save pink lives." A few of these words lingered on my mind: *kinga* (S., guard), *prevent, protect, rescue, save, sure*. But also, relatedly: *risk, anal sex, HIV, homophobia,* and *heshima* (S., respect). Announcing discursive logics that connected this room to its social and political economic conditions of existence, these words also gestured to what I call *intimate rescue*, if perhaps in ways I could not yet have imagined then.

Sitting at her desk, Rose began to gently peel a hard-boiled egg. "This is my breakfast," she said matter-of-factly, looking up from behind her computer screen. "I don't like to eat much in the morning. Usually, I only have one egg. Sometimes I also have *chapati*. But not today." I had only known Rose for a few days, but I quickly came to enjoy her company. She was not only friendly and witty, but she also spoke of routine mundane tasks, such as her breakfast, with an interest that was contagious (the following morning, I too made myself a boiled egg). When she interacted with the organization's "beneficiaries"—mostly men who identified as *gay*, *kuchu*, or *MSM*—she treated them with warmth and respect. KEMRI's Mtwapa office carried out medical research on HIV infections and mental health among these men and tried to "sensitize" town residents to their struggles. The organization also offered STI screenings and treatment to MSM, but also to women engaged in sex work and people with drug addictions—all considered at high risk of HIV infection. When they entered KEMRI's office, Rose was typically the first person they met; at least, that is, if they arrived on days when she was not away, visiting beneficiaries at their homes to check on their treatment schedules and observe their living conditions. Just as Rose finished eating her boiled egg, a young, tall, skinny man entered the room. "How can I help you, darling?" she asked with a warm smile, gesturing for him to sit down at her desk. Then, she gently caressed his cheek with the back of her palm: "What's the matter?" The man stretched over Rose's desk and whispered in her ear. With an understanding nod, she grabbed a handful of condoms from a drawer and put them in the man's backpack.

Spending my morning in Rose's company reminded me that, as Liisa H. Malkki (2015) argues, seemingly banal mundane practices and routines can be as important to understanding humanitarian rescue as the spectacular interventions with which we often conflate it. Rose's peeling a boiled egg while describing her breakfast preferences or offering a kind word, a caress, or a handful of condoms may appear trivial when set against Kilifi County's struggle with an HIV infection rate of 4.5 percent (in 2015)[1] or its recurrent incidents of sexualized violence. That morning, sitting in KEMRI's reception room, I could not help thinking that Rose and I sat in the very building which, only seven years prior, in 2010, had been targeted by anti-homosexuality protesters. So why dwell then on the mere and the mundane? Examining how volunteers knit blankets or mail teddy bears in support of the Finnish Red Cross's international rescue missions, Malkki notes that "the inadequacies and embarrassments of 'the mere' always stood . . . against the horrifying accounts of acute emergencies and 'real suffering'" (203). Despite this contrast, Malkki insists, "one must recognize that a certain kind of power resides in objects and practices repeatedly and habitually dismissed as 'the mere'" (205). It is important to explore what forms of imagination and subjectivity such "mere" moments and things generate and sustain. Rose surely found such moments meaningful. "What I love about my job," she once told me, "is that I can help other people."

A focus on intimate rescue should not simply privilege panics, the exceptional, and the spectacular. The concept of "panics"—as in "moral panics," "sex panics," or "gender panics"—has certainly been crucial to understanding contemporary forms of governance through intimacy (Cohen 1973; Cole and Moore 2020; Fahs, Dudy, and Stage 2013; Herdt 2009; Lancaster 2011; Rubin 1984). Paul Amar (2013), for example, shows how, in recent decades, political leaders have generated and mass-mediated such panics to reproduce the state's legitimacy as a sovereign source of moral rescue and securitization. To be sure, panics do not merely respond to preexisting anxieties and fear, but also produce such emotions or channel them in new ways: in other words, they are "dramaturgical productions of fear" (Angelides 2009, 169–70; see also Irvine 2008). But the fact that panics are indeed politically mobilizable strategies of governance does not explain why they become widely meaningful social phenomena. Responding to Stanley Cohen's (1973) classic study on moral panics, Stuart Hall et al. (1978, 156) note that the question "is not why or how unscrupulous men [sic] work"—that is, it is not about the actions of leaders who incite panics—"but *why audiences respond*" (see also Rao 2020, 154). Addressing this question requires, in this case, careful attention to how a *subject of intimate rescue* emerges—to how one comes to believe that rescue is necessary or to desire that one's intimate lives be redressed and securitized. What are the symbolic, imaginary, and emotional conditions that make possible both panics and a desire for rescue? And what kind of subject-citizens do these conditions produce? I approach here the exceptional as dialectically related to the everyday. The subjectivities that emerge out of this dialectic are both continuous with and, in some regards, also distinct from state and NGO humanitarian ideals and strategies.

Examining how different troublesome objects, such as the homosexual body, figure in both mundane moments and outright panics related to intimate rescue, I wish to distill a set of *grammars* and *logics* that are central to intimate citizenship. Following Antonio Gramsci (2000, 354), I use "grammar" to describe patterns of thought sustained, in part, through language that involves "the reciprocal monitoring, reciprocal teaching and reciprocal 'censorship' . . . and . . . mimicry and teasing." Gramsci argues that "this whole complex of actions and reactions comes together to create a grammatical conformism, to establish 'norms' or judgements of correctness and incorrectness," becoming *hegemonic*, part of an unquestioned "common sense." We can think of these grammars as composed of discursive *logics*, which can enable "the coherence of hegemonic blocs," but "that can [also] be subversively undermined and rearticulated by counter hegemonic alliances" (Amar 2013, 177–78). Logics, Jason Glyons and David Howarth (quoted in Amar 2013, 178) argue, "focus our attention on the rules of grammar that enable us to characterize and even criticize a phenomenon, but they also allow us to disclose the structures and conditions that make these rules possible." Ethnographic attention to mundane practices makes more discernible, more readily graspable, the grammars and logics of intimate rescue. My engagement with different objects throughout the following chapters reveals logics constitutive of a dominant grammar of intimate citizenship.

To explore the roles that objects play in shaping such grammars, let us first consider what we can only loosely call a *subject of intimate rescue* and its relation to the political totalities of which it is part, including homes, families, villages, neighborhoods, regions, or the nation. To tease out some of the key logics that make this subject possible, I focus on a set of *intimate scenes*. I use this term to identify moments that are constitutive of what Berlant (1997) calls the "intimate public sphere," a late capitalist reconfiguration of the public sphere that entails (i) a growing public fascination with private domains of life; and (ii) the experiencing of national belonging through such domains. Intimate scenes then are moments of everyday life in which people debate, evaluate, worry about, or intervene upon intimate matters, whether in person or virtually, via radio, television, or social media.

The Truth about Rescue

One morning in February 2017, my research assistant Mary and I visited the Mtwapa office of an organization I will call the Global Institute for Sexual Reproductive Health (GISRH) to learn more about its activities. Founded in Europe in 1994, this multinational public health NGO has opened, since 2000, several offices along the Kenyan coast. With funds from the United Nations, the organization set out to respond to the AIDS pandemic by implementing so-called "behavioral change programs" focused on "sexual reproductive health." They also educated a wider coastal population on "family planning" and "gender-based violence." But, with donor priorities changing, since 2014 the organization has focused more exclusively on so-called "vulnerable populations"—social groups at the highest risk for HIV transmission. Thus, by the time Mary and I visited GISRH's Mtwapa office, women who engaged in sex work were its primary "beneficiaries." The office occupied a large, two-story house—what, I thought, must once have been an upper-middle-class family home—with a reception area, a kitchen, and a meeting room on the first floor and an office and a clinic on the second.

That morning, Mary and I joined ten women in the organization's reception lounge. We all sat on white plastic patio chairs aligned against the room's walls. The women in the room were sex workers who volunteered with GISRH as "peer educators." "On top of going out at night," the office manager told me, "these ladies also help educate their peers." That day, they had gathered for their monthly "supportive supervision meeting," where they filled out forms reporting the total amounts of condoms, lubricant sachets, and safe-sex fliers they had distributed and the number of sex workers they had referred to the NGO's clinic for STI screenings. But, on these occasions, they also shared, more informally, gossip and advice.

Besi, a thirty-five-year-old sex worker who had been appointed by the NGO to supervise the peer educators, liked to entertain these women with spicy rumors from around town. A gifted storyteller, she narrated events and dialogues with a theatricality so lively it could hold an audience captive for hours. Sitting on a chair by the entrance, Besi clutched her purse tightly with her left hand, as if she were in a hurry. But, as she started speaking, time appeared to stand still. Her right hand, holding a pen, remained suspended over the form she had been filling out until then. She spoke in Swahili about a schoolgirl whom she did not name. The girl was from Mtomondoni, a neighborhood on the western edge of Mtwapa whose residents were among the town's poorest. A police officer, Besi had heard, had accused the girl's mother—who, people said, was "insane" (S: *chizi*)—of neglecting her child. Claiming the girl needed to be "rescued," the officer placed her in an orphanage. But, when the girl's grandfather went looking for her, the girl was nowhere to be found. The officer now claimed the orphanage had "lost" her. But, Besi said, the girl's grandfather could not be fooled. He was no "common elder" (S: *mzee wa kawaida*), she said. He was a *babu digital*, a "digital grandfather," that is, a man who, though of an older generation, was well versed in using social media. "What do you think the grandfather did?" Besi asked, pausing as if to heighten our curiosity. "He found pictures of the child on Facebook and went to court." It turned out the officer had "sold" (S: *aliuza*) the girl to a white man. It wasn't clear to me whether the white man was an illegal adoptive parent or someone who had a sexual interest in children, but Besi's describing it as a sale made this distinction likely less relevant. "The court," she said, "gave the officer one week to return the child." The women in the room looked at Besi in astonishment: "Is that true?" one women wondered. "Very dangerous," said another, referring to children being kidnapped and sold. Besi ended by highlighting what she thought was the story's takeaway point: "It was the grandfather," she insisted, "who rescued [S: *mwenye alimrescue*] that child."

Besi captivated her audience not only with the evocative way she narrated her story but also because what she described resonated with the experiences of some of the women in the room. The story's plot spoke to a common perception that (familial) intimacy was a site of intensified uncertainty and insecurity. Rumors of children from poor households being stolen and sold—often with the help of corrupt state officials—were common at the coast. In these rumors, children's vulnerability was not only the product of broken marital and filial relations but also of a state that, instead of protecting familial intimacy, extracted value from its alleged breakdown. These rumors also echoed stories coastal elders told about the nineteenth-century Indian Ocean slave trade, when local families similarly lost children to an extractive global economy. For some women present that day at the NGO's office, Besi's story hit close to home. Doty, a thirty-year-old, told me that a few weeks prior, neighbors had taken her seven-month-old infant to an orphanage. She had left the child alone in her one-room home to go buy fresh milk. Because he started crying, women living on the same residential plot assumed Doty was neglecting her motherly duties. They took the infant to the police station, where they described the mother as a "prostitute" (S: *malaya*) who abused alcohol and drugs. Doty insisted that, being HIV-positive and unable to breastfeed, buying milk was essential to caring for her child. Even so, the judge who later heard the case placed the child in an orphanage and promised Doty she would be able to retrieve him only if she changed her lifestyle. Doty now tried desperately to improve her economic situation to convince the judge she was a competent mother. But she also worried that in the meantime, her infant could disappear from the orphanage—a danger that Besi's story poignantly underscored. That children disappeared under the pretense of being "rescued" heightened distrust and suspicion of neighbors, state agents, and NGOs. For, as women tried to secure their children's futures through whatever means available, others deemed their livelihoods "immoral" to produce and profit off uprooted children.

Tying intimacy to the need for rescue, Besi's story echoes and reworks humanitarian anti-trafficking logics that are probably as common today at the Kenyan coast as in many places across the world. Since the 1990s, NGOs and state institutions have been extensively preoccupied with how sexual economies associated with coastal beach tourism and its growing afferent urban areas have affected in particular women and children: how sex work, drug addiction, and AIDS have undermined motherhood and familial intimacy;

how growing up amidst the sex trade children have been lured into pursuing "quick money" and thus become prematurely sexualized; and how wealthy foreigners have taken advantage of coastal poverty to exploit women and children. And so, a transnational "rescue industry" (Agustin 2007)—a coalition of state, non-governmental, and other civil society groups—also grew its presence at the coast, seeking to curb "sex trafficking" and rehabilitate family life. In Mtwapa, NGOs such as Heshima Rescue Center, Mtomondoni Rescue Foundation, Shekina Rescue Center, and Kenya Care, among many others, worked, sometimes in collaboration with the police and the Chief's Office, to spearhead such efforts.

For this rescue industry, the life conditions of the Child (with a capital C)—what Lee Edelman (2004) aptly describes as an abstract emblem of intimate politics across the United States and its global empire—became symptomatic of collective capacities for social reproduction and national progress. Since the 1990s, in Kenya, transnational organizations such as Plan International have played an important role in reorienting national development away from masculinist and gerontocratic imaginaries of the post-independence state and toward women and, perhaps more so, children. James Smith (2008, 200) argues that "focusing on developing humans who embodied a potential future, Plan [International] representatives hoped that people would sacrifice their own interests for the larger good that children seemed to represent, fostering a sustainable politics morally grounded in the private sphere." In Kenya's Taita Hills, Smith shows, this focus on the "sovereign child," an imagined pre-political being of sacred innocence, has generated new intergenerational and gender conflicts. It has also prompted rumors that NGOs now sold local children to sponsors abroad: if sponsors fed Taita children, so the logic went, they would eventually come and claim them as their own (200–203). Over the last three decades, then, fears over the trafficking of children have coincided with a neoliberal market logic that blames the material and affective challenges children grow up with on failed familial intimacies rather than on political economic transformations.

As neighbors took neglected children to the police station and the police, NGOs, and orphanages actively sought to "rescue" children, there emerged a problem of trust: Were claims to "rescue" truthful acts or illicit ways to extract children from local parents and sell them to foreigners? Besi's story implies that, in a context of heightened danger, insecurity, and distrust, each person had to become some sort of a grassroots humanitarian in matters of intimacy and familial life. The story's hero, the "digital grandfather," takes over the securitizing function of the state to protect his granddaughter from the very same state agents meant to perform this role in the first place. Pursuing his family's safety, the grandfather thus becomes a good citizen. Besi did not explicitly criticize dominant discourses that blamed insecurity on citizens' intimate domains of life. Nevertheless, she drew attention to how state agents undermined families instead of protecting them, thus raising questions over the wider political and economic context in which intimacy appeared under the sign of rescue.

Two aspects of what I call intimate rescue are evident in the scene described above. First, the deployment of a grammar of rescue in relation to intimate life does not simply involve humanitarian elites, such as NGO, state, or religious leaders, but also those who are, initially at least, "beneficiaries" of such humanitarian interventions—in this case, sex workers. This striking insight allows us to think further of what Toni Morrison (1992, xxv–xxvi) describes as the debt incurred by the rescuer on the rescued (see the epigraph of this chapter), whereby "the rescuer wants to hear his name, not mimicked but adored" (xxvi). Such adoration presupposes that the rescued adopts the language of the rescuer and thus "loses his [sic] idiom, the language of his culture" (xxxvii). Adoration in Morrison echoes Frantz Fanon's (2008) "desire for lactification," the colonial subject's desire to become white, to adopt a white culture, which can help explain how the grammars of "rescue" come to be adopted so eagerly. Yet there is another aspect to this adoration, one that Morrison does not mention. Through the very act of rescue, the rescuer may also come to experience what Lacan (1977) calls the "desire of the Other"— the recognition of a wider community of like-minded people—here, a community of rescue. Thus, Besi and the women with whom she shared her story were not only beneficiaries of a humanitarian NGO, but, having already adopted and reworked some of its *modus operandi*, imagined themselves as part of a community of rescue.

Preoccupied with how sharp inequalities and extant forms of exploitation undermined rescue efforts, these women also wondered whom they could trust or not to bring about such moral redress. And this is my second point. The "digital grandfather" did not trust the police officer; Doty did not trust her neighbors, the court, and the orphanage; and Besi's very story emphasizes that instead of trusting others' salvational promises, people should become grassroots humanitarians on their own. Part of such a grassroots initiative would be precisely, as the "digital grandfather's" deeds suggest, learning to distinguish genuine from fake rescue. Despite this growing contestation of rescue, Besi did not simply do away with the term and its logics. Instead, she repurposed their meanings: for her, a more ethical or authentic kind of rescue was indeed possible *and* necessary. For her, *pace* Morrison, rescue could generate more than a dyadic relation (i.e., rescuer-rescued). If, on the one hand, rescue had the potential to bring about violent extraction and indebtedness, as Morrison suggests, on the other hand, it also produced moral forms of collective attachment: a community of rescuer-citizens. The challenge now was precisely learning to distinguish between real and deceptive forms of rescue in a context oversaturated with such salvational claims.

Intimate Rescue as Subjective Orientation

Listening to Besi, I wondered how the term "rescue" and its association with intimate domains of life may have become meaningful to her and to the women who listened to her story that day. In *Developing Partnerships*, Kate Bedford (2009) argues that, since the mid-1990s, intimacy has acquired globally new significance as a site of reformist interventions. The World Bank, the International Monetary Fund (IMF), and other international funding institutions have, in part, prompted this shift. Experts working for these organizations became aware that free markets with minimal government oversight, structural adjustment programs, and government cuts of social services have not led, as initially intended by the Washington Consensus of the 1980s, to economic growth. Instead, these reforms further exacerbated poverty. And so, international funding institutions urgently needed an alternative approach to development. They needed to involve states more actively, along with civil society groups, in building social safety nets to grapple with dilemmas of social reproduction.

Intimacy—a historically longstanding site of biopolitical governance (Stoler 2002)—became, once more, of ultimate importance to actualizing political economic transformations. World Bank experts, for example, sought to alleviate recent shifts in gender dynamics that had left women solely responsible for the unpaid labor of social reproduction and sidelined men altogether in development initiatives. Funding the reform of gender roles and relations, they hoped to redefine development as a "harmonious partnership," if mostly for heterosexual couples (Bedford 2009, xviii). Distinctive of this new approach, Bedford argues, are the "invocation of empowerment, self-government, and responsibility, and . . . attempts to engender changes at the highly intimate level of individual subjectivity as a condition for market success" (xv). Drawing on examples from Latin America—a "laboratory" for the Bank's new reformist interventions—Bedford shows that "complementary love within sharing couples is a central . . . part of the Bank's push to embed markets in more sustainable ways" (xii). "Poor people's intimate autonomy," says Bedford, "is hereby being reimagined . . . to cultivate particular attachments to resolve economic crises" (xxix).

If international funding institutions such as the World Bank and the IMF have set the stage globally for an ideology of intimate rescue, the proliferation of this ideology can certainly not be attributed solely to these institutions' top-down policies. Indeed, a salient push for intimate rescue has emerged also as part of a global backlash against such policies and globalization more generally. By the late nineties, having experienced the chokehold of structural adjustment programs for nearly two decades, leaders across the world came to see national intimacies as needing rescue, this time not *through* but *from* international donors and global markets. Amar (2013, 6) describes the ensuing pushback as having given rise across the Global South to the "human-security regime," a new mode of governance defined by "the forcible protection and moral rehabilitation of the citizenry, restoring dignity and 'humanity' to certain communities marked by gender, sexuality and culture and seen as menaced by the 'perversions of globalization.'" Rendering particular sexualized populations hypervisible and criminal, Amar argues, such initiatives have generated "new subjects of sexual rescue and emancipation around which this new brand of sovereignty and species of coercive governmentality coalesced" (31). Promising to secure morality and restore "traditional" gender, sexual, and familial arrangements, elites have sought to legitimize state capture, investments in state militarization, and various capital-building endeavors.

To a large extent, governance through intimate rescue is not new. Indeed, its intelligibility and symbolic currency for a wider national public rests precisely on its historical ties to the colonial civilizing mission and the central role intimate reforms played in nationalist struggles for independence. Colonial governance worked extensively through sexualization and securitization, whether in "black peril" scares, campaigns against polygyny, "free love," genital cutting, widow inheritance, and more (Hoad 2007; Magubane 2004; Stoler 2002; Thomas 2003). So, too, emerging nationalists sought to counter older racist colonial attributions of sexual perversion to the colonized by adopting modes of intimate governance premised on Christian or Islamic notions of respectability (see, for example, Ivaska 2011). What is new about intimate rescue in the present is perhaps the extent to which its performative claims have amplified—in part through mass mediation. New too might be the extent to which intimate rescue has become a key condition of good citizenship.

However, if intimate rescue is not just about the top-down policies of transnational organizations, it cannot also be reduced to the discourses and interventions of elites and leaders, whether past or present. Its cultural logics, as I have already suggested, have long embedded themselves in the mundane. Thus, a distinct kind of subject—what Malkki (2015, 2) describes as "*a humanitarian subject* characterized by a desire to help"—has long proliferated. This is, in part, a subject made by the state and NGOs but also one situated, partially, beyond these institutions' purview. Subjects of rescue reinvent themselves, Malkki argues, through "a gift *of* the self to an imagined other, but also a gift *to* the self," which allows them to be part of something greater than themselves, whether the nation or the world (9–10). Amidst the disorientations emerging with late capitalism's political economic transformations— new forms of mobility, consumption, and speculation—the subjective orientation of intimate rescue promises to anchor people in various nested totalities of belonging through the very act of transforming private life. Everyday experiences of intimacy become thus key scenes for the production of such attachments. So, as Clare Hemmings (2012, 130) aptly suggests, rather than disinvest from the intimate, "our current late capitalist political economy of misery and immiseration for those on the economic bottom re-invests the intimate sphere with a significance that it is always bound to fail to deliver." It is no surprise, then, that since the 1990s, in Kenya, intimacy has taken an ever-more-central position in public discourse (Spronk 2011)

Grewal (2017) argues that, in the United States and as part of its global imperial presence, the humanitarian subject comes to constitute the basis for "exceptional citizenship": "Naturalized as entrepreneurial and aspirational but also fearful and insecure," exceptional citizens "believe they can do more than the state and save the empire and the world" (4). These subjects seek out the state, even though they are suspicious of it, to secure privileges associated with good, respectable citizenship. By making the intimate into a perpetual scene of rescue, good citizens at once do the work of the state and defer conditions of personal gratification (material, sexual, emotional) to an indeterminate future (Berlant 2011). The logic runs something like this: *If I work hard to save intimate attachments in the present, I too may enjoy a good life one day in the future.* Grewal (2017, 120) discusses a fascinating American example of this type of subject-citizen: the "security mom," a woman who, for her family's safety, supports state securitization initiatives, including the "war on terror" or the "soft power" of U.S. humanitarian imperialism abroad. Notably, then, intimate rescue remains tied to the security state, while, at the same time, moving beyond it to involve complex forms of self-making and subjectivation across myriad sites and scales.

The grammars of intimate rescue then have a complex, multilayered genealogy: they emerge at the intersection of international funding organizations' discourses and those of ethno-nationalist institutions and leaders; and they draw on longstanding imperialist concerns with saving colonial Others as well as the late capitalist rise of humanitarianism, anti-trafficking, and securitization. What they then offer is a subjective orientation that does not exist in the abstract but is itself shaped dialectically by the historically specific scenes and objects that it animates and that may involve the Child, the homosexual, and the fake rescuer, among others. The pervasive intelligibility of the language and logics of "rescue" in humanitarianism, international economic policy, and thus also in people's everyday life makes intimate rescue meaningful and efficient—indeed, an important subjective orientation of late capitalism's zeitgeist.

When the Rescued Becomes the Rescuer

During the months Mary and I spent with Besi discussing our research or, over lunch or drinks, talking about her work, life, and plans for the future, we came to learn about how her experiences with the local rescue industry have shaped her sense of the self. Besi had moved to Mtwapa in 2000 at age eighteen. Because she had become pregnant before being married, her parents, respected Christians in the western Kenyan town of Eldoret, chased her away from home. She traveled to the coast to find her older sister, who had moved there a few years prior. But when she arrived in Mtwapa, her sister, who had secretly been engaging in sex work and did not want her family to find out, no longer picked up the phone. "There I was," Besi remembered, "standing with my bags at the Bondeni stage [minibus station] in Mombasa, asking people if they needed a maid." Besi found domestic work, but she soon learned that it was poorly paid (Ksh2,500 [about US$25] a month) and involved long working hours. Moreover, employees often abused domestic workers verbally or even beat them. So, Besi left this work after only one month. "I started making friends with women my age," she recalled. "So, I followed them and entered prostitution [S: *nikaingia umalaya*]." She had remained in Mtwapa ever since.

Besi's involvement with different NGOs began around the same time as her sex work. By 2003, she was the beneficiary of a German faith-based organization (FBO). Its Mtwapa branch was run by a Catholic nun who sought to "reform" female sex workers. Operating primarily with an anti-trafficking framework, this FBO offered religious education, attended to women's health, and provided small loans and micro-financial training for them to start various businesses. In 2009, Besi began collaborating with a smaller FBO, launched by a white evangelical couple from the United States. They too sought to rehabilitate sex workers through religion and microfinance projects. And, starting in 2014, Besi worked for GISRH, where—satisfied that, as she put it to me, laughing, "these ones no longer want to reform me" (S: *hawa hawataki kunireform*)—she was known as an exemplary peer educator and women's leader.

Besi's relationships with these organizations were ambivalent. On the one hand, she benefited from them. "The work that I've been doing with NGOs has saved my life," she told me on several occasions. During the seventeen years she spent in Mtwapa, numerous women she had been close to, including her older sister, died with AIDS. But her involvement with NGOs had allowed her to learn about HIV prevention early and protect herself. Furthermore, NGOs also offered her intermittent income opportunities. When I met her, Besi was earning likely as much money, if not more, from her collaborations with different NGOs as from sex work. Her income sources included workshop travel allowances, training funds, or payments for mobilizing sex workers for various research projects, a service that she has also offered to provide for Mary and me. On occasion, her connections to members of these organizations also allowed her access to medical care. During my fieldwork, Besi's younger sister discovered she was HIV-positive and, later on, Besi's teenage daughter secretly pursued a "roadside" abortion that left her severely ill. On both occasions, I saw Besi call her acquaintances at local NGOs, who, in turn, helped her family members with medical care.

On the other hand, Besi was also growingly disappointed with the elites leading these NGOs. She considered most of them corrupt and hypocritical, accumulating wealth while their "beneficiaries" continued to live in poverty. Her perception resonates with Eglė Česnulytė's (2020) research findings about the NGO sector attending to sex workers at the Kenyan coast. This sector, Česnulytė argues, "is built on the same structural inequalities that have pushed women into such occupations in the first place," and, therefore, "many NGOs either do not succeed in improving the lives of sex workers or manage to do so to a very limited extent" (29). When the American FBO had enrolled Besi as its beneficiary, she recalled, she had tried to meet their expectations. She stopped going out at night, attended church service regularly, fasted, and even began a small business with a micro-loan they had offered her. "But, at the end of the day," she said, "I would return from church and 'sleep on an empty stomach' [S: *nililala njaa*]." As if that were not enough, she often spotted the pastor, his wife, and the other NGO leaders eating at expensive restaurants along Mtwapa's main road. "I told myself: 'If this is how it goes, let me just go back to my work on the street and forget all about the church and the organization.'" So, Besi sold off her business, used the money to pay up her rent for several months in advance, and never set foot in that organization's office again. During my fieldwork, one of the leaders of this FBO recalled Besi to me paternalistically as "a good girl," but one who "struggles and slips back a lot."

Amidst this ambivalent relationship with humanitarian organizations, Besi crafted her own subjective orientation and sense of ethical obligation. It is thus that she now employed the term of "rescue" and its logics in ways that related more strongly to her sense of right and wrong and less to the elitist projects of the NGOs that had employed and trained her. Her repurposing of rescue is an instance of what Lorway (2020) observes as Kenyan sex workers' growing "entanglement" in—resistance to and reworking of—the scientific, technocratic, and humanitarian repertoire of public health organizations. But, if in some regards Besi's efforts were continuous with and premised on the grammars of global humanitarianism and the security state, they were also not simply reducible to them. Indeed, her mundane deeds, desires, and deceptions expanded and reworked these logics in unexpected ways.

Throughout the months I spent meeting with Besi, she told many stories in which she depicted herself as having "rescued" members of her community. On one occasion, she found out from a teen boy who lived in her residential plot that an older man had paid him money to watch porn in his company. Besi decided to give the boy Ksh100 (US$1) to take her to the man's house and help set him up so that the police would catch him in the act. Besi understood this as a way to "rescue" the boy and protect other teens from sexual predation. On another occasion, she "rescued" two gay men from an angry crowd in Mtwapa that wanted to lynch them. Neighbors who found the men having sex in a room on their residential plot had called for "mob justice." Scandalized that gayism now occurred in residential plots where families raised their children, they too sought to "rescue" their community. For, as Edelman (2004, 28) argues, "the sacralization of the Child . . . [often] necessitates the sacrifice of the queer." Yet Besi had a more compassionate view. Not only were many gay men her fellow sex workers, but, she reasoned, "these men did their own thing without abusing anyone. What business do people have killing them?"

What different people considered worth rescuing was highly contested. If Besi, for example, saw her saving of the two gay men from the angry crowd as "rescue," those neighbors and others who beat them saw their actions through a similar prism. The residential plot was a quintessential intimate scene, where poor families lived close to one another, often without the privacy of middle-class homes. Many perceived this proximity as dangerous. Such proximity threatened the Child, as an emblem of futurity and rescue efforts. Certainly, with heightened distrust among neighbors and toward NGO and state agents, the authenticity of "rescue" was itself uncertain.

But, despite this, what is interesting to me is precisely the *common sense* that, indeed, today, *intimate life needs rescue*. This is a permeating logic that various social actors shared despite the sharp differences in how they imagined the directionality or authenticity of different rescue efforts. The logics of rescue involved all sorts of objects—the Child, the homosexual body, and so on—producing, in turn, subjects growingly preoccupied with the qualities and potentials of their intimate lives. Intimate rescue, I now turn to show, has also become meaningful to how people imagined themselves as part of various political totalities, whether residential plots, villages, neighborhoods, regions, or the nation itself.

The Nation as a "Community of Affliction"

Meeting Besi reminded me of Meja Mwangi's (2000) *The Last Plague*, an intriguing Kenyan novel I had recently read. Like Besi, the novel's main heroine, Janet, relates to the community where she lives and works through everyday acts of intimate rescue. In the face of the 1990s AIDS pandemic, Janet seeks to share scientific medical knowledge about sexual behavior, risk, and prevention with people in her rural town. She seeks to intervene in their domestic arrangements where, as she sees it, masculine entitlement, polygamy, and widow inheritance have helped spread HIV with catastrophic outcomes. Hired by the government to distribute condoms, Janet walks daily from one homestead to another, often only to be chased away by locals who feel insulted by her claims, as a woman, to a new, superior kind of knowledge about sex. Yet Janet persists. And her persistence is central to the novel's moral message: that good citizens must continuously seek to rescue others, even when faced with doubt, suspicion, or hate.

Set in a generic rural town, suggestively called Crossroads, the story unfolds against a backdrop of sheer intimate disorder and decay. And it is this context that makes Janet's efforts both meaningful and urgent. "The imminent end of Crossroads," we learn, is approaching "like a runaway juggernaut, crashing down and breaking up everything that lay in its path" (Mwangi 2000, 4). "Most of the lodgings and the shops and the bars had long closed down, moved elsewhere or simply died in anticipation of death" (4). "The plague destroyed everything," the narrator says.

> It ate into relationships and severed unseverable bonds. It exploded havens of faith and trust and caused mayhem and anarchy in all abodes of hope. Aids [sic] was the greatest confounder Crossroads had ever known. And because few people understood it, the fear it instilled was irrational as it was terrible.

Wives distrusted their husbands and husbands suspected their wives. Whole families accused one another of witchcraft. It seemed there was no purpose to life anymore. (55)

"Severed unseverable bonds," "mayhem," "anarchy," and "fear" describe a context in which intimacy—the "abodes of hope," couples, and families—are growingly disoriented by distrust, suspicion, and mutual accusations. This context echoes Macharia's (2020, 566) notion of "intimate disorganization"— a longstanding colonial trope in the rendition of Black Africa as backward, premodern, "belated" to the global scene of modernity. Like in Besi's case, Janet's own familial arrangements had also broken down. Disapproving of her marrying a Christian, Janet's parents, recent converts to Islam, cut off all ties with her. Abandoned then by her husband who ran off to Mombasa to chase dreams of quick riches, she is left to care alone for her three children. Only Janet's grandmother, a conservative elderly woman, is left to remind her daily that, without a man by her side, she will have failed as a woman.

Interestingly, however, despite the state of intimate disorganization she inhabits, Janet does not figure in the novel as a failed woman. Quite the contrary. She is the novel's heroine precisely because she seeks to redress this state of affairs. She is adamant that "Crossroads can and will be saved" (42). Rescue, for her, is a way to pursue intimate order in a time of intimately perceived disorganization, disorientation; it is a way to be a good citizen. But in whose eyes is Janet a good citizen? What is her community of social value, if, in Crossroads, she appears to be, if anything, a lonely, stigmatized fighter? Where is the Big Other, to use Lacan's term, that is, the place whence springs the recognition that renders Janet's deeds legible, legitimate, and morally meaningful? What makes Janet a good citizen is not her obeying or working for the state. The state is otherwise absent in the novel, as it has been, throughout the nineties, in many Kenyan rural settings. If the state indeed provides Janet with the condoms she distributes, it is not responsible for the passion and persistence with which she not only distributes them but goes beyond her mandated duties to help and educate others. Neither does the moral recognition of her deeds spring solely from the small community of support she eventually builds around herself. One realizes eventually that it is precisely the reader who is invited—or, one might say, interpellated—to be such a source of recognition. This is most likely an educated, middle-class Kenyan who is already well familiar with the language and logics of postcolonial humanitarianism. Like Janet, the reader must see rescue as modern, rational, and necessary and, therefore, imagine her as a member of a national community which, in turn, values her deeds as acts of good citizenship. "Exceptional citizens," let us recall Grewal's (2017, 4) point, are those who "believe they can do more than the state and save . . . the world." It is not Crossroads then but an imagined national public that bestows upon Janet such recognition. In other words, if Janet's subjectivity is a desire for the desire of the Big Other, it is precisely the national public that represents this Other. For this public, Crossroads and its intimacies exist merely as peripheral, abject scenes in need of intimate rescue. In intervening upon and helping reform Crossroads, Janet's deeds are indeed also acts of nation-building.

Janet also invites the novel's readers to be part of something greater than themselves—in this case, the nation not only as an "imagined community" (Anderson 1991), but also a community constituted through the afflictions to which its good citizens attend. The nation becomes thus a "community of affliction." Victor Turner (1968) uses this term to describe a set of cults meant to redress bodily and social life among the Ndembu in Northern Rhodesia. During Turner's fieldwork, in the early 1950s, British colonial occupation, land dispossession, and labor crisis posed new challenges for the authority of Ndembu chiefs and their matrilineal kinship relations. Says Turner, "It was as though the whole community was in recoil from a sharp blow to its self-esteem" (1968, 93). This sense of crisis manifested, in part, through all kinds of bodily and societal afflictions. Revisiting Turner, Brad Weiss (2004, 2) describes these cults of affliction as "collective, ritual acts aimed at recapturing the lost, occluded, or ensnared powers of full social participation and reproduction." In Mwangi's novel, as in the contemporary Kenyan context, "communities of affliction" that rescue and redress bodies and intimate domains of life ultimately revitalize collective attachments.

If good citizens, like Janet (or Besi), are people who pursue rescue, then the nation itself comes to be imagined as a "community of affliction." This perception is evident across Kenyan popular culture and religious life. Children's storybooks with names such as *Resuscitating Kenya: United Nations to the Rescue* (2012) or *Tumi to the Rescue* (2020) (see fig. 4) depict respectively Kenya as a "happy patient" of Global North political rescue efforts or, reversely, good Kenyan citizens (like Tumi, a young Somali Kenyan girl) as superheroes who rescue others. Kenyan movies, such as *Mission to Rescue* (Foxton Media 2021), celebrate the state's militarized counterterrorism efforts as ways to "rescue" its citizens from Al-Shabaab violence. And the list could go on. Across these examples, the subject of intimate rescue is the emblematic national citizen—people like the "digital grandfather" in Besi's story or Janet in Mwangi's novel, who take it upon themselves to redress collective life. Echoes here also of the rising popularity of Pentecostal modes of self-making in the present: here, as Barbara Bompani and Caroline Valois (2018, 19) argue,

FIGURE 4. Kenyan children's storybooks featuring "rescue" as good citizenship.

"the relationship of the Christian citizen ultimately does not reside with the state, [but] rather with the greater objective of establishing a biblical model of a reborn nation, thus validating their duty to act as agents of change not for the postcolonial state but for the prospective nation."

Sexualized Peripheries, Spectral Cores

To become a good citizen in Kenya was, in part, to act as a subject of rescue in a national geography of various imagined moral peripheries that needed such rescue, places such as the fictional Crossroads in Mwangi's novel. "Tell me something about Maralal," Rose said. By then I had already been waiting for nearly one hour at KEMRI's reception to talk to the organization's director. When he had introduced me to Rose a few days prior, she had asked me where I had learned to speak the Swahili language. I told her then that I had lived and done research in Maralal, the headquarters of Samburu County. Rose, like most non-northerners I knew on the coast, had never been as far up north as Maralal. Many Kenyans associated Samburu County with an inhospitable environment and harsh living conditions. "Heee, that place is very far," Rose said. "And I hear there is a lot of HIV there. Those pastoralists, they have high rates of HIV. You know they have those morans and they spread HIV."

Rose's comment drew on longstanding colonial stereotypes of ethnic sexuality that have associated the indigenous population of Samburu County with promiscuity, hypersexuality, and STIs. British colonialists had deployed such discourses to legitimize morally their militarized occupation of pastoralist land, the near incarceration of Samburu people in a closed ethnic enclave, and various other biopolitical interventions (Kasfir 2007, 46–58; Meiu 2017, 40–56; Straight 2020; Waweru 2012, 161–71). The morans that Rose mentioned, young men of the "warrior" age grade, have been at the forefront of such reformist interventions since the 1920s. Colonial administrators and missionaries blamed cattle raiding, interethnic wars, and homicide on the morans' allegedly excessive carnal desires, on their desires to impress women and gain their sexual favors. And so, if controlling Samburu meant disciplining morans, morans, and, through them, Samburu ethnicity, became sexualized. Following Kenya's independence in 1963, this imaginary continued to mark Samburu as a sexualized periphery of the nation. Since the early 2000s, this imaginary has also prompted numerous development workers, including middle-class Samburu, to identify the region as a "hotspot" for humanitarian work with a focus on HIV/AIDS, orphans, child sexuality, and teenage pregnancies.

But sexualized stereotypes also framed the coast, and especially Mtwapa, as a moral periphery of the nation. Mtwapa's spectacular growth from a cluster of three fisher villages of a few thousand residents in the seventies to a town of 51,000 inhabitants by 2010 was largely a product of Kenya's rising beach tourism and its sexual economies. Kenyans knew Mtwapa as the country's "sin city," the "Kenyan Las Vegas," or the nation's "Sodom and Gomorrah." Since the nineties, male and female retirees from Switzerland, Germany, and Italy moved more permanently to Mtwapa, where they built houses and lived with Kenyan partners. All along, the town's ill repute grew and fascinated. A Kenyan journalist describes how "at night, the town comes to life with sin that can put Sodom and Gomorrah to shame."[2] "If you visit Mtwapa," *Business Daily* warns, "you are encouraged to toss any sanctimonious morality crown you may be wearing into a dustbin . . . The most outstanding social element of this town . . . emanates from a lack of a morality . . ."[3]

So ingrained were stereotypes about Mtwapa that my very working there often raised eyebrows among elite friends and colleagues. In 2017, when I attended an event at a university in Nairobi, the university's vice chancellor came to greet me enthusiastically, having heard I was, at that time, a professor at Harvard. "Where in Kenya do you live?" he then proceeded to ask me courteously. I told him I lived in Mtwapa. Speechless, he bit his lower lip all-too-knowingly, nodded politely, and—without another word—moved on to talk to other people. A graduate student who noticed our interaction later advised me, laughing, that in the future, I should simply say I lived in Mombasa. "Mtwapa has a very, very bad reputation," she said.

But the sexualization of places like Mtwapa or Samburu County was not simply about downright moral condemnation. People also knew Mtwapa as a place of exceptional tolerance. Gay friends in Nairobi and Mombasa, for example, pointed out to me in 2010 that *California*, at that time one of Kenya's only two gay clubs, was located in Mtwapa (the other, *Gypsies*, was in Nairobi). Similarly, those of them who knew I worked in Samburu County often teased me to "admit" that same-sex intimacies were common in the age grade of the morans. "You mean to tell me that those morans who stay at cattle camps for months without girls don't do things with each other?" they would say. "Bro, please!" By contrast, others romanticized Samburu as a customary heteronormative haven. A straight colleague, who knew I was gay, warned me in 2009 that in Samburu, "a moran will take out his *panga* [machete] and cut you with it if you only as much as look at his ass." Regardless of whether the place was imagined as tolerant or intolerant, a "homoromantic" precolonial haven or a bastion of customary heteronormativity, such discourses reproduced sexualized national peripheries as what Ghassan Moussawi (2020) calls "fractal Orientalism."

Sexual stereotypes have, no doubt, shaped political economic circumstances. In Samburu, such stereotypes have served as ideological alibis for the government to defer indeterminately investment in infrastructure, schooling, health and the well-being of the indigenous population. Bad or inaccessible roads, poverty, and illiteracy have also meant that elites could extract commodities and labor from northern regions at very low costs, while importing foreign goods to Samburu at much higher prices than elsewhere in Kenya. Northerners, to be sure, perceived their region's ongoing marginality as an extension of colonialism, a deferral of their full citizenship in the Kenyan state.

In Mtwapa, the political economy of sexualization worked somewhat differently. Because the town brought in significant revenues, government administrators had interest in both tolerating its sexual economies and protecting its revenues. In this context, Mtwapa's sexual ill repute worked as a strategy of surplus value extraction: sex workers, cab operators, bar and brothel owners, and others had to pay bribes to officials and police to have their activities temporarily exempted from the rule of law. Such bribes, as Besi once told me, were known as *kakitu cha macho*, "something small for the eyes," or perhaps better translated as a payment "for closing one's eyes." But there was also a striking similarity between Samburu County and Mtwapa as sexualized moral peripheries of the nation. In both places sexualized stereotypes rendered "legitimate" the rapid expansion of a rescue industry that involved NGOs, CBOs, FBOs, churches, charities, and government offices and actors. For these institutions, what they saw as the *exceptional* situation of intimate and sexual life in these places underscored the urgency of reformist interventions and also made obtaining international funding easier.

It is important to ask, then, what moral positions did *posing* such sexualized peripheries produce? This question is central to understanding the subject of intimate rescue as a "good citizen." The "core" in relation to which these places figured as moral peripheries was not a stable locus. If, to some extent, this "core" could be imagined as the capital city of Nairobi, the country's middle class, or its nationalist elite, I want to suggest that we think of it more complexly. This "core" is rather a shifting, subjectively assumed moral position. Assuming this position represents a claim to national belonging and citizenship. Although norms and aspirations of intimate rescue can be loosely recognized as Christian and "middle class," and although many of those who spearheaded humanitarian projects in both Maralal and Mtwapa were in a middle-class income bracket, others were not. Those engaged in various mundane intimate projects—sex workers like Besi, for example—were, in fact, poor. Indeed, many poor embraced intimate rescue as a way of self-making, of pursuing value and belonging through means widely recognized as respectable.

Throughout this book, the reader will encounter the "middle class" as a spectral position, one constantly haunted by that which it disavows as peripheral, as beyond itself. On the one hand, middle-classness comes to be associated with particular styles, commodities, milieus, and normative attachments (Spronk 2012; Stoll 2018). On the other hand, being middle class is haunted by a sense of existential uncertainty. TV shows on Kenyan national television such as *Auntie Boss* or *The Real Househelps of Kawangware* illustrate this beautifully: key dramas here are the danger of the maid that seduces the husband or the teenage son of the middle-class household that employs her; the threat of the bodaboda (motorcycle cab) driver who sleeps with the mother of the middle-class home; the village cousin who brings bad (sexual) manners into the house of his/her urban kin; and so on. These TV shows draw their humor from this shared existential uncertainty over being or becoming middle class, a topic to which I return in chapters 3 and 5. Other programs, such as the moral advice show *Bi Msafwari* on Citizen TV, guide middle-class heterosexual couples on how to manage their relationships to each other, maids, garden boys, bodaboda, and others to secure themselves from the dangers that lurk in their intimate lives.

✶

At a very basic level, the subject of intimate rescue is premised on the opposition between those who help and those who need to be helped in situations of intimate trouble. This opposition requires myriad, shifting moral peripheries and objects against which those who perform various acts of rescue may position themselves as occupying a moral core. This orientation is fractal: rescue could be directed toward whole regions or towns known as morally peripheral or simply toward particular moralized social categories, such as sex workers. But intimate rescue is not merely premised on a dyadic relationship between the rescued and the rescuer. In fact, it is very much a threesome, as it were, one that also involves the perceived gaze of a national public for which intimate rescue is emblematic of good citizenship. Like the Lacanian Big Other, the imagined national community—here, a community of affliction whose main role is to redress and securitize normative intimate arrangements—informs mundane acts of rescue, making them meaningful. But rescue, as we shall see, is a way to both bring various sexual Others into the normative arrangements of a heteropatriarchal nation *and* assert their Otherness as a mode of normative self-making. This then is also a central paradox of the subject of intimate rescue.

3

"Male-Power":
Virility, Vitality, and Phallic Rescue

> ... the phallus, as the central signifier of power and the prerogative of male domination, has been radically undermined ... In the cultural cartography of the end of the twentieth century, we find ourselves confronted with a phallic dynamic which, more than before, is a field of multiple mobilities.
>
> ACHILLE MBEMBE

"I saw I had a certain weakness," said Kevin, a forty-year-old Uber driver, in March 2017, as he drove my partner and me to a shopping mall at Mombasa's north coast. We had met Kevin two months prior when we moved to Mtwapa and, since then, had relied on him for transport. "Sometimes, when ladies ask you to give them a ride at night," he continued, "they can try to seduce you to sleep with them." Nightlife along the Mombasa-Kilifi highway, on which Mtwapa is located, attracts numerous tourists, businessmen, migrants, and sex workers. Working at night allowed Kevin to earn relatively well. But night shifts had their pitfalls, he said. "When you drive these ladies back home, they can even tell you they don't have any money to pay. So, they want to give you that other thing instead." Sex, he meant. "I saw that this weakness of mine can affect my family," he added. "So, I had to do something about it." A few weeks prior to our conversation, Kevin enrolled in a course that a Pentecostal church offered for men. "These are lessons about how to live your life as a good Christian, a good man ... You come to realize what it is that you are doing wrongly, and you try to change."

Sex-for-money exchanges of the kind Kevin described are common at the coast. Taxi drivers and motorbike cab operators, so-called *bodaboda*, routinely engage in sex with female passengers. As one bodaboda explained to me, this is "a way to find pleasure after a hard day's work." For some women, men in the transport business are also attractive because, as one woman put it, "though they're not rich, they handle a lot of money every day." But such relationships also attract social opprobrium. "It is these *malaya* [prostitutes] that are destroying our young men [S: *wanaharibu vijana wetu*]," Fatima, a middle-aged development worker, protested in Swahili. She and I were among some twenty participants in a workshop on young men's struggles, hosted by a community-based organization in March 2017, in Mtwapa. A participant interrupted Fatima, pointing out that it was wrong for her to use the derogatory word *malaya* to refer to sex workers. She smiled dismissively and continued: "Women are coming here from all over the country. And they go out at night and seduce men. And they go for low prices. So, they are causing a lot of trouble." She sighed. "Our young men have become very weak," she said. To highlight her last two words, she switched to English: *Very weak*. Fatima's reasoning resonates with narratives I heard among other development workers, political leaders, and religious reformists. These narratives depict men who continuously pay women for sex as becoming "weak" and blame women for "destroying" them. Sex workers I interviewed said that drivers and bodaboda actively asked them for sex in exchange for rides. Yet they commonly took the blame for men's "weakness."

Being seduced by women, people said, drains men of *nguvu*, energy or power, and prevents them from building decent livelihoods. Kevin agreed with this common sentiment. He had moved to the coast in 2005 from a village near Kakamega, western Kenya, in search of work opportunities he knew he could not have found upcountry. For the past few years, he worked as a taxi and, more recently, Uber driver, earning some Ksh30,000–40,000 (ca. US$300–400) per month. This income allowed him, his wife, and their three daughters to lead what can be described as a "lower middle-class" life. They rented a self-contained one-bedroom apartment, sent their children to public schools, and occasionally took family vacations at their rural home near Kakamega. Kevin, however, aspired to earn more money in the coming years. For one thing, he hoped to purchase a car. Like most taxi or Uber drivers at the coast, he had been driving someone else's car for a percentage of the generated income. Driving his own car, he thought, could make him more money. But, Kevin said, struggles with sex and alcohol had slowed him down. To realize his dream, he had first to work on himself. So, encouraged by his wife and the pastor of their Pentecostal church, he enrolled in a course that sought to rehabilitate men struggling with "addictions" (S: *uraibu*).

In recent years, the idea that men have turned weak has become widespread in Kenya. Many Kenyans blame the "destruction of men"—their becoming depressed, unable to work, or, some claim, impotent—on excessive sex, alcohol, drugs, gambling, or various ways of chasing quick money. In response, different churches, NGOs, and community organizations have initiated courses and workshops to rescue men. For example, a flyer that circulated with the *Daily Nation* in 2015 advertises courses offered by the Wells of Hope Ministries, a Christian NGO (fig. 5). It promises "to rehabilitate and impart skills to our men [who are] on the verge of destruction." Two images

FIGURE 5. Flyer advertising a fundraiser and course to rehabilitate men. Wells of Hope Educational Ministries, Kenya, July 2015.

on the left side of the flyer depict the decadent state of contemporary men: one shows a presumably drunk man lying on his back in a puddle of mud; the other, a group of men sitting bored in what looks like a roadside bar. They sip cheap alcohol, through straws, from shared plastic containers. Similar images in the national press and on social media portray emaciated male bodies in dirty clothes, sitting idly or lying on the ground, as emblematic of men's vital depletion. In sharp contrast to the first two images, two portraits on the right side of the flyer depict men in upright positions, wearing elegant suits and ties, and smiling contentedly. Juxtaposing these two sets of images, the ad promises a radical transformation: "from this . . ." ". . . to this." "Return my image (Man) to my position," pleads the male beneficiary imagined by the ad, "and I will restore Kenya." Good citizenship, the ad implies, starts with men working on their vices and vitality.

Rescuing men, in this context, means claiming gender roles that have been central to national ideologies of masculine authority, citizenship, and reproduction. This process often involves women as much as men in running male rehabilitation programs. Interviewed by the *Daily Nation*, Joyce Mugambi, the director of Wells Hope Ministries, said that Kenyans "have lost many men to illicit alcohol and drugs," a trend that risks "to finish [off] generations." "I have decided to reverse all this," she said, "and to rebuild [men's] ego and position of authority and return [them to] leadership in the family." Women like Mugambi play leading roles as what Grewal (2017) calls "security feminists"—"exceptional citizens" who undertake the work of the state by securitizing gender, morality, and intimacy. In recent decades, Pentecostal—but also, perhaps to a lesser extent, Catholic and Anglican—churches have played a pivotal role in reforming men in Africa and elsewhere (Boyd 2015; Burchardt 2018a; Sommers 2001; Thornton 2016; Van Klinken 2013). Kevin's family participated actively in the Sunday programs of a Pentecostal church in Mombasa, and, as I found out when I visited their home later that year, his wife was studying to become a minister. Encouraging Kevin to enroll in classes for men, she hoped he would "find strength" to avoid "temptations" and provide better for his family. Like churches, NGOs and government offices also ran public health and vocational training programs to restore ideals of respectable masculinity.

Beyond institutions, rescue logics have come to play a central role in everyday life, with men working on themselves by helping to rehabilitate others. "Now, when I pick up a lady at night," Kevin said, "I just drive her home or to where she wants to go and try not to think about those things. I can even tell her that what she is doing [i.e., sex work] is not good and help her see that there are other ways." Because, clearly, not all his customers were willing to discuss their livelihoods with him, Kevin devised another way to communicate with them: he played gospel music in his car. "Some of these ladies laugh at me and tell me to turn it off. They come from the disco. They say: 'What kind of music is that?' So, I have to turn it off." In such cases, Kevin, who kept copies of gospel music CDs in his car, offered them as presents to his customers at the end of the ride. "These songs have very good messages," he promised.

After Kevin shared his personal struggles with my partner and me, I wondered why he might have chosen to do so. Although we had already known him for two months, at that point, we had shared little of our own lives with him. For example, he most likely did not know that we were gay or a couple, things we preferred to share only with close friends or other gay people. Although Kevin knew that I was a university professor doing research on gender and sexuality and that my partner was, at that time, a researcher at the same institution, he might also have seen us as two unattached, straight, cis-gender white men. That we spent time in Mtwapa could have meant that we, like numerous white male tourists and expats, were there for women and sex. Indeed, Kevin often picked me up with his car from bars and cafes known for sex work, where I would meet with research interlocutors. Sharing his intimate struggles with us, Kevin might thus have tried to help us reform ourselves too. I cannot know this for sure.

But narrating his experience was probably also pleasurable and energizing because, in helping others, his confession also claimed and performed good citizenship. Confessional narratives such as the one he offered are common techniques of subjectivity and citizenship in both evangelical Christianity and humanitarian rescue (Burchardt 2018a; Grewal 2017; Lorway 2014). "Telling the truth about oneself," Marian Burchardt (2018b, 173) argues, "replete with instances of leaving behind or moving out of states of ignorance or blindness and seeing the light of truth and wisdom, unfolded as staged and highly dramatic performances of authenticity in which powerful claims to subjectivity and personhood were made." By helping restore a gender order widely recognized as foundational to national citizenship, it is possible that Kevin recognized himself in—and thus felt himself desired by—the current zeitgeist: a time when the state, religious and humanitarian organizations, and citizens find a common ground in the moral rehabilitation of men and their intimacies.

What do preoccupations with men, their alleged "weakness" or vital depletion, reveal about intimacy and citizenship today? How are vitality, vigor, strength, and life force gendered in this context? And why does male vitality revolve so strongly around questions of sex and sexual potency? So-called "male-power" (S: *nguvu za kiume*) refers to a distinctly gendered energy that pivots centrally around genitality: a man's ability to sustain an erection, have sex, and produce offspring. Indeed, weak men often figure in public discourse as impotent, unable to sire children, build families, and gain respect. It is also in relation to anxieties over depleting sexual virility that male-power has become a prominent commodity: bottled liquid, powder, or pills on sale with herbalists, witch doctors, or physical therapists. Flyers advertising medicinal male-power hint to how, in this context, men's ability to have an erection is metonymic of their bodily strength and vitality as well as of their capacity to build a future (see fig. 6).

It is this objectified vitality I take on as my queer object in this chapter. If, in some instances, male-power appears as an obvious object—a thing you can buy or sell—in other instances, its objecthood is less obvious, yet legible from the materiality of men's bodies and the various tokens of their productive and reproductive labor, their wealth and well-being. In yet other instances, male-power, often ambivalent and indeterminate, may shift its locus across signifiers as varied as guns, motorbikes, cars, engines, clothing styles, the body in motion, or, ultimately, the very act of rescue. Akin to what Lacan (1985) calls the "phallus"—the dominant signifier of a subject's social desirability—male-power becomes a hegemonic object in citizens' quests for self-fulfillment. Its rescue, cultivation, and maintenance are thus central avenues to good citizenship. Thinking of male-power with postcolonial feminist critiques of the

FIGURE 6. Flyer advertising *Nkoma Power* brand of medicinal male-power, circulating on Kenyan social media platforms in 2019.

phallus, I suggest that this object is pivotal to what Alexander (2005) calls "heteropatriarchal recolonization": attempts by the postcolonial state, elites, and civil society actors to secure power by redeploying—if in new ways— older, colonial investments in heterosexuality. Male-power reorients citizen desire toward particular gender and sexual hierarchies and legitimizes an image of the nation as founded on gender-conforming citizens engaged in patriarchal, heterosexual forms of intimacy.

Like the other queer objects discussed in this book, male-power is not "queer" in itself. If anything, it remains a key fetish of national heteropatriarchy. But, at the same time, following this object across the different social terrains in which it is being cultivated and contested reveals how the sexual subject of national ideologies is itself fragile, prone to failure: this object's elusiveness, its ability to shift unexpectedly, to leak, or to empower and enliven women over men, poor youths over powerful big-men, demonstrates that it remains in excess of heteropatriarchal logics, an excess that rescue projects often try to surveil, police, contain. Along the way, as we shall see, such quests for a normative kind of vitality also co-opt—and manifest through—anxieties over generation, ethnicity, gender, and homosexuality, among other things.

"Weak Men": A National Dilemma

"Kenya's young men are now the weaker sex," writes Kimani wa Njuguna for the *Daily Nation* in 2015.[1] Many people, he adds, speak of young men as "Blue Band boys," a phrase that invokes the name of a well-known Kenyan brand of margarine, which the current generation of young men grew up consuming. Unlike foods deemed traditional, like roasted meat, which is believed to strengthen men's bodies, margarine is a modern, urban food said to soften them. Indexing fluidity and malleability, margarine signifies a particular state of bodily duress: the *lack* of vigor, virility, strength, or assertiveness. Referring to adult men as Blue Band boys is, no doubt, infantilizing and emasculating. But the phrase also captures a distinct material property of "weakness" that men's bodies appear to share with margarine. Similarly, in Samburu County, I encountered the term "*mutuma* boys," coined in the 1990s to designate young rural men said to waste their time in towns, drinking millet porridge (S: *uji*) from large-sized cups known as *mutuma*. Like the Blue Band boys, mutuma boys were said to be weak, strengthless, and lazy, sharing in the fluid properties of the porridge they consumed. Both porridge and margarine then were metaphors of a certain liquification, a loss of bodily firmness or containment. Poor parenting, absent or unreliable father figures, and the decline of family values, wa Njuguna suggests, are responsible for rising numbers of weak men. "The current crisis facing the boy child," he warns, "is a national one."

Depleting male vitality also liquifies what appear to be otherwise lasting material tokens of authority and prestige, including land, cattle, monetary savings, or real estate. In 2017, in the *Standard*, Martin Muthai describes a man from Nakuru County, who had been laid off from work, "a weak bone who couldn't match up . . . energy sapping work. . . . gave up and turned to idling at the local pub and drinking himself silly." One day, Muthai recalls, the man's wife walked into the pub to find him treating his friends to alcohol after, unbeknownst to her, he had sold the family's land.[2] What makes the story interesting for its intended audience is how the loss of men's vitality also renders fluid seemingly durable media of wealth, leaving families poor: land turns into alcohol, further weakening men's bodies. So, if the body's normative firmness should anchor both property and men's authority, losing this firmness means exponentially losing everything.

In 2015, *Daily Nation*'s Magesha Ngwiri decries:

> [A] whole generation of youth has gone to waste, and the whole [central] region has become "a village of the damned." The evidence is there for all to see, for the number of drunken zombies staggering all over is proliferating at an alarming rate. Young men are no longer doing any productive work; nor are they siring offspring, for they can rarely rise to the occasion, and even if they did, they have no means of looking after their families . . . The only saving grace is that they are too weak to mug, rob, or do much more damage than steal chickens and sugarcane, for which they are routinely jailed.

For Ngwiri, men's loss of vitality has catastrophic implications for the wider social totalities to which they belong, including their generations and local communities. Too "weak" to work, steal, or reproduce, young men, he suggests, have turned into "drunken zombies," "a generation gone to waste," "a village of the damned." Most notably, for Ngwiri, men's inability to reproduce— "to rise to the occasion"—is metonymic of a more general depletion of their vigor. In recent years, some Kenyans have referred to this vital lack as *maisha bila steam*, "life without steam," speaking of weak men as *wenye wameishiia moto*, "those who are out of energy" (S: *moto* also means "fire"), a phrase commonly used to describe discharged mobile phones. In principle, "steam," "fire," or even "electricity" (S: *stima*) can designate the vital energetics of both male *and* female bodies. However, in my experience, these phrases are used more commonly with reference to men, thus inextricably tying vitality to virility, the energies of the male body to those of youths (S: *vijana*) and the nation (S: *taifa*)—the latter two categories, as we shall see, highly masculinized.

With late capitalism, across the globe, discourses on a so-called "crisis of masculinity" have made impotence emblematic of men's rapidly transforming social positions. Afflictions of male virility have come to express collective anxieties over a wider political economy, in which men's capacity to work and reproduce appears strained (Bonhomme 2016). Everett Zhang (2015), for example, shows how, in post-Maoist China, claims of an "impotence epidemic" have captivated the national imagination, giving rise to new genres of medicine, food, and literature meant to help men regain their virility. "Impotence," Zhang argues, "was experienced as a disturbance resulting from multiple forces of social transformation," including market incitements to consumption and pleasure and men's inability to respond to them (12). In Mexico, Matthew Gutmann (2007) shows, men struggle to negotiate and cultivate virility amidst the growing medicalization of their sexual lives, HIV/AIDS, and transformations of social reproduction. This is made more difficult, Gutmann argues, by a dominant tendency in public reproductive health to "totemize" men's sexuality—to assume its assertiveness as natural—and render pathological the lack or diminishment of their libido. Concerns over men's sexual potency have also proliferated across Europe, North America, Latin America, and the Middle East (e.g., Inhorn 2012; Kilshaw 2009; Wentzell 2013).

In Kenya, this global trend has intersected with older colonial and postcolonial discourses and tactics of power. From the early days of British colonial rule, anxieties over men in general and young men in particular have been central to the making of the state. As Paul Ocobock (2017, 15) shows, "very intimate conversations took place between the state and young men about acceptable forms of manliness, sexuality, and maturity as well as the outlets through which to express those feelings," including, among other things, "sports, hard work, education, and marriage." Colonial reformists instituted white bourgeois and Christian notions of respectable masculinity as "universal" to the imperial regime of power. In response, African customary institutions of socialization, including initiation or age-set rituals, either declined or became construed as dangerous, insurgent forces (Maina 2017; White 1990). For example, because colonials saw East African warrior traditions as driven by men's excessive desire to impress women and gain their sexual favors, controlling men became tantamount to controlling their sexuality (Meiu 2017, 50–56). Kenyan elites reemployed this assumption in their own reforms of poor men's sexual desires.

Following independence, a new type of masculinity came to be both celebrated and vilified in the national imaginary. Tom Odhiambo (2007) shows that between the 1960s and 1970s, urban men who engaged in "eating leisure" (S: *kula raha*) by consuming sex and alcohol excessively occupied a central stage in popular imaginaries of what it meant to be Kenyan. Men who fought for independence, Odhiambo argues, came to overshadow women's contributions to the anti-colonial struggle and claim the nation as a quintessentially masculine domain. In response to a colonial regime that had extensively policed and regulated African mobilities and intimacies, sexual and consumptive indulgence became a way, for men, to enjoy liberation. Revisiting Kenyan novels of that time, Odhiambo observes that their male protagonists are "in perpetual search for self-gratification and appear to be 'out of control'"—indeed, "wild men" (2007, 652). If, on the one hand, theirs were "attempts . . . to cope with [an] ever-changing social reality" (662), on the other, men's desire for self-gratification further tied normative masculinity to sexual assertiveness.

Since the 1980s, a new dominant narrative of masculinity has emerged. Mary Amuyunzu-Nyamongo and Paul Francis (2006) suggest we understand this narrative as part of a context in which structural adjustment programs have led to a decline in agricultural production, and, I add, drought and receding national meat markets have deteriorated pastoral livelihoods. These transformations conspired with growing unemployment to undermine severely avenues to cash in a labor market that, up to that point, had been dominated by male workers. Drawing on 710 interviews with men and women in rural areas across Kenya, Amuyunzu-Nyamongo and Francis show that men's eroding opportunities coincided with a growing feminization of labor: women received training, through NGO and state programs—including the famous national campaign *Maendeleo ya Wanawake* (Development for Women)—to be "better placed to adapt to livelihood changes" (228). Amuyunzu-Nyamongo and Francis note that, if these programs encouraged women to take on leadership positions in their communities, they also left men feeling disempowered, lifeless, weak.

Since the 1990s, the iconography of HIV prevention has been pivotal in shaping ideas of male weakness and vital depletion. Cartoons and political art in the national media from the early 1980s did not yet depict the prototypical lazy, idle man as skinny and weak. Rather, he was still a corpulent man, who, lacking the material means to become a "big-man" (S: *bwana mkubwa*), maintained a deceptive appearance: large, yes, but without means to sustain his largess. Unlike rich big-men who circulated resources across vast networks of exchange and clientage, he was a corpulent man in a state of stasis, sitting idly, without work. It is around this time perhaps that urban youths, using Swahili *sheng* slang, began addressing male friends or referring to their fathers as *Budangu*, my Buddha, echoing an image of seemingly immobile corpulence. Public health posters depicting AIDS as bodily wasting away must have then inspired imaginaries of male vital depletion, although HIV infection rates have been much higher among women (for a critical discussion, see Mojola 2014).

The early postcolonial image of the "wild man" now coexisted with that of the "weak man." Their coexistence informed the idea that, in the absence of other means, sex remained an ultimate way to prove one's masculinity (Mojola 2014; Wyrod 2016). "Possessing no means to change their economic situation," Margrethe Silberschmidt (1999, 8) argues, "many men seem to translate their frustrations into other forms of behavior: sexual activity with many partners being one of them, an activity that seems to boost male identity." This then exacerbates a downward spiral, in which sex and death become intertwined, and men's bodily depletion sets the nation on a dooming path.

In this "climate of anxious virility," as Julien Bonhomme (2106, 34) calls it, rescuing men and their vitality becomes important to securing the nation. Several governmental and non-governmental institutions have taken on this challenge in recent years: the Family Caucus in Parliament has advocated for the restoration of traditional family values led by a male breadwinner; the National Youth Service hoped to rehabilitate men's strength through military training; *Maendeleo ya Wananume* (Development for Men), a conservative "men's rights" NGO, sought to rescue the "boy-child" from being marginalized by women; Man Enough, a Christian organization, taught men in villages, slums, and prisons about respectable sexuality and fatherhood through economic success; and the Save Our Men Initiative sought to "save the family, save youth, save Kenya" by, among other things, preventing the spread of homosexuality. In Mtwapa, local organizations taking on similar projects included the Chief's Office, the Youth Office of the local Administration Police, as well as different evangelical churches and public health NGOs and CBOs.

Thinking of "male-power" as the "phallus" demonstrates how a certain political overinvestment in this object is central to utopias of the nation, ethnicity, and generational well-being. For Lacan (1985, 82, 84), the phallus represents a "privileged signifier" of "the desire of the Other," the thing one wants to have or actualize in order to attract the love and recognition of an outer world (or, the social world; what Lacan calls the "Big Other"). Such desirability and recognition promise fulfillment, wholeness, plentitude. Distinct from the penis, the phallus shifts across different signifiers, including bodies, objects, and practices that promise to restore the subject to its lost totality. Postcolonial feminist scholars have critiqued Lacan for failing to show just how central the apparent universality that psychoanalysis has attributed to the phallus has been to the colonial project. Stopping short of questioning its universality has also meant occluding the role of other bodily signifiers: "carrying all the force of ethical law," Jan Campbell (2000, 4) argues, the phallus has been "colonizing all other imaginary tales under one symbolic" (see also McClintock 1995; cf. Nzegwu 2011). Rather than employ it as a universal analytic, then, these scholars show, it is important to name and critique it as part of a particular symbolic repertoire of colonialism and its global exportation of a distinct form of heteropatriarchy.

Masculine vitality is phallic in that it promises to actualize the full potential of political totalities through the assertive energetics of men's bodies in ways that are continuous with colonialism. The following three sections demonstrate how the phallic quality of male-power figures in struggles over ethnicity and regional citizenship, urban youth's attempts to claim recognition, and humanitarian attempts to rescue intimacies. The phallus shifts here between different objects, including bodies, penises, statistical fertility rates, motorbikes, clothing styles, and ultimately the very practice of rescue as such, all of which become new potential sources of male-power.

Vital Lack: Gender, Ethnicity, and Male-Power

In April 2015, Kenya's National Bureau of Statistics released the results of a new Kenyan Demographic and Health Survey, revealing that Central Province[3] now registered some of the lowest fertility rates in the country, with 2.3 children per woman in Kirinyaga County and 2.7 in Nyeri and Kiambu Counties. This took leaders, journalists, and the public by surprise. On July 1, 2015, the *Star* notes that "fertility rates in Central Province are noticeably dropping as a result of alcoholism among men, which has led to rising impotence."[4] "If the current trend continues," the newspaper warns, "Central Kenya might witness a loss of an entire generation to alcohol and its devastating consequences." Associated with Kikuyu, the largest ethnic group in the country, the region has played an important role in electoral politics. At that point, three out of the four presidents since Kenya's independence had been Kikuyu from this region. Uhuru Kenyatta, who was president at the time when these statistical figures were published, was one of them.

Disturbed by these statistics, in a public speech on July 1, 2015, Kenyatta directed MPs, senators, and women's representatives from Central Province "to lead the war against illicit brews in their constituencies."[5] He also immediately called for an outright military rescue operation. He ordered the General Service Unit (GSU), a paramilitary branch of the National Police Service usually responding to severe security threats, "to move from door to door closing all outlets selling illicit drinks and destroying those in the process of manufacturing . . . [such] drinks."[6] He also ordered the National Youth Service, a governmental organization offering young men military training, "to start a parallel campaign of rounding up drunk and addicted youth to put them in special centers for rehabilitation."[7] "These young men are most affected," the president said. "They must start a new life."[8] Local leaders quickly responded to the president's call.

Kenyan political leaders have long invoked alcoholism to express anxieties over young men. Thus, the idea that alcoholism *caused* male sexual potency to decline has long been a dominant, albeit contested, narrative.[9] This time, however, something else seemed to concern politicians. "It is Kikuyu men that politicians are worried about," a university professor from Nairobi explained to me. He and I discussed the events in Central Province, over a drink, in June 2018. "This is about Kikuyu masculinity, specifically," he said. "They worry about young men because they are the future of Kikuyu and, for a long time now, Kikuyu have played a leading role in politics." My colleague urged me to explore why the only other people about which there is so much concern among leaders were the Somali. As I looked through national newspapers from 2015, I learned that, while the Central Province recorded the lowest fertility rate in the country, Kenya's northeastern counties, a predominantly Somali region, registered the highest rate (with an average of 6.4 children per woman in North Eastern County and 7.4 in Wajir County).[10] These statistical findings resonated with Kenyan middle-class discourses about Somalis' alleged sexual promiscuity and aversion to family planning. "Kikuyu politicians worry about this," my colleague said. "They say Somalis reproduce fast and will soon be too large a population."

In the national public, statistical numbers reflective of fertility took on a phallic quality, rendering masculine productive and reproductive capacity a "dominant signifier" of an ethnic group's potential for assertion in the national political arena, its desirability and legitimacy in the eyes of the nation. In nationalist imaginaries, big-men and male elders have been key to imprimaturs of power and sustained the idea that the nation-state was male (Blunt 2019; Odhiambo 2007). By extension, during elections, struggles between different groups of political patronage to capture the state apparatus have figured, in part, as phallic contests between similarly gendered ethnic groups. The president's response to "his" province's low fertility rates illustrates this phallic battle for male-power—a fragile object, foundational to both ethnicity and the nation.

When government officials decided to rehabilitate men in Central Province, the region's residents had long been confronting their own challenges with men, sex, and alcoholism. Grace Njoki Maina (2017) shows how what appears in the present as a distinct "crisis of masculinity" in the region is the product of a history of the *long durée*. Since colonialism, men have been emasculated as white settlers appropriated their land, as new Kenyan elites marginalized and demeaned them, and as women came to dominate regional affairs in response to men's labor migration. A boom in the coffee economy between the early sixties and the late seventies gave men access to resources through which to claim authority and respectability. But the crash of the coffee market in 1978 has left them without these means and with a distinct sense of lack. "Without coffee to give men a source of income," a Kikuyu elder told Maina, "men felt emasculated. As a result, many were depressed and had to turn to alcohol and idleness as defense mechanisms to cover their weakening status" (2017, 97).

In the months leading up to Kenyatta's militarized intervention, rural women across the region demonstrated against alcohol breweries and against men's drinking. Widely featured in the national media, these demonstrations remained different from the state's rescue attempts: if the latter was a quintessentially masculine, military show of force, the other represented a grassroots form of women's collective action with a much longer history in the local culture of politics.[11] Women marched in groups of ten to fifty, holding small green branches, a customary sign of protest. They hit card boxes rhythmically with their palms to make noise and announce their presence. Entering bars and roadside breweries, they grabbed men by their clothes, dragged them out in the streets, and whipped them with branches, calling them weak and impotent. Such protests continued for over a year. The *Star* describes, for example, how, in November 2016, fifty women, members of the Destiny of King'eero Women's Group, "rained slaps, kicks and blows on drunk men at a den in Kabete."[12] One participant told the newspaper: "Many young men have been affected . . . They do not bring anything home but still ask for food . . . Women have been miserable."[13]

If, for the most part, national media applauded the president's military rescue intervention, it depicted Kikuyu women's protests as deviously masculine—that is, as making an anomalous claim to the phallus. Indeed, what made the scandal over men in Central Province a national sensation was not merely that men had allegedly become weak, but—more importantly—that women suddenly appeared too strong; stronger, that is, than their husbands. Consider a cartoon from 2015 that captures this predicament evocatively (fig. 7): "What kind of garbage is this?" a woman says in Swahili as she upturns an alcohol barrel, while the other beats a skinny, weak man, admonishing him: "You drank alcohol until your transformer died!! You think children can be conceived over Bluetooth?" The metaphor of the "transformer," a common euphemism for the penis, figures here as the medium of an otherwise absent male-power. Meanwhile, the sticks women hold firmly in their hands to descend with force on the emaciated man indicate a phallic energy inherent in the very act of rescue, an aspect to which I shall return.

This seeming gender inversion—or leakage—has sparked extensive debate among middle-class Kenyans, with some decrying it as an effect of women's empowerment programs and others claiming that men are also victims of "gender-based violence." "I hear they [Kikuyu women] started a long time ago," one blog post reads. "Ask the *wazee* [elders]. They chose to keep quiet due to embarrassment. Now the young boys are crying . . . Tell them to look for wife-material, not marry a man like themselves." If, according to this logic, strong women become men, weak men become more like women, adopting women's styles, demeanors, and traits. Notably, a fear of homosexuality (e.g., "tell them . . . not [to] marry a man like themselves") has haunted anxieties over the liquification of male-power, the fluidization of the gender binary. During her fieldwork in Nyeri, Maina (2017, 108) notes growing concern that

"MALE-POWER"   73

FIGURE 7. Women protest men's alcoholism. "What kind of garbage is this?" a woman asks. "You drank alcohol until your transformer died!!" the other admonishes. "You think children can be conceived over Bluetooth?" Cartoon by Kourier. *Standard,* July 6, 2015.

"the traditional African man was reduced or else reduced himself to a 'wife,'" that "men [have] become gentle." Summarizing local views, Maina says:

> Idle young men turned to the internet and television programs as the source of consolation. They started imitating what they saw and heard in television programs. With such, some men ended up dressing in female attires, others even began plaiting their hair and wearing earrings and jewelry like women. Fashion and modernity emerged as a force and stimuli behind men adopting feminine traits. These men . . . thus discard the African socialization into manhood. (2017, 109)

The de-calibration of a gendered distribution of vitality appears to threaten a gender binarism that remains foundational to ethnic and national power. If male bodies turn feminine, female bodies, energized by the very act of rescuing their communities, appear to turn masculine. I do not wish to suggest that this gender fluidity is merely a product of late capitalism. Since the 1960s, post-independence leaders in Kenya, Uganda, and Tanzania have repeatedly banned men from wearing long hair and jewelry and women from wearing trousers (Ivaska 2011; Kintu 2017), policing thus the threat of gender fluidity or leakage. However, historical transformations have amplified this perceived threat. Growing numbers of female politicians and, since the late 2000s, rising debate among politicians over the "one-third gender rule" in Parliament—an affirmative-action rule asking that one-third of the seats in Parliament be occupied by women—have accentuated a sense that state rule is no longer simply male. So too have anxieties over what, since 2000, appears as a rising "pandemic" of gayism. In nationalist discourses, homosexuality has become emblematic of an active quest to liquify and leak gender, a key cause for the loss of male-power (see chapter 6). These discourses emphasize, for example, that men engaged in receptive anal sex lose their virility and ability to have erections.

If the liquification of male bodies generates gender leakage, it also redistributes vital energy in ways that undermine heteropatriarchal claims to ethnicity and the state. Achille Mbembe (2020, 297) suggestively describes these sovereign claims as a "sexual potentate," "a structure of power and an *imaginaire* of life, body, and pleasures that gives a prominent place to a unique signifier: the phallus." Because the phallus is never concrete or fixed, because it can never be fully pinned down, actualized, Mbembe argues, it "exposes the potentate himself [sic] and proclaims, paradoxically, his vulnerability in the very act by which he claims to manifest his omnipresence" (297). It is this instability of phallic power that, Jane Bryce (2011) argues, is at stake in popular concerns over the loss of male virility. "The loss of [male] potency," she argues, "is a metonymic device for the representation of the unstable relationship between manhood and the state" (12). Observing how, since the 1970s, across West Africa, hegemonic forms of masculinity have been rendered virtual—appearances emptied of content—Bryce suggests that "the over-insistence on phallic imaginary conceals a lack, in which substance has been replaced by sign." It is an astute awareness of this lack, in turn, that drives efforts to the phallic rescue and rehabilitation of male-power.

A few incidences in Nyeri County in 2015 stood out as particularly suggestive of this phallic struggle. Already in the months prior to the president's intervention, several cases occurred in which individual women separately cut off the penises of their husbands as a form of protest against their alcoholism and idleness.[14] These cases became emblematic in the media of Kikuyu women's demonstrations. "We will just continue cutting [men's penises]," *Art Matters* quotes a woman from Nyeri as saying. "Even if they arrest and imprison us, we will come back and cut again; because men have become totally useless. Their work is just to drink and they don't bring anything home. And when they come back, they want food."[15] Not all women supported such claims. KTN news showed a woman who, in response to one such incident, confessed being horrified: "For the man, this [the penis] is the most meaningful thing.

So now, she went and destroyed [S: *ameharibu*] that thing; she destroyed it completely." The woman concluded with a most evocative statement: "*Sasa, ile sehemu ndyio nyumba*," she said. "Now, that area [of the body] is the house," meaning the source of procreation, of a couple's ability to build a home, a family, a future. "So, if you cut that thing, what will you do?" Journalists, opinion pieces, and talk shows agreed: "The chopping off of men's genitals is also a threat to procreation and the family unit. Without procreation there will be no future generation." To cut off a penis—what, after these incidents, came to be known in Swahili as *kubobbit*, from a similar 1993 case in the United States that involved one John Bobbitt—encapsulates a more general fear of castration, of women's appropriation of the phallus. In this instance, however, the phallus the women appropriated was not the penis as such. It was the strength—the male-power—with which they went about "rescuing" their communities, a vigor that, in turn, rendered penises dispensable—signs without substance—further dissociating them from the phallus. In discourses about these incidents, the sticks women used to beat men or the knives with which they cut them signify precisely this phallic strength.

Under the witty hashtag #Nyeriwives, memes and social media posts have depicted these incidents as spectacular but also comical forms of gender inversion. Jokes began circulating on social networking platforms, such as the following:

> They say that if a man goes to our home in Nyeri being called Dickson and does something wrong, he will come back only being called Son.
>
> Nyeri is now called *-ri*, because women cut off its *nye-*.
>
> Marrying a woman from Nyeri is like going to preach peace in the unpredictable Somali capital, Mogadishu.
>
> Kenya should deploy women from Nyeri in fighting the Somali Al-Shabab terror group instead of using its armed forces.[16]

What made such jokes entertaining was, on the one hand, the implicit, yet salient, role of ethnicity: the fact that these incidents took place among those who have long claimed to be the leaders of the nation, that Kikuyu men were emasculated, indeed beaten and castrated by women. This was a way to ridicule what Rasna Warah (2019) has called "Kikuyu supremacy." On the other hand, it was ridiculing women's strength: The first two jokes explicitly point to women's appropriation of the phallus through their very strength to overpower men. The last two jokes compare this strength to that of military forces—epitomes of masculinity now appropriated by "Nyeri wives." In this instance, the attribution of virility to women works, as Mehammed

Mack (2017, 23) notes for women of color in Paris's suburban gangs, to render women devious, deviously masculine. In this context, devious Kikuyu women and weak Kikuyu men not only liquify the gender binary but, in doing so, also undermine Kikuyu claims to state leadership.

As a queer object, "male-power" and the struggles that it has generated demonstrate that what sustains the very distinction between men and women is not bodily biology as such. Rather, it is a particular distribution of vitality. Oyèrónkẹ́ Oyěwùmí (1997) and Ifi Amadiume (1987), among others, have shown that a biology-based gender binarism originates in a Western bourgeois ideology that has served as the basis of colonial rule in Africa. If this binarism has become foundational to African nationalisms, however, it has remained irreducible to the *bio*-logic of sex. Indeed, a focus on vitality demonstrates how the energetic de-calibration of bodies leaks gender, undermining the claims of particular ethnic groups to citizenship or the control of the state apparatus.

Vital Excess: Bodaboda and the Fleetingness of Male-Power

Bodaboda—motorbike taxi operators—offer an evocative counterexample to the figure of the man who depletes his vitality through alcohol consumption, a counter case to what the national imagination construes as phallic loss, lack, depletion. Bodaboda appear in the national public in the late 2000s as men who embody vitality-in-excess. Elites devalue these men as excessive and unable to hold on to their vitality, wealth, and well-being. Central to elite discourses but also to these men's styles of self-fashioning is the notion of "the rush" (using the English word or the Swahili *haraka*). Analyzing these performances and discourses reveals another important presumption about male-power, namely that, to be converted into lasting forms of value, it must be divorced from speed, excess, or the rush; sustainable vitality cannot come in bursts. The logic of excess, it turns out, devalues and marginalizes bodaboda masculinities.

Motorbike taxi operators emerged in urban spaces across Africa in the early 2000s and their numbers grew quickly (Agbiboa 2018). Several factors played an important role in shaping this economy, including growing urban areas and populations in need of cheap transport; rising numbers of young men seeking work in towns; and the influx into the East African market of affordable Japanese motorcycles. Soon, the social and cultural milieus that bodaboda crafted became meaningful spaces for young, unemployed men from poor households—alternative avenues to desirable, dignified masculinities. Bodaboda men I interviewed in Mtwapa in 2017 were primarily migrants and migrant settlers from coastal or upcountry villages. Many of them had dropped out of high school. They found working as bodaboda more lucrative than pursuing an education which no longer guaranteed employment. Most bodaboda were between ages eighteen and twenty-five, and a few were in their thirties or forties. There were over 1,000 bodaboda operators in Mtwapa alone, waiting for customers in groups of five to twenty at every street corner.

"The nice thing about the bodaboda," Kahindi, a twenty-five-year-old motorbike operator, told me in July 2017, "is that there is quick money [S: *pesa ya haraka*]." He joined the bodaboda in 2010, when he was eighteen. After failing his high school entrance exam, he looked for work to support his single mother and younger brothers. Originally from a coastal village, he had come to Mtwapa to work as a bodaboda for a businessman who owned several motorcycles. When I spoke to Kahindi, I was familiar with the phrase *pesa ya karaka*—translating literally as "money of the rush." I had encountered this phrase in derogatory references to "quick money," cash one did not actually work for and that existed in moral opposition to "money of sweat" (S: *pesa ya jasho*) (Meiu 2017, 140–43). But Kahindi seemed to be using this phrase differently, so I asked him what he meant. "This is 'money of the rush' because a person comes to you: 'I want you to take me to Majengo [a Mtwapa neighborhood] because I am late.' So, your rides are 'of the rush' [S: *ya haraka*], not 'of the sleep' [S: *ya kulala*]." In other words, bodaboda operated in and profited from the rush as opposed to waiting or idling. Rather than understanding the rush negatively, Kahindi suggested, it is the rush and one's ability to navigate it efficiently that represented bodaboda's main sources of income. Claiming the rush, bodaboda distinguished themselves sharply from the "weak men" said to wait around, bored—a form of masculinity somewhat emblematic of late capitalism (Jeffrey 2010; Mains 2011; Masquelier 2019; Ralph 2008).

Because of the rush, another driver told me, "A bodaboda never lacks money . . . If he wants to eat meat, he eats . . . It's not like a salaried person who gets paid monthly, goes to work by foot, or takes [food] on loan from the shop . . . Bodaboda don't have those issues." Money rushing through bodaboda's pockets was held to revitalize their bodies—"if he wants meat, he eats." It is no surprise then that the notion of the rush was also essential to their own style. Driving quickly, overtaking cars and trucks along the road, taking shortcuts through small back alleys, outsmarting traffic police, or competing in elaborate choreographies involving standing on one wheel or spinning in circles are ways to claim the rush as their distinct style. These performances are premised on speedy mobility—a surge of energy or excess vitality—something they share, in part, with men in the *matatu* or public mini-bus industry (Mutongi 2017; Wa-Mūngai 2013). The distinct style of bodaboda also involved performing a set of highly sexualized verbal games with explicit and, for some, quite vulgar references to sex (Obudho 2019). "Being bodaboda requires talent," Kahindi said. "You need to be strong. Not any idiot can do it." This is why, he added, "being bodaboda has become idealized work."

"Ladies love their style," said Fred, an NGO worker in Mtwapa. "The bodaboda comes [on his motorbike] and stops, standing up on one wheel, and then he races off. And he plays love music. And his motorbike is new, completely refurbished. That attracts those schoolgirls very much." Young women's fantasies and desires enable bodaboda masculinities, a point that Stella Nyanzi et al. (2004) also make for Kampala, Uganda. "A bodaboda can be even more desirable than me," Fred said, pointing to his clothing style as an educated, employed man. "Even if I am smart and I tuck my shirt in, he will be loved more because his money flows fast [S: *pesa inaflow kwa haraka*]. He gives you and he'll get more quickly." Thus, if schoolgirls desire bodaboda, many schoolboys desire to become motorbike taxi operators.

To understand the centrality of the vital rush to their sense of self, consider, for example, a set of ritualized acts bodaboda performed at the funerals of fellow operators. Within a few years from their emergence as a social category, because of high road-accident fatalities, such funerals had become common and acquired a distinctly elaborate protocol. On the day of the burial, hundreds of bodaboda arrived on their motorbikes at the mortuary to pick up the deceased. They then formed a procession that led the coffin to the grave. As part of the procession, they honked their horns loudly, maneuvered their motorbikes in dangerous twists and spins, and blocked traffic along highways for long periods of time. "If anyone dares challenging us or hitting a motorbike with their car in that situation," one bodaboda told me, "we can even break his windscreen and burn his car down." Outside this ceremonial context, police stopped bodaboda daily, confiscating their keys until they came up with the requested bribes. Meanwhile, truck and car drivers often hit them carelessly, leaving them disabled, unable to work for long periods of time. The funeral ceremony inverted these everyday quandaries. Bringing the highway to a standstill, bodaboda claimed excess vitality from an infrastructure that otherwise marginalized or killed them. To signal this excess vitality, at funerals, they tied red ribbons around their foreheads and wrists, as Kahindi told me, "to warn others to stay away from us."

In this mode of self-styling, the motorbike itself, a bodily extension of the driver, congealed male-power—a phallic object generative of vitality, speed. Commercial ads for motorcycles in Kenya invoke this cultural logic, depicting their products as able to impart "power" (S: *nguvu*) to their male owners.

That these ads feature exclusively men as potential owners confirms that the power they reference is "male" (S: *ya kiume*). This is also confirmed by the fact that my bodaboda interlocutors saw the only young woman who worked as a motorbike taxi operator in Mtwapa as having "turned male": "If you look at her closely," Kahindi said, "you see she looks like a man though she is a *dem* [young woman]." Like the Kikuyu women protestors, the bodaboda woman had appropriated a clearly phallic strength, a strength that, in this case, inhered in the motorbike as such. The phallic quality of the motorbike is also evident in stories Mtwapa residents told me about the violence that groups of bodaboda have inflicted on motorbike thieves. Motorbike thefts prompted operators to mobilize in large numbers, catch thieves, and kill them on the spot. Notably, they left their bodies in the street, naked, sodomized with their own severed limbs. While this violence is certainly horrific, it is important to remember that bodaboda understood its distinct mode of expression as commensurate with the *act* of motorbike theft. *Both*, then, were severe forms of emasculation, castration, phallic alienation.

An extension of their claim to male-power is also what bodaboda see as their "rescue work" (S: *kazi ya rescue*). Over the past decade, they have also acted as neighborhood vigilantes. Because they were able to move quickly and congregate in large numbers very fast, they were the first to respond to muggings, burglaries, thefts, or sexual assaults. Some Mtwapa residents referred to them mockingly as "pretend ninjas"—*wamejifanya maninjas*. A sitcom on national television channel KTN, entitled *Boda Boda*, dramatizes this style of rescue: men who, like ninjas, Superman, or Batman, intervene to save people in danger, bring perpetrators to justice, and secure the city's collective good. "Bodaboda are a very good rescue team," said Kahindi. "They provide very nice security. Because there are now many of us, crimes are decreasing." Bodaboda I spoke with emphasized that their work was critical at a time when most urban residents did not trust the police. Appropriating and reworking the promise of rescue and militarized securitization from the state and private security firms, they claimed it as a countercultural phallic identity. It is perhaps no coincidence then that the National Youth Service and the police, while highly critical of bodaboda, often recruited soldiers from among them.

For political and religious leaders, elites, and other Kenyans, bodaboda embodied a vital excess that undermined not only state sovereignty and the rule of law, but also national values associated with development, respectability, and the life course: they invoked that bodaboda do not value formal education; that they were impatient and chased quick money; or that they caused accidents and acted violently. Some bodaboda I interviewed explained that only younger operators who "have power without brains" (S: *wana nguvu bila akili*) were responsible for violent rescue interventions. But others agreed that speeding up or taking shortcuts were more than vital excesses; they were key modalities to survive in an economy that valued speedy speculation.

Not surprisingly, perhaps, much of the dominant discourse on bodaboda's energy-in-excess was a discourse on their sexuality. In an article entitled "Of Bodaboda Sex Predators on High School Girls," the *Standard* derides a common pattern:

> Just Ksh100 [less than US$1] or "chips" is enough to lure the girls into their traps. You will always meet them in the evening waiting for the young girls to step out of school offering them lifts. As if that is not enough, some operators have in some cases disappeared with the girls only to resurface after they have conceived. At this point, they drop them . . . Action should be taken against these bodaboda men to bring the practice to an end.

By seducing and impregnating schoolgirls, bodaboda, who were already said to prefer taking shortcuts over the normative life course, appeared also to derail young women from the pursuit of respectable futures.

So common were these relationships that numerous educational posters and cartoons warned against them. A cartoon by Said Michael that has circulated online (fig. 8) shows how a schoolgirl's social paths close after becoming pregnant to a bodaboda. Expelled from school, her dreams of graduation vanish, her "parent" (S: *mzazi*) has chased her away, and her bodaboda lover rejects her: "Me," he tells her, "I gave you a lift and you then helped me [i.e., offered sex in return]. Let's not know each other, young lady." Rejected and crying, she walks down the only path left to her: *mitaani*, to the neighborhood—a euphemism for sex work, nonbelonging, and disrepute. Although the cartoon addresses primarily schoolgirls, its discourse is also about bodaboda sexuality: a sexuality premised on irresponsible mobility, a rush or excess vitality that disrupts women's lives. Unlike sex workers who, as I suggested at the beginning of this chapter, were often held responsible for "seducing" taxi and bodaboda drivers, schoolgirls were construed as their victims, in ways that effaced more complex sex-for-money exchanges (Mojola 2014, 159–61; Nyanzi et al. 2004; see also chapter 4 in this book).

According to these narratives, bodaboda also disrupted heteronormative domesticity, seducing housemaids, married women, or becoming "kept boys" to wealthy single women. Elite and middle-class Kenyans claimed these men's sexual mobility led to their eventual illness and death. National newspapers reported a rapid loss of "male-power" and erectile dysfunctions among bodaboda, mainly *because* of their sitting for long hours on motorbikes. Like their

"MALE-POWER" 81

FIGURE 8. Once pregnant, a girl is expelled from school, chased away by her parent (S: *mzazi*), and abandoned by her *bodaboda* lover. "Me," he tells her, "I gave you a lift and you then helped me out [with sex]. Let's not know each other, young lady." Cartoon by Said Michael, circulating on Kenyan social media in 2020.

laboring capacity or wealth, their sexual potency also appeared temporary, fleeting. Sooner or later, so the story went, they lost it, turned HIV-positive, and died; that is, if they didn't die in road accidents first. One news outlet reports that bodaboda "end up wallowing in poverty as they get easily persuaded by women instead of sticking to earn their living."[17] A bodaboda, therefore, "will go home without money in his pocket but with disease in his body."

If for bodaboda excess vitality or male-power was the phallus, that which makes them desirable, respectable men for the national public, this excess also was what undermined the durability of their bodies and wealth and cut their futures short. Construing bodaboda as excessive, leaders, elites, and the media devalued their styles and delegitimized their claims to the phallus in a national arena. Unable to acquire the right quantity or quality of phallic vitality, they remained "youths" (S: *vijana*) unable to become men. In contrast to them, as the next section shows, leaders, elites, and development workers now sought some sort of "middle-ground" of vitality—a particularly balanced, gendered distribution of male-power that would reactualize the lost ideal of the heteropatriarchal nation.

Vital Middle-Grounds? Rescuing Male-Power

"A man is someone who can sire children [S: *kuzalisha*]," said Amos, a development worker. "There can be many factors [that make a man]. But that's the most important one." The Swahili verb *kuzalisha* is masculine, meaning "to cause to birth," distinct from the feminine *kuzaa*, "to give birth." Over drinks at a restaurant in Mtwapa, I asked Amos and his colleague Mosi to help me understand contemporary challenges over masculinity. The two men, both in their early twenties, ran a community-based organization (CBO) that provided sex education to young men and women in Mtwapa. "What does it mean to be a man?" I asked them. "A real man," Mosi said, "must not discriminate by gender. He cannot only educate his sons and not his daughters." He echoed a common discourse in NGO feminism. But Amos cut him short. "Before we even get to children's education," he said, "the most important thing for a man is to sire children." To illustrate his point, Amos told us of his uncle, a pious Anglican, without children. "He was an important man in the church. But, without children, he was not respected." "He went mad [S: *alienda cheesy*]," Amos said, meaning severely depressed. "Why is it so important to sire children?" I asked. Amos explained: "When you walk down the street with your boy or your girl, holding their hand, that is already an identity . . . [it shows] that you are fertile." "Male-power" or fertility, he said, are no joking matter. They are central not only to men's respectability but to the core of their identity. Without "male-power," good work and wealth alone could not sustain respectability.

If "male-power" was essential to men's respectability, Amos and Mosi explained, men had to carefully cultivate it through particular choices in lifestyle, intimacy, and sex. "Young man who drink or gamble become weak," Mosi emphasized. Consequently, their ability to sire children and provide for them diminishes, as does their respectability. In the workshops Amos and Mosi offered as part of their CBO's sex education programs, they encouraged their young beneficiaries to cultivate a certain "middle ground" (S: *sehemu ya kati*), a middle range of vitality: not too much, not too little. Sustaining such a middle ground ensured they would pursue respectable paths. Certainly, development workers, public health workers, and church reformists did not fully agree on what this respectable middle ground should look like. If Amos and Mosi, for example, believed that sex education was central to it, many church leaders feared that sex education would cause teen promiscuity.

Overall, however, they agreed that respectability revolved around the figure of the educated, decently employed male figure of middle-class aspirations.

Like others, Amos and Mosi also saw their work as rescue. But they also claimed that their kind of rescue was superior to others' because it was premised on scientific knowledge. In 2013, they opened their CBO under the patronage of a coastal NGO working on HIV prevention with funds from the United Nations Population Fund. In a rented two-story house in Mtwapa, their offices hosted educational workshops and theater sketches for the town's youths. They educated their beneficiaries on patterns of HIV transmission among heterosexual couples, condom use, and STI-testing possibilities. Beginning in early 2017, as the U.N. reshuffled funds to prioritize "key populations" in the transmission of HIV—mainly sex workers and "men who have sex with men" (MSM)—Amos and Mosi's CBO lost all funding. With the help of Mtwapa's state-appointed chief, they relocated to a small room in the town's hospital, where they worked pro bono, hoping that other NGOs would employ them in the future. As they waited for such opportunities, they shifted their sex education programs to social media platforms—Facebook and WhatsApp—and also began producing and circulating low-cost educational videos. These films featured them and their friends, enacting scenes of everyday life which, for them, required careful moral judgment.

The Party!!, a two-minute video they produced in 2016, portrays the "dangers" of group sex and drug addiction. It opens with six men and three women, all in their early twenties, dancing, smoking, and drinking at a supposed party. At one point, the group decides to play Spin-the-Bottle. "When it lands on a chick," one man explains in English, "I get to kiss her." "What if it lands on a dude?" another man asks. "Are you gonna kiss him too?" Everyone laughs. "No," the first man replies. "We spin it again." As the game heats up, one man stands up, screaming: "Stoooop!!!" "What's your problem?" the others ask, annoyed. His answer comes as the film's educational message:

> My problem is: When are we gonna stop all this? Look at the life we are living: partying all the time, engaging in group sex, doing drugs... Can't you see that we are at a risk of contracting HIV and other STIs? Do you want us to become a class of drug addicts? We need to change. It's high time we live a healthy life.

The "healthy life" invoked here is one devoid of sexual and consumptive excesses, one unaffected by sexual risks. The film implies that knowledge and education about HIV/AIDS and sexuality help balance life choices and maintain a middle-ground vitality.

Rescue work (including teaching safe sex) became thus a space for claiming "mid-range" masculine vitality—a wise masculinity. For Amos and Mosi, that was what made them desirable and respectable among their peers. For them, then, the rescue of sexuality was the very source of phallic revitalization. It is important to note also that, although their films addressed both men and women, in the videos I watched, only men speak. Thus, even as Amos, Mosi, and their colleagues supported a certain NGO feminism (e.g., equal opportunities for the girl- and boy-child), they nonetheless relied on heteropatriarchal notions of gender, sex, and family, long associated with the middle class. For example, not only did they condemn homosexuality, but Mosi also told me that he had participated, along with numerous bodaboda, in the anti-homosexual protests of February 2010 in Mtwapa, which made global headlines (I return to these in chapter 7). Indeed, the Save Our Men Initiative, among other similar Kenyan NGOs, launched the *Zuia Sodom Kabisa* ("Prevent Sodom Completely") campaign to "rescue" men from homosexuality. The middle-ground vitality that development workers sought then presupposed foreclosing the so-called "perversions of globalization," including pornography, group sex, and homosexuality.

The *middle* in "middle ground" designates and brings together several orders of meaning. First, it can refer to the middle point between mere vital lack and vital excess—on the one hand, the men of Central Province and, on the other, the bodaboda. NGO workers sought to help others cultivate, temper, and sustain such vitality, by inscribing it in a Protestant ethic of self-care and work and by tying it to heteronormative sexual respectability. Second, the *middle* may also refer to the middle class, not as a class in itself, but as a fantasy lifestyle associated with the moral values of both nationalism and neoliberalism. Amos, Mosi, and Kevin (the Uber driver I introduced at the beginning of this chapter) had livelihoods that could be described as lower middle class. Middle-class belonging, however, was fragile. Sustaining such lifestyles was uncertain. As Amos and Mosi, for example, lost their salaries with the global reorganization of public health funding, their ability to consume in ways associated with the middle class also decreased suddenly. Nonetheless, their strong investment in rescuing and securing forms of intimacy associated with middle-class respectability promised to relaunch their careers: ultimately, so they thought, it would be for the work they did and the values they held, and not for their economic standing, that other NGOs would eventually hire them. Third, the *middle* can also refer to a bodily middle zone: genitality as a key domain of intervention and vital rescue. To cultivate and sustain masculine vitality—at least, in its mid-range, middle-class forms—was to control sexuality (as genital intimacy). Recall, for example, Kevin's decision to enroll in an evangelical class for men to deal with his "weakness" for excessive sex, or Amos and Mosi's efforts to help their peers with the desire for group sex.

Sexuality here held the key to a more holistic revitalization of men, bodies, class, and even the nation itself.

Martin F. Manalansan, Chantal Nadeau, Richard T. Rodríguez, and Siobhan B. Somerville (2014, 1) argue that a broadly conceived category of the "middle," often associated with the normative (e.g., the rural U.S. Midwest as representative of American national values), may nevertheless offer "a queer vantage—a troubled, unstable perch" to understandings of sexual subjectivity. "We believe," they argue, "that such instabilities are productive of alternative ways to approach space and time and to reimagine routes and paths, contours and shapes, directions and teloses of queer lives, practices, and institutions." So too is the case of the phallus: an object that is queer in that, though it continues citing its initial associations with genitality and the middle (the law of the Father in bourgeois ideologies) as the origin of colonial heteropatriarchies, it also undermines these associations. It shifts, inflates, and depletes in ways that require the hard, continuous work of rescuing and placing it securely within normative parameters.

✶

To be sure, in Kenyan debates over "male-power," there is no uniform set of norms defining a middle-ground sexuality and vitality. As Kenyans reflect on extreme manifestations of vitality—its depletion and excess—they seek to understand what such a middle ground would look like in the first place. NGO workers like Amos and Mosi believed that middle-class values should be dictated, in part, by medical knowledge, while Kevin coupled these values with being a "born-again" Christian. And, to the extent that the idea of the *middle* is but a hegemonic orientation, it is also shaped by the desires of men like the bodaboda who, according to its logics, are excessive, devious. It is thus that some bodaboda sought to distinguish themselves actively from operators they too saw as impulsive. Kahindi, a Pentecostal, for instance, told me that sex, alcohol, and drugs undermined bodaboda men's health and vitality as well as their efforts to save money. A bumper sticker common on bodaboda's motorbikes in Mtwapa read: *Nguvu kijijini, mjini akili*—"Power [belongs to] the village, wisdom in town," a claim some distance from the initial style that associated these men with excess and the rush.

Across these contexts, as I have shown, rescue itself became revitalizing. Attending to the qualities and quantities of vitality, one's own and others', generated the conditions for a middle-ground vital flow that was healthy, life-giving, respectable. The rush to secure and rehabilitate oneself and one's nation and to produce thus good citizens was a quest for the phallus that promised respectability, fulfillment. But because rescue—the quest for the phallus—was revitalizing not only for men but also women, ambiguities inevitably emerged over gender leakage. Thus also, it is no coincidence that state rescue interventions took the form of militarized action, further masculinizing the state, asserting its phallic power; nor that Kikuyu women's demonstrations and female bodaboda were deemed deviously masculine.

It is important to distinguish between narratives and imageries that depict men as "in crisis," "weak," or "lacking" vitality, and the wider political economic context that has left many men and women without the normative means to provide for others or consume. If this wider context has generated numerous kinds of non-normative masculine subjectivities, including the bodaboda, the discourse of "weak men in need of rescue" has worked to disavow these plural subjectivities and maintain desire within monolithic (hetero)normative parameters. Rescue has made the stereotypical "weak man" emblematic of an era, a region, or a social category, and invested him with apocalyptic qualities—the destruction of generations, communities, the nation itself. Similar qualities, as I will show later, came to characterize the homosexual body, except that the latter was also imagined to vampirically feed on the male-power of other men, by seducing them to sex. These apocalyptic visions, in turn, mobilized efforts to rehabilitate men, their male-power, and, through them, intimate citizenship.

4

Bead Necklaces:
Encompassment and the Geometrics of Citizenship

> Encompassment denies the other the right to be different, and it demands that the encompassed others define themselves by the very same features as those defined by and defining the encompasser.
>
> GUIDO SPRENGER

The previous chapter took as its queer object the otherwise fleeting substance of bodily vitality, energy, or life force which has been important to how at least some Kenyans have imagined and contested the gendered body and polity in recent years. This chapter turns to an object that introduces a related preoccupation: namely, a concern with how families, state institutions, NGOs, ethnicized regions, and the nation should efficiently enfold, encircle, or enclose bodies and their vitality to produce and sustain a desired polity. The object introducing this preoccupation with what I call "encompassment"—a key logic of intimate citizenship—is a seemingly trivial one: bead necklaces worn by Samburu women in northern Kenya. Focusing on encompassment reveals how the sexualized indigenous body—just like, as I will later show, the homosexual body—becomes unassimilable ontological difference, a thing that can subvert the nation's nested circles of belonging.

In 2010, in an article provocatively entitled "Samburu Women See Red in Their Stunning Beads," journalist Tabitha Nderitu writes: "A Samburu woman in traditional attire is perhaps one of the most well-known images of tourism in Kenya. Millions of travelers . . . are struck by the young nomadic women who . . . give them a preview of the cultural extravaganza that awaits them in the East African nation." "But," says Nderitu, "no visitor can ever imagine that the aesthetically beautiful beads that the Samburu women wear are in reality part of an atavistic rite of passage that robs the young girls from the community . . . of their youth."[1] Nderitu refers to a custom that women-empowerment NGO workers called "girl-beading" and which, throughout the following decade, would make national and international headlines. According to a local elder, Nderitu explains, "upon a girl being beaded, which literally means being adorned with necklaces by a Moran [young man], her parents are required to build her a house, where the Moran, usually a relative, is allowed to engage in sexual activity with her." "In our community," a local development worker tells Nderitu, "a girl-child is considered to be an object. It's time our people discarded outdated practices such as beading, which have no value in the modern world."

In 2015, Coexist Initiative, a Nairobi-based NGO that advocates for gender equality, reports that although "beads form a great part of the Samburu people's way of life . . . the attachment to beads in the community has resulted in the worst forms of human rights violations, including exposing girls as young as twelve to life-threatening situations through informal marriages and the consequences attributed to it."[2] Beading, Coexist insists, is "socially licensed sexual abuse," part of "treacherous cultural, societal, and customary norms that shape and govern the perceived entitlement of men and boys at the expense of women and girls' vulnerability."[3] Therefore, the report claims, "beading is an affront to all development efforts as defined by . . . millennium goals and Kenya's own Vision 2030"[4]—a government program launched in 2008, which, according to its website, aspires to make Kenya "a newly industrializing, middle-income country providing a high quality of life to all its citizens."[5]

Associated with an ethnic custom variously condemned as "life-threatening," "socially licensed sexual abuse," an "atavistic rite of passage," or a "human rights violation," bead necklaces are clearly troublesome objects. On the one hand, Nderitu says, they are "aesthetically beautiful," globally recognizable artifacts that have efficiently branded Kenya's "cultural extravaganza" for tourist consumption. Because tourism has been the country's second largest source of foreign revenue, its successful marketing is important to financing national progress. On the other hand, the journalist and the NGO workers said, unbeknownst to foreigners, these necklaces hid a dark side that undermined the nation's progress, slowing down or deflecting its movement toward a better future: for necklaces mediated sexual intimacies that involved girls in their early teens and morans probably a few years older. Beads were then outrageous things because they sustained a custom in which sex between children or teenagers was permissible and rural parents condoned rather than condemned it.

In November 2011, Samburu Women for Education and Environment Development Organization (SWEEDO), a women's empowerment NGO led by middle-class Kenyans, published a catalogue featuring the organization's new focus on "girl-child beading." Under the prominent title "Beads of Bondage," the cover describes beading as "one of the worst silent contemporary form[s] of sex slavery" (fig. 9). The cover image depicts a girl in her early teens looking away from the camera. Her large red bead necklace, enclosed in text that frames its meaning, anchors the cover design. The signifier "bondage" plays a central role in this interpretative framing. Echoing caricatured depictions of BDSM (bondage, domination, sadism, masochism) in national and international media, "bondage" highlights the apparent irrationality of some sort of pleasure in submission: "young girls do not mind being beaded," the cover says, ". . . turned into tools of sexual pleasure or sex slaves." "Speaking from ignorance," these girls then need rescue. In the title, the bright coloring of the second syllable in "bondage"—AGE—suggests that what makes beading unacceptable is the young age of these girls: children, the catalogue explains, should not be sexually active. But "bondage" also refers here to "enslavement" *in* and *by* a "patriarchal" ethnic culture. The cover image suggests this by locating the girl with the beads in a cattle kraal, a setting which—on tourist postcards (Kasfir 1999), for example—has long been emblematic of Samburu as a rural, pastoral people. Accordingly, bead necklaces become objects through which an ethnic culture subjugates its women.

The aesthetic choices on SWEEDO's cover reveal a set of ironies that reflect wider contradictions in the humanitarian discourse on beads and beading. First, bead necklaces figure at once as media of outrageous sexual intimacies *and* central visual means for advertising the NGO's humanitarian project for potential Euro-American donors. The latter are very likely to recognize the scene depicted on the cover from tourist advertisements and to read the body of the girl through racialized colonial imaginaries of East African ethnicity and pastoral cultures. Emblematic of ethnic and cultural Otherness, the bead necklace makes such a marketable reading possible. Notably, SWEEDO's own brand logo (visible in the lower-left corner of the cover, next to the logo of the International Work Group for Indigenous Affairs [IWGIA]) depicts a Samburu woman with a large bead necklace framed in a map of Kenya's national borders. This brand logo affirms the NGO's goal to rescue Samburu women by pulling them, forward in time, out of their "backward" ethnic culture and integrating them into the modern nation. All while capitalizing further on the visual spectacularism and marketability of bead necklaces as ethnocultural artifacts.

Second, a closer look at the textual and aesthetic modalities of the cover reveals the NGO's assertive effort to establish firmly the meanings of these necklaces as sexualized artifacts. Black cassettes containing sharp phrases that cite the language of transnational NGO feminism point, like arrows, at the image of the girl's necklace to uphold steadfastly what this object is all about: "a silent sacrifice," "a tough life," "ignorance." One might even argue that if, according to the NGO's discourse, the bead necklace encircles or encompasses the girl, tying her down or binding her to a patriarchal culture,

FIGURE 9. Cover of the *Samburu Girl Child Magazine*. Samburu Women for Education and Environmental Development, Kenya, November 2011.

the cover's design performs a similar encompassment: it enfolds the girl and her beads in its own humanitarian language and ideology, thus making her a legitimate object of rescue. It is therefore important to think further about how, for different social actors, bead necklaces might perform various gendered encompassments—sexual, ethnic, national, humanitarian—while respectively enchanting or appalling different publics.

I have been gathering articles and reports like the ones described above since around 2010, when "girl-beading" became a salient focus of reformist interventions in northern Kenya. At that time, my research in rural Samburu explored other topics and I did not pay close attention to "beading"—other than, that is, archiving these texts as part of my effort to understand how development discourses sexualized ethnicity (Meiu 2017, 58–63). What eventually made me determined to study this issue was not the spectacularism of the bead necklaces as such or the sensationalism with which the media and NGOs discussed beading. Rather, I was struck by the discrepancies between the content of NGOs' widely circulating representations of rural Samburu and what I was learning about gender, intimacy, and social life in the same region. For example, NGO workers claimed that the custom of beading was preventing girls from going to school, that it was causing high numbers of teenage pregnancies, and that, because rural Samburu considered illegitimate children unpropitious, it led to abortions. Rural youths and their parents have indeed spoken to me about a rise in "girl pregnancies." But most of these pregnancies, they said, occurred in schools, away from home, and had nothing to do with what they called "bead giving" (M: *aisho saen*). Indeed, teenage pregnancies were rising across the country.[6] So, the phenomenon was by no means specific to rural Samburu. Furthermore, over the last ten or so years, as the local government expanded its surveillance networks in rural settings, police and humanitarian workers more strongly enforced anti-abortion laws. Fearing arrests, parents preferred to forego abortions and let their daughters give birth to "inauspicious children" (M: *ngursuneti*), even if they thus jeopardized their familial "life force" (M: *nkishon*). And so, contrary to NGO claims, the number of abortions had actually declined.

A more striking incongruity for me was that, during my fieldwork, I had never encountered the custom of "beading" as described by NGO workers, except in my interlocutors' nostalgic recollections of the past. Elderly people remembered the custom as an efficient way to prevent promiscuity, avert unwanted pregnancies, hold young people responsible toward each other, and prepare girls and morans for marriage. Although beads remained important in the intimate exchanges of rural young men and women, their relationships resembled those between youths in schools and urban areas. Such relationships also involved gifts of mobile phones, airtime, perfume, clothes, and cash, among other things, and were negotiated by the young without the direct involvement—or even the knowledge—of their parents (see, for example, Mojola 2014). By the 1990s, in most highland villages, mothers had stopped building the special *senkera* house associated with the custom. They often complained that, as a result, they could no longer control their daughters' whereabouts or know who was responsible for their pregnancies.

NGO workers also asserted that beads and beading were symptomatic of a more general objectification and oppression of women among "pastoralists" like the Samburu. But gender oppression, as a rich feminist anthropological literature on East Africa shows, cannot be seen as the prerogative of an anachronistic pastoral culture. Rather it has been, in part, an effect of the *idea* of such a culture. In other words, as colonialists, missionaries, nationalists, and development workers have deployed the stereotype of patriarchal pastoralists in their reformist work among Samburu, Maasai, Turkana, or other pastoral indigenous people, they have occluded and suppressed women's myriad modes of political expression (Broch-Due 1990; Hodgson 2001, 2005, 2017; Straight 2007; Talle 1988). Certainly, women in northern Kenya—like elsewhere—often experienced different kinds of oppression and violence (Ott 2004), and I by no means wish to diminish or deny that fact. But it is important to emphasize that the construct of inherently powerless pastoralist women has been an ideological means for governing ethnic populations (see also Magubane 2004, 14–39).

Discourses on Samburu beading posit an ethnic and sexual Other whose contemporaneity with a modern nation that claims to be invested in human rights and gender equality must appear accidental, aberrant, abhorrent. I see these discourses as part of a worldwide ideological formation that Sara R. Farris (2017) calls "femonationalism." The term refers to the deployment of feminist tropes within a national public sphere to blame the "culture" of immigrants, indigenous people, or various ethnic or religious minorities for gender oppression and call for their mandatory cultural reform. Such interventions posit the nation as having already overcome patriarchy and gender inequity and allow the state to incorporate minority women into particular— usually low-paying—niches of the national economy (2017, 74, 147–82). In Western Europe, Farris shows, femonationalism has brought right-wing activists, corporations, and women's equality groups together in otherwise racist, anti-immigrant campaigns. Similarly, in East Africa, humanitarian workers sometimes employ the language of transnational feminism in ways that reproduce colonial stereotypes of race and ethnicity to reform and govern particular populations. Writing about NGOs among the Maasai of Tanzania,

Dorothy Hodgson (2017, 126) argues that "Racialized assumptions about the inherent vulnerability and victimhood of rural, illiterate African women have now also become class assumptions, evident, not just in the content of laws that criminalize certain cultural practices, but in the campaigns to enforce them."

Building on the work of Farris and Hodgson, I argue that NGO campaigns against "girl-beading" produce an ethnicized and sexualized noncitizen through and against which leaders, reformists, and other elites can claim and perform good citizenship. What puts rural Samburu families outside the space and time of the modern nation—and therefore also beyond legitimate claims to citizenship—is the unbearable intimacy of which the bead necklaces are a sign, a means, and a symptom: children's and young teens' erotic desires and pleasures. In *The Fear of Child Sexuality*, Steven Angelides (2019, xxii) argues that "the latter part of the twentieth century has witnessed further moves away from notions of childhood and adolescent sexual precocity and agency—and the possibility of a diversity of youth *sexualities*—to notions [and fears] of premature sexualization more generally." This, Angelides shows, has required a "homogenous child . . . produced through parameters of *age* that define what universal childhood is and against which then racial, ethnic, and other childhoods can be pathologized" (2019, xv; see also Bernstein 2011). Making child sexuality unthinkable and unbearable lends force to public outrage directed at rural Samburu. National fear over infantile sexualization thus becomes "legitimate" xenophobic sentiment. For example, in response to an article on Samburu beads as "sex objects" in the *Star*, one commenter suggests that "A shock therapy needs to be administered to pull a few communities still in their tribal medieval phase into a nation."[7] If this commenter sees rural Samburu as existing outside the time of the modern nation, another commenter on the same article blames beading on the nation's own moral failure: "Archaic customs that romanticize sexual predation . . . very diabolical. But then what else would be expected from a 'kinyeshihole' [shithole] nation?"

How do bead necklaces come to congeal the unbearable or unthinkable sexuality *against which* to imagine a national future? What does it mean to be a good national and ethnic citizen in terms of one's orientation toward bead necklaces and beading? And what do such discourses occlude and produce? I began focusing more systematically on the politics of this custom in 2015, when Samburu elders in different rural communities began organizing ceremonies to put death curses on different girl-empowerment NGO workers and activists—most of them elite women who were themselves Samburu. I wanted to understand what led elders to curse these women, knowing very well that the curse was a religious and political act that they only employed in extreme circumstances. As I pursued this topic through field and archival research, I learned that Samburu necklaces came to congeal anxieties over rural kinship, ethnic sovereignty, national belonging, and child sexualization. The necklaces' material form and relationship to the body, what humanitarians saw as "bondage," determined me to think further about *encompassment*— bodily and ideological—and how different social actors imagined the links between different bounded social and political totalities, including the homestead, the clan, the ethnic group, and the nation. Various forms of gendered political encompassment have resonated with and found expression in the politics of Samburu necklaces. Ambiguous objects, such necklaces constitute an important site for distilling proper national sexuality from intimate noncitizenship. Tracing these gendered geometrics through the trajectories of sexualized beads demonstrates the central role of ethnic hierarchies to national citizenship.

Bead Necklaces in Northern Kenya

In December 2010, I asked Nolkulal, a Samburu woman in her eighties, where beads came from. "They are being brought by white people," she said. "They belong to the whites. We always give out money to buy them." Although I knew that the plastic beads Samburu use to make necklaces and bodily decorations are industrially produced—imported primarily from the Czech Republic—Nolkulal's answer took me by surprise. While most of my interlocutors preferred to describe these objects as quintessentially autochthonous, Nolkulal gestured to their inextricable entanglement in the history of white colonialism and globalization. Beads made of ostrich eggshell, seeds, or glass have been used for centuries in the region. But plastic beads only became prominent, gradually, throughout the twentieth century, having thus "always been modern," as Vanessa Wijngaarden (2018) argues (cf. Kratz 1994; Njoroge 2016; Straight 2002).

In northern Kenya, plastic bead decorations were important means to perform and identify social distinction along lines of ethnicity, gender, age, marital status, residence, and class. Although both men and women wore bead jewelry among Samburu, only women wore necklace bundles— so-called *lchatat*. These bundles grew exponentially from childhood until marriage, changed components as a woman moved through different stages of the life course, and then became smaller and simpler as she aged. Since the 1950s, bead necklaces have marked an important distinction between women engaged in pastoral livelihoods and those educated in mission or district schools. Carolyn Lesorogol (2008b) shows that Samburu have distinguished between schoolgirls—so-called *naarida*, "those of the tight clothes"—and "girls of the home" (M: *ntoyie ee nkang*) or "girls of the beads" (M: *ntoyie ee saen*), that is, girls who herd livestock. In this distinction, bead necklaces marked the proximity and attachment of the latter to the *nkang*—a word that means both "home(stead)" and "family." Meanwhile, the absence of necklaces among schoolgirls signaled the ensuing distance between them and their rural kin. Rural Samburu also used *naarida* to refer to women in towns, whom they saw as different from themselves as "women of the beads" (M: *ntomonok ee saen*). Such distinctions often occurred within the same family, as some daughters attended school and moved to towns while others did not. Yet schooling and residence were not stable markers of distinction. Indeed, some educated women chose to become "women of the beads," finding this rural form of femininity more desirable and respectable.

Since the early 2000s, the distinction between *naarida* and girls and women of the beads has been further complicated by elite and middle-class Samburu women in towns who began wearing necklaces, on special occasions, to claim ethnic identity. At weddings, church services, political rallies, and NGO conferences and workshops, these women wore bead bundles similar to—though typically less voluminous than—those of rural women. Overall, their style remained distinct from that of rural women, in that they also included tailor-made neo-traditional dresses, purses, high-heeled shoes, and elaborate hairdos (unlike rural women, who mostly shave their heads). In her memoir, *The Colorful Bead Necklace of My Mother Tongue*, Maasai journalist Lorna Sempele (2017) explains why bead necklaces have become important to her, as an elite Maa-speaking woman. Raised in Nairobi, she recalls summer vacations in her grandparents' village of Siyiapei, where she learned to speak Maa. "Slowly, and sometimes elusively," Sempele (2017, 4) writes, "I picked up one Maa word at a time and formed a beautiful language necklace that I wear with pride today, as it gives me identity as a Maasai woman." The metonymic relation between the words of the Maa language and the beads of a necklace makes the latter an important visual and material anchor of identity. Similarly, for elite Samburu women, bead necklaces were means to perform and situationally claim attachment to a rural "home(stead)" (*nkang*) as a genealogical anchor of identity.

If, for elite women, the necklace expressed a claim to ethnic belonging, for rural women its size, shape, and individual strings also attested to the intensities and qualities of their social relations. At age six or seven, a girl began to receive coils of wired red beads from parents and relatives. By the time she turned twelve or so, her necklace bundles, the *lchatata*, should have already been large and bulky. On top of it, she would add a string of aluminum coins (M: *nkomesha*) or strings of alternating black and white beads (M: *lopon* or *nkerre*) that she received from her boyfriend (see the necklace in fig. 9 above and Nakamura 2005, 72–74). Girls without boyfriends received these beads from parents and kin, further complicating NGO claims that beads were merely signs of sexual relationships. For a girl to grow up without beads was tantamount to being orphaned, socially undesirable, or lacking social ties. In 2011, Nabaro, a woman in her thirties, recalled coming of age in the early nineties, as a foster child to a rural family:

> That elder [the foster father] had two wives. The wife I was living with was the big one [first wife]. Now, she was a very bad woman. The small [second] wife was better. But the big one was bad. She had a daughter my age. She gave her beads to wear. There were so many times the daughter would go out to dance with the other girls. But me, I couldn't. I was ashamed. I had no beads, no nothing. Me, I was just being called a "boy." So, in that homestead, I was staying like a boy. No person would look at me and see me as a girl. That is, I was not given anything. I had no beads. And, you know, those girls [from the village], even if they were younger than me, they had beads. But me, I did not even have one [string] like this. I was living a different life.

Markers of motherly love, kinship, and social desirability, bead necklaces, Nabaro suggested, were central to embodying femininity successfully. Mistreated by her foster mother, Nabaro could not have been recognized as a girl. For, without beads, she displayed her lack of social ties for everyone to see in a way that left her misgendered and ashamed.

But necklaces also represented a girl's nubility, erotic desirability, her being loved. Bilinda Straight (2004, 274) shows that in rural areas, beads have played an important role in signaling "healthy separations" between specific social categories with important implications for norms of sexual access and avoidance. Consequential separations include those between initiated and uninitiated youths, married and unmarried people. Unmarried girls could engage in legitimate intimate and affective relations only with morans, that is, unmarried but initiated young men. To display their compatibility, members of these two categories of age and gender wore the most elaborate bead decorations. And it was precisely the eroticization of bead necklaces in such relationships that educated and urban women disliked. Lesorogol (2008b, 567–68) notes that "When educated girls and women emphasize that they do not wear beads and that they do not sing at night . . . they are making reference to the 'bead relationship,' which they view as morally suspect. . . . They are often disdainful of these relationships, calling them a waste of time and useless." Thus, girls of the beads and schoolgirls, it was assumed, subscribed to different sexual norms. Bead necklaces were emblematic of this difference, further sexualizing rural girls in the eyes of educated women: according to the latter, village girls who always wore bead necklaces also subscribed to a form of femininity invested in a promiscuous teenage sexuality.

Rescuing "Beaded Girls"

In May 2011, CCN broadcast a "rescue mission" organized by activist Josephine Kulea. Accompanied by CNN reporter David McKenzie, the cameraman, and two Kenyan soldiers, Kulea travels to a Samburu village in Isiolo County to pick up three pregnant girls aged roughly twelve to fourteen. Upon arrival, McKenzie stands in front of a small traditional house, with a group of villagers looking at him puzzled. Holding up to the camera a large bundle of red bead necklaces, he explains: "They call it beading and what happens is that a close family relative will come to the mother and father and then bead the girl, place it over her head, and effectively the adult can have sex with girls as young as six." The bead bundle appears to weigh down heavily on the reporter's arm, its material heaviness metaphoric of the psychological weight it carries for those made to wear it. "Beading," McKenzie says, "has gone on for as long as they can remember, but it is against the law in Kenya." "This is our culture," the father of one of the girls explains. "But Kulea, a Samburu herself," McKenzie retorts, "says this is a bad cultural practice." In her interview with McKenzie, Kulea links beading to unwanted teen pregnancies and abortions. The report ends dramatically with the activist and the soldiers pushing the three crying girls into a military van to take them to a shelter. "Staying," McKenzie quotes Kulea as saying, "would be a worse fate." Notably, in this last scene, the girls no longer wear their necklaces. They have already been *un*-beaded.

The collaboration between McKenzie, a white American journalist, and Kulea, an elite Samburu activist, is based presumably on their shared horror for child sexuality and aversion to gender inequality. McKenzie's description of the bead necklace rehearses imaginaries of this object as a means of "bondage" and "enslavement" in culture: by placing the necklace on a girl, he says, a man owns her. Describing beading—authoritatively, yet incorrectly—as involving sex between six-year-olds and adult relatives, McKenzie associates it with both pedophilia and incest, thus imploding the outrage he expects his audience to feel. This incendiary depiction of beading, in turn, renders the act of *un*-beading and the rescue of the girls at once meaningful and urgent. The discarding of the girls' necklaces represents here an act of ultimate liberation from cultural patriarchy—girls being quite literally unbound.

Women's empowerment NGOs have been present in northern Kenya since the 1990s, promoting education and microfinance projects and preventing "female genital mutilation" (FGM) and "forced marriage" (Cloward 2016, 97–154). But it was only around 2010 that they also launched anti-beading campaigns. Transnational feminist organizations, UNESCO, the International Work Group for Indigenous Affairs, and private donors, among others, funded these projects, prompting a growing number of local NGOs to focus on beading. These included the Samburu Girls Foundation (SGF) that Kulea founded in 2011; but also Samburu Women Trust (SWT), founded in 2009; Coexist Initiative Kenya, an older NGO that, since 2015, has also worked on preventing beading; and others.

To rescue girls from beading, activists working for these organizations deployed different tactics. First, they used judicial means. Invoking the 2010 Constitution, they argued that beading infringed on national and international child rights agreements and was a way to discriminate against women.[8] In collaboration with the National Gender and Equality Commission (NGEC), a national government office established in 2011 to implement the new Constitution, they have carried out "audits" in Samburu villages to identify what an NGEC representative described to me as "girl brides"—a trope commonly deployed in feminist humanitarianism focused on "forced marriages" (Tambe 2019). Some activists went even further, seeking to make beading—a specifically Samburu "problem"—into a nationally recognized category of discrimination in law, a project taken on, for example, by Zeina W. Kombo's thesis "Beading: The Undefined Offence in Kenya" (2016) (see also Lpatilan 2014). Second, NGOs also deployed punitive measures. Although I do not know of elders, mothers, or morans who were actually arrested for beading, "rescue operations," such as the one featured by the BBC, in which NGO workers and the police removed beaded girls from their families and placed them in "safe houses" or orphanages, had indeed been common in the early 2010s. By 2015, in just five years of operation, SGF claimed to have "rescued" over 200 girls in this manner. Third, NGO workers also organized "sensitization" sessions to "educate" rural residents about the "negative effects" of beading, but also FGM, teen pregnancy, and abortion. In recent years, this became their preferred strategy because it antagonized villagers less than more punitive measures.

However, by far the most prominent tactic NGOs deployed was to generate discourse that made anti-beading campaigns meaningful and urgent to a wider public in Kenya and beyond. Discourse production has been also central to obtaining funding to sustain these organizations. Development workers carried out pilot research projects, compiled data in elaborate reports, and produced elegantly designed catalogues, posters, websites, and films that detailed their findings for foreign donors, transnational partners, and government offices. The CNN feature that Kulea participated in, for example, was part of such a discourse-production effort—what NGO workers called "raising awareness." It sought to demonstrate that beading was a particular instance of what women's rights advocates opposed as "gender-based violence" and "sexual violence." But, in detailing the myriad cultural implications of beading for non-Samburu, English-speaking audiences, local NGO discourses also produced the practice anew through legalistic, feminist, nationalist, and class politics frameworks.

What is notable in the CNN feature—as in other NGO reports on beading—is what Carole Vance (2012), writing about humanitarian sex-trafficking prevention efforts, calls a discursive "melodrama": "Melodrama achieves maximum effect through the equation of parts with the whole, severe decontextualization, the juxtaposition of tangential or irrelevant examples that aim to shock, and a sustained effort to mobilize horror and excess. . . . [Such discourses] draw on a one-hundred-year-old tradition of melodrama to structure their narratives, using images of female sexual innocence virtually unchanged from late nineteenth-century European, British, and American social purity campaigns in their crusades against white slavery" (2012, 203). Indeed, the CNN feature melodramatically equates beading with pedophilia, incest, rape, and teenage pregnancies, all inherent to an unchanged, violent "pastoral culture."

When I first watched the CNN segment featuring McKenzie and Kulea, I wondered what their "rescuing" and un-beading the three girls might have meant for the girls' parents and families. Colonial administrators, police, and missionaries have also—sometimes violently—removed necklaces from girls' necks by way of ending the "beading" custom. Straight (2020, 14) says that "Samburu who had experienced the enactment of bans [on beading] reported that colonial police had literally cut beads from girls' necks, an action tantamount to violent abduction during pastoralist warfare." Let us remember that for rural women, necklaces materialized the social ties in which they were embedded. So, in the interethnic raids of the old days, to kidnap young unmarried women, raiders first removed their necklaces, thus severing their existing kinship ties and making them available for assimilation in their own lineages. Similarly, Straight argues, in un-beading girls, "the colonial government was raiding the Samburu."

The "raiding" of children by settler colonial states has been a common mode of governing indigenous, ethnic, and marginalized populations over the past century. Invoking incest, early pregnancies, early marriages, circumcision, and "improprieties" of a people or culture, states have legitimized incursions on indigenous land and disrupted indigenous relations of kinship and social reproduction. Throughout the twentieth century, this has been the case among Aboriginal Australians (Darian-Smith 2020; Povinelli 2006); the First Nations of Canada (Simpson 2014); the Sápmi of Scandinavia (Herranen-Tabibi 2022); indigenous families in Peru (Leinaweaver 2008); and others. To understand what is distinct about the Samburu case, it is important to dwell further on the symbolics of bead necklaces in relation to kinship, belonging, and citizenship.

The Queerness of Custom

Far from being the recent invention of feminist NGOs, the sexualization of Samburu bead necklaces emerged, as already suggested, through colonial interpretations of Samburu intimacies, especially the policies of British administration and the Anglican and Catholic missions in northern Kenya. Between the 1930s and World War II, colonial administrators tried to ban specific bead necklaces that the Samburu used in beading relations. They saw "girl beading" as the primary cause for cattle raiding and interethnic violence in the region. Believing that morans engaged in violence to impress girls with their bravery and thus gain their sexual favors, administrators collaborated with Samburu elders to ban also, on several occasions, the custom of beading as such (Kasfir 2007, 188–90; Meiu 2017, 50–52; Straight 2020). In 1936, for example, a British district commissioner informed the colonial government that "elders . . . issued orders forbidding the eating of meat in the bush, or the giving of beads to maidens by the new morans." Often, he explained, "a young warrior gives beads to his girl, she sings about him, she taunts him to deeds of bravery and so he goes off to blood his spear."[9] Elderly Samburu recalled that colonial police arrested girls found wearing particular kinds of beads known as *somi* (received as gifts from morans) and forcefully removed them from their necks (Kasfir 2007, 190; Straight 2020, 14).[10] Older women have also told me that girls recruited to mission schools were forced to leave their necklaces behind as a way to embrace a modern, Christian femininity.

I interpret the persistence of necklaces and bead-giving among Samburu in defiance of colonial rule as an instance of what T. J. Tallie (2019) describes as customary domains of queerness. "If settler colonialism itself is presented as a form of orientation," Tallie argues, "of making a recognizable and inhabitable home space for European arrivals on indigenous land, then native peoples and their continuous resistance can serve to 'queer' here attempted forms of order" (2019, 7). In such contexts, Tallie suggests, "customs, practices, and potentially the very bodies of indigenous peoples can become *queer* despite remaining ostensibly heterosexual in their orientation and practice, as their existence constantly undermines the desired order of an emergent settler state" (7). In KwaZulu-Natal (South Africa), for example, the indigenous practices of bridewealth and polygamy, Tallie shows, have constituted "the worst fears of . . . settlers" (21). Tallie's argument also echoes recent engagements with the "queer customary," a term that refers to "those practices and desires and their representations that reference (while inhabiting and inflecting) the heteronormativity of customary categories" which hold a potential for "political pragmatism" (Fiereck, Hoad, and Mupotsa 2020, 365).

Echoing these scholarly arguments, in northern Kenya, bead relationships can also be said to have been "queer"—indeed, instances of the queer customary. Despite being media of heteronormativity, they have also troubled the imagination of a white settler colonial order. And this saliently so since 1931, when the government accused Samburu morans of murdering a white settler in the Laikipia highlands and launched campaigns to confiscate their spears and eradicate beading (Simpson 1994, 518–72; Straight 2020; Waweru 2012, 155–66). Over the twentieth century, the queerness of this custom extended from the initial relations of rural Samburu with colonial officers, missionaries, and settlers to those with nationalist elites, middle-class Kenyans, and, later, humanitarians, including educated elite Samburu. All have seen beading as undermining national norms of sexual propriety and tried to distance themselves from or eradicate the intimacies that these necklaces signaled.

If the custom of beading can be seen as queer, then necklaces further congeal and amplify this queerness. To think of bead necklaces as queer objects is to emphasize the contradictory historical forces that continue to animate their social deployments. At once indexical of child, teenage, and premarital sexuality *and* emblematic of marketable ethnicity, at once abhorrent things that derailed progress *and* valuable artifacts that enabled it, bead necklaces maintained a generative tension that made them ambiguous and hence, potentially, also troublesome.

There is also another key paradox at play today in sustaining the contradictions associated with bead necklaces, one that might expand how we think of the relationship between queerness and the customary. This paradox involves humanitarian depictions of beading that reproduce an anachronistic colonial vision of the custom. Strikingly, such depictions haunted rural Samburu at a time when the alleged custom either no longer existed or had long changed, offering a causal explanation for girl victimhood at the expense of more nuanced engagements with the social, economic, and political inequalities in which this custom was alleged to persist. The disjoint or disconnect between the discursive reification of beading and the historical circumstances shaping intimacies and social life in Samburu is itself queer: it troubles normative humanitarianism from within its representational claims. NGOs might thus entail the seed of their own undoing, a subversive queerness inherent in their own normative discourses.

In July 2015, while in Lorosoro, a highland Samburu village where I had been doing fieldwork, on and off, for a decade, Jackson, a friend, research assistant, and village resident, told me that a girl-empowerment NGO had recently built an office there. When he mentioned its name, I recognized the organization as one involved in preventing beading. So, I asked Jackson about the custom. He had not heard of it taking place, he said, in over two decades. The last *senkera* house he remembered in Lorosoro existed until the early 1990s. Together, we speculated that the expansion of schooling and public health interventions related to HIV prevention had possibly led to the custom's abandonment. Even so, bead necklaces continued to circulate and remained important to rural women's identity. To learn more about this custom, Jackson suggested that we talk to Nadinia, a woman in her eighties. Like other rural youths, Jackson saw elderly people as repositories of local culture and history. Moreover, as a classificatory "grandmother" (M: *ngoko*) to men our age (we were both in our early thirties then), it would also not have been inappropriate for her to discuss sexual matters with us. The next day, Nadinia visited us at Jackson's house.

"It is a mother's duty to teach her child what to do and not to do," she said when I asked her what "bead giving" had been all about. She stopped every now and then to sip the hot sweet milk tea Jackson had prepared for us. "The thing a mother fears most," she continued, "is her girl becoming pregnant."

"Why is that so bad?" I asked.

"It's very bad for Samburu," she said. "It's because of the *nkorno* of her father." Nadinia referred to a particular ritual act during a girl's initiation, when her father smears fat known as *nkorno* across her face to bless her and make her a full member of his homestead. Uninitiated children did not belong quite yet to the homestead and lineage. "If a girl is broken [M: *ketoroyie*]," Nadinia said, meaning if she becomes pregnant before initiation, "a father cannot do that. If he puts *nkorno*, he will die."

> The mother had to prevent the daughter [from becoming pregnant]. She would make a *senkera*. It was just a small house with a bed and fire, nothing else [was] there. She built this house right next to hers . . . so she could see who goes there. Then, when the girl received beads, the mother made sure she did not become pregnant. She told the moran: "That girl, she has a father, so

watch out." She also went to the morans of their subclan [M: *ntipat*] and told them: "Tell that moran who gave my daughter beads to watch out not to do bad things."

"The moran should watch out for the girl's period," Jackson intervened to clarify, "not to impregnate her." "In the past, before condoms came," he later told me, "morans used to pull out [before ejaculation]." Older men recalled that, until the 1960s, bead relationships involved non-penetrative sex—sex "between the thighs"—which suggests that the sexual practices associated with the custom had long been changing too.

According to Nadinia, intimacies mediated through the giving and receiving of necklaces and through the construction of *senkera* houses were ways for mothers to prevent daughters from becoming pregnant. Pregnancies among uninitiated girls were held to jeopardize the father's homestead, a homestead to which the daughter belonged. Therefore, the necklace and the *senkera* house formalized these relationships. Bead relationships, Nadinia said, were called in Maa *nkyama dorop*, meaning a "short marriage"—or, temporary marriage. If actual marriage had to follow clan exogamy, "short marriages" involved members of the same clan, something NGOs construed as incest to further outrage their audiences. In fact, rural Samburu notions of incest (M: *surupon*) were much more expansive than those of NGO workers (Meiu 2019, 157–61). A girl's moran lover was indeed a man of her clan (M: *lmarei*) but never of her subclan (M: *ntipat*). A subclan included all descendants from a common fourth or fifth great-grandfather who were classificatory "brothers" (M: *lalashera*) (for an earlier anthropological account of these relationships, see Spencer 1965, 112–13).

In stark contrast to the English "beading" used by NGO workers, Nadinia spoke of "giving" (M: *aisho*) or "receiving beads" (M: *atum saen*). If the English verb presupposes a unidirectional motion and is used to depict men as active (they "bead") and women as passive (they are "beaded"), the Maa verbs presuppose a more dynamically negotiated exchange. Nadinia said that if, in some cases, mothers pressured girls to accept a particular suitor, it was ultimately the girls themselves who accepted or refused gifts of beads or terminated a relationship by removing their necklaces and returning them to the moran. "But nowadays," Nadinia said, "those relationships no longer exist. Those *senkera* [houses] . . . none are left."

I do not wish to offer Nadinia's words and Jackson's reactions as more accurate or authentic alternatives to the narratives of the NGOs discussed above; although, I must admit that my own friendships with and long-term fieldwork among Lorosoro residents tempt me to do precisely that. To be sure, even if "short marriages" were meant, as Nadinia said, to be ways of preventing pregnancies and offering legitimate circumstances for erotic pleasure, they did not foreclose the possibility of violence or abuse. Neither, for that matter, do sexual intimacies of any kind, anywhere. If anything, Nadinia offered a more nuanced understanding of bead relationships to the pathologizing humanitarian discourse. What is interesting, however, is precisely the disjunction between Nadinia's narrative and the discourses of the NGOs. No doubt, Nadinia's nostalgic recollection was driven by a wider context, in which, as we shall see, the very possibility of reproduction and belonging was undermined by new economic inequalities with central implications for questions of intimacy, kinship, and belonging.

Kinship as Encompassment

Nadinia prompted me to think also of the role of filiation, clans, and the homestead in bead relations, and of how the forceful removal of beads could have been tantamount to kidnapping young women. The more I thought of what I had learned over the years about local kinship and belonging, the more central appeared the form and materiality of bead necklaces to be therein.

The necklace's material form—a set of nested circles of wired beads—strongly resembled the geometrics of local kinship reckoning, offering important clues about how rural Samburu imagined familial encompassment and attachment. When explaining to me how their families related to others within wider groups of patrilineal descent, elderly Samburu often took a stick and scratched a few nested circles on the ground. The circles stood for houses and settlement enclosures in an imagined ideal-type village which served as a symbolic matrix for genealogies of patrilineal descent. A basic relationship of marriage could be imagined thus: one circle standing for a house (M: *nkaji*) and/or the woman who always built and owned it; and another circle, containing the first, representing the fence of the homestead (M: *nkang*) and its gateway (M: *ltim*), both nominally associated with the husband. Within the homestead circle was an additional circle representing the cattle kraal—the *boo*, a word also used to describe patrilineal unity. If the house represented a woman's fertility and life force, the kraal represented the fertility and life force of the patriliny. A polygynous marriage was represented thus (fig. 10a): a circle for each wife's house, ordered clockwise by their seniority around the circle of the kraal and encompassed in the husband's homestead circle. Symbolically speaking, a woman's house was an extension of her womb, containing her children as a unit of belonging: children born to the same mother described themselves as "children of one womb" (M: *nkera ee nkosheke nabo*) or "of the same house" (M: *le nkaji nabo*). Siblings by the father's other wives described themselves as of "the same gateway" (M: *le ltim obo*).

To refer to higher orders of kinship, the imagined setup was slightly more complex; more often verbally rather than graphically depicted, though with an uncontestable visual imaginary in mind. A settlement including several polygynous units belonging to different "brothers" (male members of the same lineage) was depicted as a large circular fencing representing the lineage and containing several "homesteads"—or marital units—each of which has its own gateway. Note how what, at a lower order, is a marital unit circle (fig. 10a) becomes, at a higher order of inclusion, a slice of a larger circle (fig. 10b). Here, the number of gateways indexed the number of husbands within that enclosure, while the number of houses indexed the number of wives. This enfolding of marital units reached its highest level in a clan settlement known as *lorora*. Once every ten or so years, for the initiation of a new age set of morans or its graduation to elderhood, local clan groups built such settlements (for a satellite view of a highland age-set graduation *lorora* from 2012, see fig. 10c). Although a *lorora* dissolved within a few months, its geometrical forms and the concrete position of each family in it, as a "slice" positioned in order of relative seniority, continued to inform how people imagined and described their kinship relations: they invoked the spatial organization of their clan's *lorora* to specify their precise genealogical position.

Although my interlocutors did not compare explicitly the circles of the bead necklace (fig. 10d) to the circles of the homestead or the *lorora*, I suggest that these play similar roles in crafting kinship. Interestingly, necklaces could actualize not only relations of patrilineal belonging but also other forms of relatedness. If many necklaces in a girl's bead bundle were gifts from her parents or moran lovers, who are of the same clan as her, others were from her maternal kin or female friends from different clans, and so on. If in an actual marriage, the husband's compound encompassed the wife's house, incorporating her in his patrilineage, the bead bundle contained different necklaces that also encompassed a young woman in myriad competing and complementary kinship relations.

The link between necklaces and the circles of kinship reckoning was not merely representational, but also material. People related through the mother's house, the father's gateway, or through bead necklaces came to share bodily substance with each other *and* the actual objects that emblematically described their relationships (Straight 2007). For example, if a person died while visiting another, the body could not be taken out through the gateway of that compound lest the whole "gateway"—meaning the husband, all his wives, and all their children—be polluted with death. Here, the gateway was

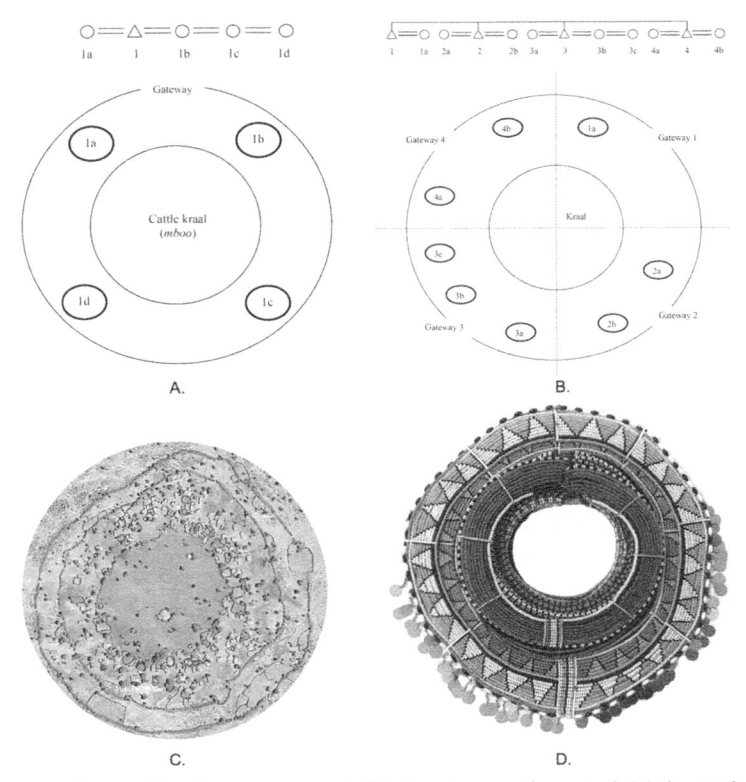

FIGURE 10. Circles of kinship encompassment: (A) the polygynous homestead; (B) the patrilineage; (C) satellite image of a *lorora* ceremonial clan compound (Google Maps); (D) a women's bead necklace, author's collection. Photo by George Paul Meiu.

not only a symbol of the patrilineal polygynous unit but also materially continuous with its members' bodies. (In this case, another makeshift gateway had to be made through the fence to remove the body.) The circles to which one belonged contained the life force of the members of that specific kinship unit. Similarly, by wearing each other's beads, people made kinship in that they became materially entangled in each other's embodiments (see also Straight 2007).

Encompassment, as a symbolic and material process, is therefore important to understanding local kinship. The encompassment involved in bead giving and rural kinship, more generally, may resemble partly how NGOs imagined beading. But it is not the same as "bondage." In rural kinship, encompassment certainly reflected gender hierarchy: at one level, a settlement has complementary male and female centers of influence (the patrilineal kraal versus the female house), while at another, the male circle of the compound contains the female circle of the house. This is, however, a perspectival issue, similar to how Marilyn Strathern (1988) describes objects and relations in Melanesia. For, at yet another level, a woman's house also encompassed and stood for all her male and female offspring. Over time, as lineages grew and split into different, named lineages, they always took the names of the women to whose houses they traced descent (so that most Samburu lineages have ancestral women's names). In this kinship ideology, encompassment is not absolute but relational, perspectival. Furthermore, as Guido Sprenger (2004) argues in an insightful critique of Louis Dumont's (1980) understanding of the term,[11] encompassment is better seen as a *discursive* strategy that people deploy performatively for specific purposes. Thus if, at one moment, male elders may perform patrilineal encompassment by insisting on the circles of descent, at other times other people might exchange beads to perform alternative encompassments.

Encompassment as a performative claim to different forms of kinship was important to the politics of belonging in the region. Rural families who, in the highlands, mostly lived on collective group ranches without title deeds had repeatedly been pushed off their land by private farmers, corporations, and state administrators (Lesorogol 2008a). Lacking means of livelihood, lineage members migrated to towns in ever larger numbers, further undermining patrilineal unity. Meanwhile, elders who continued to live in villages called forth this clan unity in ritual practice, political action, and other efforts to resist the state's, NGOs', and corporate incursions on their land (Meiu 2016). NGO workers who removed the bead necklaces of girls and took them out of their patrilineal compounds rehearsed a longer colonial and post-independence history of breaking kinship circles and, by reforming rural families, re-encompassing them in the nation.

One year after my discussion with Nadinia and Jackson, while in the United States, I received a text message from Jackson: "The elders, one hundred of them, have gathered on the football field in Lorosoro." He said they "put a death curse [M: *ldeket*] on Jasiti," the woman who led the anti-beading NGO that had recently bought land in the village.

Child Sexuality and Ethno-National Encompassment

The conflict between NGOs and rural families invoked older struggles over ethno-national encompassment, in which the sexual intimacies of children have been saliently debated. In British East Africa, nationalist elites concurred, in part, with white colonials in imagining proper sexuality as hetero-patriarchal reproduction. But what this meant was highly contested. State administrators, courts, missionaries, elders, and others have debated premarital pregnancy, abortion, birthing, circumcision, and marriage as ways to control girls' and women's intimacies (Kanogo 2005; Shadle 2006; Thomas 2003). If, for colonial reformists, sexual regulation had to maintain racial boundaries and ensure the reproduction of a black labor force for a white settler population, African nationalist elites sought to interrogate the racist premises of sexual control.

An important question of these debates was how to educate children and youths and control, contain, and reorient their sexual desires. In *Facing Mt. Kenya* (1938), Jomo Kenyatta describes his own Kikuyu culture to critique racist colonial paradigms of socialization and imagine a modern African nation anchored in ethnic custom. A leading figure of Kenyan nationalism and, later, the country's first president (1964–1978), Kenyatta wrote this book as a student of anthropology at the London School of Economics, supervised by Bronislaw Malinowski (Berman and Lonsdale 2007). His discussion of *ombani na ngweko*, a customary intimate practice between young unmarried people, is particularly illustrative of how he saw sexual regulation as a condition for the stability of ethnicity and the nation. Similar to Samburu bead relations, *ngewko* took place in a special "boys' hut" called *thingira* (a noun similar to the Maa *senkera*, suggesting that versions of this custom were common in the region). There, groups of boys and girls engaged in fondling and "sex between the thighs," penetration being strictly forbidden. This practice, Kenyatta argues, counters colonial notions of African promiscuity: "In order not to suppress entirely the normal sex instinct," he suggests, "the boys and girls are told that . . . to keep good health they had to acquire the technique of practicing a certain restricted form of intercourse" (149). Unlike the abstinence missionaries preached, *ngweko* acknowledged the erotic desire of children and youths as "normal" and molded it for future marriage, an argument that Nadinia also made about bead relations. For Kenyatta, *ngweko* is an example, then, of how custom can shape child sexuality to produce good citizens and a stable nation-state.

Revisiting Kenyatta, Keguro Macharia (2019, 123) argues that his "emphasis on 'technique' and 'practicing' indicates that *ngweko* is a discipline designed to produce heteronormative, ethnic citizens." This presupposes, among other things, erasing the practice's homoerotic possibilities (e.g., the fact that older girls also practiced *ngweko* with younger girls) and relegating its "function" to securing marriage and reproduction, to "solder[ing] intimate performance to ethnic continuity" (124–25). Kenyatta's work was continuous with Kikuyu elites' efforts to "manage the gendered and sexual disruptions occasioned by colonial modernity," with schooling, migration, and urbanization (96). "Amid the many changes of colonial modernity," Macharia notes, Kenyatta "tried to make sex and gender stable concepts and practices that would ground him" (96). Recuperating *ngewko*, he pursues "an embodied reaffirmation of belonging" (123) and "a model for ethnicity as intimate practice" (119).[12]

Heteropatriarchal ethno-nationalism has been foundational to state leadership. But it has also offered a model to ethnic groups like Samburu to mobilize against their marginalization by Kikuyu state leaders. With the decentralization of the national government in 2010, Samburu were able—for the first time ever—to elect their local government leaders. In this context, an elite-driven Samburu ethno-nationalism expanded and intensified. But, if mostly educated and relatively wealthy, town-based Samburu ran for local government offices, rural residents were not too quick to offer them their votes. To make sure they would have direct access to government resources, elders in different regions sought to elect members of their own clans. Meanwhile, elite politicians who needed rural votes made clans central modes for mobilizing electoral support. And thus, kinship and descent became foundational categories of Samburu ethno-nationalism. This animated rural and elite efforts to reclaim attachment to the circles of patrilineal descent and involve urban Samburu more actively in the affairs of the rural homestead (Meiu 2016; 2017; 2019). As part of these efforts to imagine Samburu as an ethno-nation, concerns with rural children's and youths' intimacies proliferated. If rural elders sought to solidify the circles of patrilineal control by preventing incest or adultery, some elites turned to humanitarian girl-empowerment projects to criminalize particular forms of rural intimacy.

I should mention here that imaginaries of ethno-nationalism in Kenya, more generally, have redeployed ethnic modes of genealogy and kinship reckoning to make the nation continuous with the segmentation of patrilineal descent. The nation was thus merely another, more encompassing circle, continuous with the nested circles of ethnicity, the clan, and the homestead. Indeed, in nationalist discourse this higher order of encompassment appeared as the *boma*, a Swahili word meaning "compound." In the national public, *boma* has been used at once to speak of a person's family and home (e.g., S: *kwa boma yangu*, "in my family/homestead") and of the nation as an all-encompassing mega-homestead or compound. This is evident, for example, in the national project *Bomas of Kenya*, a large national park in Nairobi containing prototypical traditional houses for the nation's various ethnic groups. It is also evident in the national "Boma Project," a humanitarian organization focused on women's empowerment across the country. Interestingly, the latter's logo uses a Maa bead necklace instead of the letter O in BOMA, thus further confirming the metonymic relationship between the respective encompassments of necklaces and of the ethno-nationalist compound. "A boma," the Boma Project website explains, "is a livestock enclosure. . . . It symbolizes sanctuary and protection." In this sense, the boma gives a particular weight to what James Ferguson and Akhil Gupta (2002) describe as the paradigm of "vertical encompassment" in topographies of the nation-state, the idea that the state includes civil society, community, and family through a series of ever-widening circles.

The securitization of children and youths against early sexualization has become an important aspect of the logics of ethno-nationalist encompassment in recent decades. Throughout the first half of the twentieth century, discourses on child sexualities, such as Kenyatta's, engaged more deeply with the reality of desires and pleasures.[13] Later discourses, however, categorically denied child sexuality, fetishizing child innocence instead. This has been part of a global trend. Growing sex panics and legal reforms in the Global North shaped, via transnational NGO feminism, conditions for understanding child sexuality globally. Angelides (2019) argues that "a move away from positive portrayals of sexual behavior to its darker, negative, traumatic side" occurs in the 1970s and 1980s with the legal codification of childhood as "age-of-consent" and the advent of the "anti-child-sexual-abuse" movement. This shift directly informed legal reforms in Kenya—including the passing of the Children Act (2001) and the Sexual Offences Act (2006)—as well as across much of the African continent (see also Kangaude and Skelton 2018).

Uncertain Encompassments: The Elders' Curse

On June 18, 2018, I talked to Sempele, an elderly man from Lorosoro. Jackson had told me that Sempele had participated in the ritual that put a death curse on Jasiti, the local NGO's leader. So, I wanted to learn more about what happened.

"There were many, many elders there," Sempele said, recalling the football field by the village school on the day of the curse in 2016. "There were over one hundred elders. We talked and talked. Then we said, things are not good. What is happening is not right. So, we threw twigs."

Throwing twigs refers indirectly to cursing; it names a key act integral to the ritual. As one elder recites the curse, others call out rhythmically *Nkai! Nkai!* (God! God!), each holding up a small dry twig. When the recitation ends, each elder breaks his twig in half and throws it in the direction of the sunset. The verbal curse itself ends with the punchline *todorie ndama*, "set with the sun," an unequivocal incantation of death. The dried twig, devoid of life, substitutes here for the body of the cursed person while the sunset represents their temporal regression into nonbeing. Sempele could not recall the exact words of the curse. All he remembered was the following line: "If you made me so that I cannot smear *nkorno* on my child, may you set with the sun."

Nkorno, as discussed above, refers to the fat that a father smears across the face of a daughter at her initiation. This ritual brings the novice into the circle of the patrilineal compound. The more specific symbolics of this ritual act are particularly interesting. The father, using his right hand, smears fat by tracing a continuous line from the middle of the novice's forehead across the right cheek, and ending close to the chin. The resulting semicircle may represent a fragment of the ideal-type circle through which Samburu reckon descent: a fragment cut off from the main lineage circle, which, drawn across the novice's face, expands the original circle to encompass her as a new member. According to Nadinia, bead relations were important in preventing teenage pregnancies that would otherwise render fathers unable to smear nkorno on their daughters' faces, lest they risk dying.

But how, I wondered, did Jasiti and her NGO prevent fathers from smearing nkorno on their daughters? Bead relations, as we have seen, all but ceased to exist in Lorosoro long before Jasiti opened an office for her NGO there. Moreover, Jasiti could not have been responsible for what was indeed a rise in pregnancies among uninitiated girls. Elders were aware that Jasiti advertised her work as preventing "beading," but explained that that was, as Sempele put it, "to make white people give money to her projects." Invoking beading, according to him, was a way to capitalize on colonial stereotypes to fund other NGO initiatives in what had otherwise become a highly competitive market of funding for women's empowerment. Beading might have offered just the distinction NGOs needed to stand out with donors.

Jasiti's other projects pertained to FGM prevention, the schooling of girls, and the distribution of sanitary pads. Of these, FGM prevention was probably the most controversial among Samburu in Lorosoro. Jasiti, Sempele said, "told people here: 'You should stop cutting girls or you'll be arrested.' She came with the police officers and arrested people." As I understood Sempele's reasoning, Jasiti sought to prevent at any cost elders' efforts to maintain customary separations between initiated and uninitiated girls, raising the likelihood of "inauspicious children" (M: *ngursuneti*) born in the homestead and jeopardizing its well-being.

What rural Samburu called "girls' cutting" (M: *emuratare entoyie*) had been a contentious issue since colonialism (cf. Hodgson 2017; Thomas 2003). In Lorosoro, for example, the meanings and timings of girls' initiation had changed many times throughout the second half of the twentieth century. For example, in the 1950s and 1960s, parents initiated girls before their marriage, so they would not run away with moran lovers. Since the late eighties, many opted to initiate them before they went off to schools, so that if they became pregnant, they would not give birth to inauspicious babies. In recent years, Jasiti in collaboration with Amref Health Africa also enforced anti-FGM laws. But she was hardly alone. Government offices, churches, the police, and even neighbors often intervened to rescue girls meant to undergo genital cutting. This had long driven the practice underground. Families initiated girls in the middle of the night, so that neighbors would not report them to the police. Elders now referred to girls' initiation as "stealing" (M: *amirita*): "you steal from the government," as Sempele explained, having internalized the effects of their *lkereti* being criminalized. But, while Jasiti spearheaded some of these changes, she could surely not be held solely responsible for them. Indeed, more was at stake.

Much of the elders' anger with Jasiti was actually about something else altogether, namely land. Elders of the Lorokushu clan, Lorosoro's dominant population, saw themselves losing land to wealthy elites, such as government officials, humanitarians, and town residents, who purchased land in Lorosoro. After the advent of the new administrative order, since roughly 2013, more and more non-Lorokushu Samburu elites had obtained individual land title deeds there. The area's high rainfall and green pastures made the village particularly attractive to elites who wanted to build cattle farms or cultivate corn. Meanwhile, Lorosoro's elders, including Sempele, still shared one collective "group-ranch" title which, with a growing local population, had now become nearly impossible to subdivide (Lesorogol 2008a). If the elites' quest to criminalize rural customs and intimacies was a way to undercut their very ability to sustain key life-giving circles of social life, expropriating land was akin to a collective death sentence.

Simon, a good friend of mine and a wealthy Samburu politician working for the county government, complained to me in 2018 that Lorosoro elders had become particularly hostile to him after he purchased land there. "Because I am Lmasula [by clan], they say I should not be there," he explained. "That is Lorokushu land. 'But are we not all Samburu?' I asked them." Simon depicted a conflict over economic inequality and political authority, as "clanism." But he also admitted to me that clans now played a very important role in county politics.

Like Simon, Jasiti used her NGO's capital to purchase a large piece of land in Lorosoro, although she was originally from a lowland village and belonged to a different clan. For elders, then, her reformist interventions in—and criminalization of—their intimate lives offered an ideological alibi to marginalize them further and weaken their claims to land. The alienation of their land meant, if anything, losing the ultimate means in which they had anchored their continuity and authority, the homestead and the patrilineal clan. This, for Lorosoro residents, was colonialism by other means: this time not by white British colonials, nor by the post-independence Kikuyu elites, but by their own "sons and daughters." It is this wider context, I think, that the elders invoked when they suggested Jasiti had prevented them "from smearing *nkorno* on my child." If encompassing one's child in the patrilineal homestead, through initiation, had become difficult, it was not merely because NGOs called for the abolition of FGM or a beading custom that no longer existed as such, nor because it used beading discourses to sexualize rural Samburu and amass capital. It was rather because they used that money to further displace rural families from their land. Together with other elites, they thus undermined local livelihoods and attachments in a direct affront to rural lives.

Local NGO workers, like Jasiti, often described elders' curses against them as cultural relics or a patriarchy's self-defending response. Yet it is important to understand the elders' curse as political in another sense. Elders' attachment to particular forms of belonging was hardly the stubborn traditionalism that NGOs, media, and the government attributed to rural Samburu. Rather, it was something like a decolonial commitment against elite and corporate rule, a means through which to re-encompass their offspring within the life-giving circles of kinship.

Bead Necklaces and Humanitarian Encompassments

In the national and international media and scholarship on women's rights and public health, NGO discourses on Samburu beading have become authoritative accounts of the practice and its meanings. Local NGOs were not merely replicating the language and logics of transnational feminist organizations, but actively brokering them, such as to *encompass* young rural women, ideologically and materially, in their reformist practices and institutions. Encompassment did not only occur through the actual physical removal of girls from their families, their un-beading, or internment in schools and "safe houses." It occurred simultaneously through the discursive production of bead necklaces as humanitarian objects—indeed, "sex objects"—that made girls' rescue imperative.

Attributing sexual violence to the ethnic Other while construing girls as "innocent children," these discourses produce the ethnic "girl-child" as what Farris (2017, 140) calls "the ideal type [of] the victimized object." For this, the girl had to remain "innocent"—a pre-political entity; her subjectivity inaccessible to the point of non-existence. Thus objectified, hollowed out of a point of view or agency, the girl can only come into subjectivity through her re-encompassment in the humanitarian apparatus. For girl-empowerment NGOs to be able to produce confident girls with self-esteem, their young beneficiaries must first be made into voiceless figures, lacking confidence, posture, and self-worth (Moore 2016).

To foreclose the slipperiness of its own interpretation, much of this NGO discourse then stamps what it sees as an exploitative unidirectionality in sex—morans driving pleasure *from* girls—as "sex slavery," "sexual violence," and so on. This attempt at semiotic stabilization—preventing the slipperiness of its interpretation—is akin to what Lacan (1993, 263–99) calls *point de capiton*, or "quilting point." Resembling an upholstery button that prevents the foam in a couch from moving around, the *point de capiton*, Lacan says, works to prevent the sliding of a signifying chain from its intended message. Farris (2017), for example, describes "performative contradictions" in the work of femocrats and femonationalists to point out their inherent contradictions, ruptures, and slippages—various occlusions in their rhetoric or dissociations from the wider political economy of their work. To the extent that this work depends on "technologies of talk" (Gal, Kowalski, and Moore 2015), their citational practices are prone to inconsistencies or unexpected readings. I see the Lacanian *point de capiton* as the semiotic "safety pin" that keeps a certain interpretative framework in place. In this case, the bead necklace constitutes this quilting point, at once facilitating a particular humanitarian understanding of beading as "bondage" or "sex slavery" and branding NGO projects with an otherwise seductive ethnic brand.

Both beads and beading were ways to brand a particular niche of NGOs as feminist indigenous institutions concerned with a particular "exotic" ethnic sexuality. This gave them a relative advantage in a competitive market of development funding earmarked for the prevention of gender-based violence, FGM, and forced marriage. Writing about the political economy of anti-FGM NGOs in Ghana, Saida Hodžić (2017) shows how discourses condemning cutting have become more prominent precisely as the practice's prevalence declined. The proliferation of discourse about it, Hodžić shows, legitimizes the need to reproduce the reformist institutions that deal with its eradication. Similarly, it is no accident that NGOs in northern Kenya generated a lot more discourse on beading precisely at a time when the custom had all but disappeared. For here, too, the production of discourse ensured access to resources that remained essential for other women's empowerment programs, but also to maintaining the economic and social status of the new local elites associated with development.

To suggest this is not to claim in any simple way that NGO workers like Jasiti were deceitful. Many of those I spoke to were very devoted to their work and to the young women they hoped to help. Rather, it is to suggest that a particular humanitarian ideology of rights, gender, and culture (see, for example, Chanock 2000; Grewal 2017; Hodgson 2017) has allowed them to position themselves *outside* the contexts in which they worked and to render the "problems" they addressed culturally Other. "Modernizing processes," Hodžić (2017, 6) argues, "demand that NGO workers and civil servants disidentify from these shared [social] worlds and instead construct themselves as temporally, morally, and civilizationally *ahead* of them." Considering that rural girls continued to wear beads and that bead necklaces, among other things, continued to be exchanged as presents in intimate relationships, it mattered less to local NGO workers how this might have been different from the custom of "bead giving" of the past. "For you anthropologists," a development worker once said to me, "culture is what you want to understand. For us, it is what needs to change." Reifying a static, patriarchal, pastoral culture, NGOs hoped to achieve a greater good—to liberate young women, educate them, and make them into what Moore (2016) describes as "aspirant feminists." But in doing so, they disrupted, displaced, or delegitimized rural efforts to produce kinship and, through it, belonging and citizenship.

*

An ethnographic detour focused on bead necklaces and their recent politicization illustrates an import aspect of intimate citizenship: the gendered geometrics of its competing encompassments. Encompassment poses a particular challenge: How should leaders, elites, and other citizens enfold or encircle a body, a homestead, a lineage, a clan, an ethnic group, and a nation to build an ideal political community? Ethno-nationalist deployments of these imagined nested circles have made child and teen sexuality a key criterion for separating national sexuality from intimate noncitizenship, respectable futurity from collective doom. Whether a means of "bondage" or kinship, the bead necklace's very form evoked the workings of belonging. NGO campaigns foregrounded necklaces to produce an ethnicized and sexualized Other through the rescue of which elites then claimed and performed good citizenship. But necklaces have also represented artifacts of a "queer customary" domain, through which marginalized people asserted particular forms of femininity, kinship, and ethnic belonging *against* a state- and NGO-driven heteropatriarchal recolonization.

Bead necklaces are queer objects not simply because of their initial association with a counter-hegemonic customary domain. Rather, it is because they capture key contradictions in the making of ethno-nationalism: the desire at once to repudiate beads as outrageous sex objects and to redeploy them as ethnic brands; the rush to sexualize them as media of gender oppression and to sanitize them as beautiful markers of elite ethnic attachment, and more. Necklaces sustain tensions over competing modes of encompassment and different imaginaries of belonging and citizenship at the core of which are discourses on intimacy. Such discourses work to encompass and enclose particular subjects, while placing others outside the realm of citizenship, rendering them ontologically unassimilable. Yet encompassment—like the country's borders or ethnicity's or kinship's boundaries—remains aspirational, a process of continuous reiteration, in which people draw and redraw the circles of their competing attachments, while contesting their meanings.

It is with these competing politics of encompassment in mind that, in chapter 7, I return to the Samburu "boy with beads" whom I introduced in the opening of this book. For in northern Kenya, such bead necklaces have also become productive of the homosexual body, itself an effect of early sexualization.

5

Plastics:
Moral Pollution and the Matter of Belonging

> They said that as they themselves left the field they saw that among the litter, empty cans and bottles, were many plastic snakes, and by now everyone knew that those plastic reptiles were the signature of the Movement for the Voice of the People.
> NGŨGĨ WA THIONG'O

This book, let us recall, attends to a quite unexpected aspect of the recent anti-homosexuality campaigns: namely that in everyday life, this alleged "homosexual threat" is not always easy to pin down. Making the homosexual body a more stable target of outrage or violence takes work. To make this target stick, leaders, media, civil society groups, and citizens have deployed a vast set of unlikely objects. The previous two chapters focused on objects that have foregrounded preoccupations with how Kenyans have imagined, on the one hand, the body's vitality and, on the other, its encompassment and enfolding in various nested categories of belonging and citizenship. Discursive logics associated with vitality or encompassment, as we have seen, also involve particular gendering processes. According to these logics, the homosexual body was the antithesis of the good citizen because it leaked gender by feeding on male-power and because its sexual essence, like that of the indigenous pastoralist Other, may remain unassimilable to the nested circles of national encompassment. My next ethnographic detour revolves around a type of objects that illustrates how, in the Kenyan national public, homosexuality also became akin to bodily contagion or pollution—namely, plastic.

In the last decade, anxieties over homosexuality as a "foreign import" have borrowed the language and imaginary of plastic. "In Africa," a Samburu man wrote on Facebook, "gay[i]sm has no space in the culture, looking like a fatal plastic import from the West . . . the chemistry of Africans just don't [sic] work arousing for same-sex partners." Others suggested that microplastics consumed in water caused homosexuality. And, as I will show in chapter 7, Pentecostal leaders who exorcised gayism from young men's bodies exposed it as "a snake who turned into plastic." In 2018, in an event that perfectly mirrored the Kenyan state's governance through moral securitization, the

Islamist militant organization Al-Shabaab in Somalia banned homosexual acts *and* plastic bags, making them both punishable by death. Accordingly, in East Africa, homosexuality and plastic—the latest hindrances to moral utopias—became similar, mutually constitutive, if not partly overlapping, foreign afflictions against which an ideal order could be imagined. It might not be accidental, then, that sociologist Anthony Giddens (1992) speaks of "plastic sexuality" to designate late capitalism's ever-more-fluid forms of erotic intimacy; nor, for that matter, that nationalist discourses use plastic to describe intimacies that undermine older ideals of heteropatriarchal citizenship. In both cases, plastic's very *plasticity* evokes epochal transformations that have rendered older norms of attachment highly malleable.

But to better grasp the historical stakes of plastics, it is necessary to step away from questions of sexuality *stricto sensu*. It is necessary instead to pursue these objects ethnographically across contexts in which they have recently posed problems or generated panics. Interestingly, as we shall see, this ethnographic detour should bring sexuality back to the table, albeit more complexly entangled in the politics of kinship, ethnicity, body, pollution, and contagions.

Panics over Plastics

To begin with, consider a set of coincidences. On August 28, 2017, Kenya's National Environment Management Authority (NEMA) banned the manufacture, importation, and use of plastic bags in the country. International media called this "the world's toughest ban on plastic bags."[1] Simply carrying them became punishable with fines of up to US$40,000 or prison terms of up to four years. "We will go to the extent of raiding defiant premises," threatened NEMA officials, as police inspected shops, markets, and vehicles.[2] At borders, too, "foreigners are now to be stripped of plastic bags before entering Kenya."[3] Many Kenyans met the excessive force and incendiary language of the government's infamous "war on plastic" with enthusiastic support. Journalist Pauline Kairu describes polytene bags as "an unruly monstrosity that stared at Kenyans almost everywhere"—dangerous things "woven into the fabric of our lives." "They hang on trees and trenches," says Kairu, "the winds ever so blithely unhesitating to blow them to undecided destinations."[4] And so, plastic bags must be eliminated before they destine Kenyans to catastrophic futures. Citizens also called on local governments, as one man wrote on social media, to "completely remove [any] plastic materials [from] our habitat."

The ban on plastic bags coincided with a set of rumors and scandals in which plastic figured prominently. The same year, a panic erupted over so-called plastic rice. After a severe drought had damaged crops across the country, videos circulated on social media showing rice granules melting in boiling water when cooked. "Some people are bringing in cheap and fake rice [from China]," claims a Kenyan blog, "and packaging it as if it was grown in Kenya."[5] Speculations on the rice's Chinese origin are significant when, for over a decade, the Chinese government has invested in Kenya's infrastructure, taking over responsibilities Kenyans expect their state to fulfill. In this context, plastic rice objectifies what appears as Chinese infiltration in Kenyan lives in a form other than itself. Packaged to appear homegrown, the foreign(er) now appropriates the appearance of the autochthon and, thus disguised, comes dangerously close to real citizens' bodies to poison them. It thus joins a wide set of so-called *kemikali*, or chemicals, common in local diets that are felt to "overheat stomachs" (Rahier 2021).

Plastic's association with the foreign and its afflictions is not new. As part of my research on ethnicity, sexuality, and belonging in the town of Maralal, Samburu County, I have worked with so-called "plastic boys." Plastic boys are men in their twenties through early forties who make a meager living selling antiques and plastic artifacts. If locals use the noun "boys"—a mode of reference initially deployed by white colonials in subjecting male Africans (Meiu 2015, 480)—to infantilize these men, the adjacent "plastic," as will become clear shortly, tells a more complex story. In the aftermath of Kenya's contested presidential election of December 2007, Salim, a twenty-nine-year-old who identified as a plastic boy, was evicted from his home near Maralal. Longstanding conflicts over land alienation and wage labor had broken out, across the country, in interethnic violence. "Samburu said that the land had to be shared amongst themselves," Salim recalled in 2010. "They told me to leave."

Village elders I spoke with said they had evicted Salim because he was a foreigner. To determine belonging, as the previous chapter has shown, elders now focused more strictly on patrilineal descent, emphasizing that Salim's father was Somali and overlooking that his maternal grandmother had in fact been Samburu. But they also said that Salim was a plastic boy, by which they meant a "pauper" (M: *lkirikoi*), someone without a lineage. Without ties of descent, Samburu say plastic boys—like actual plastic objects—are, by definition, non-Samburu. Salim's being a "plastic boy" might not have taken precedence over his paternal ethnicity in shaping the elders' decision. But cultural logics associated with plastic have certainly underscored his foreignness. The same week, local youths destroyed the plastic boys' shop along with those of migrant settlers in Maralal, claiming they were all foreigners. Salim told me: "I said to myself: 'I better leave lest maybe something bad happens. They can even slaughter me in the night.'"

The above examples suggest that different troublesome objectifications of plastic—bags, boys, rice, and relations—have resonated with one another and with their wider social contexts to shape belonging and citizenship. What makes plastic such an evocative idiom of nonbelonging in Kenya today? How does plastic congeal at once such "deep despair" and "utopian hope," to use the words of Anand Pandian (2016)? And what is at stake in repudiating plastic, in imagining a world without it? If plastic lends itself in evocative ways to postcolonial subjects' efforts to conceptualize belonging, new relations of belonging materialize precisely as people engage with and disavow the substance's various nefarious figurations. Indeed, the historical objectification of plastic and efforts to define belonging and citizenship shape one another dialectically. Focusing on the plastic boys as a gendered subject position, but also on objects and afflictions deemed of "plastic," I show how historical experiences with plastic's forms, surfaces, and substance informed desires for particular kinds of political order as well as the fantasies, possibilities, and limitations of people's attachments to a region, ethnicity, or the state.

How Belonging Matters

Plastic plays a central role in contemporary struggles over belonging and citizenship. Anthropologists have shown, for example, how recent efforts to tell apart foreigners from autochthons have played out, often subtly disguised, in panics over objects that seem otherwise trivial: "alien species" of fish, trees, or plants that endanger "local nature" (Comaroff and Comaroff 2001; Death 2017; Geschiere 2009; Lavau 2011). Little has been said, however, about plastic's dominant position among these objects. Concerns with plastic pollution are often about more than the substance's environmental impact. Globally overabundant, plastic is now deeply imbricated in our perceptions of space and time, in how we acquire political subjectivities and imagine futures (Barthes 1988; Davis 2022; Gabrys, Hawkins, and Michael 2013; Hawkins 2001; Meikle 1995). Amidst late capitalist political-economic transformations in Africa, as elsewhere, plastic has also become emblematic of new modes of consumption and new forms of moral disorder (Braun and Traore 2015; Weiss 1996). It is important, then, to examine what plastic's historical salience reveals about the politics of belonging today.

Heather Davis (2016, 190) argues that plastic's materiality is queer in that it troubles contemporary identity politics. Its ability to take on numerous, ever-changing forms engenders a "politics of passing": it offers "the lesson of shape-shifting, of assuming identities that defy coherent forms and change with and in response to particular contexts." Refusing to be tied to a permanent position, Davis suggests, plastic evades easy scrutiny. And so, its mutability puzzles us. Roland Barthes (1988, 92) argues that "the mind does not cease from considering the original matter as an enigma . . . because the quick-change artistry of plastic is absolute: it can become buckets as well as jewels." Recognizing plastic's distinct mutability makes it expandable to—indeed, transmutable into—a wide array of things, including perhaps afflictions ("plastic rice") or persons ("plastic boys"). However, *pace* Davis and Barthes, it is important to avoid positing plastic's materiality as universal in its perceptions and meanings. Instead, it is essential to reflect on how plastic's presence resonates with historical aspirations and anxieties in particular contexts. Exploring how Kenyans engage with plastic and how, through such engagements, they generate new attachments reveals how plastic and belonging materialize together—how they shape each other's qualities—in context. While plastic might not always "trouble" identity, as Davis (2016) claims, it certainly becomes a key means for objectifying or tackling identity's paradoxes.

Carl Death (2017, 213) argues that with intensified migration and urbanization across Africa, people commonly use environmental tropes to reflect on "foreign invasions" and what appears to be endangered "local nature." For example, in 2000, in South Africa's Cape region, a panic emerged over a new "alien" plant—the Australian acacia—that, having spread out rapidly, caused fires that destroyed vast expanses of terrain. Social anxieties over this plant, Jean and John Comaroff (2001) suggest, have paralleled xenophobic affects over labor migrants from other African countries who now competed with South Africans over otherwise scarce employment. In this context, environmental discourse and practice can restore a sense of belonging: planting trees, cleansing landscapes, or rescuing indigenous species are ways to claim autochthony, protect the familiar, and expel the foreign (Death 2017, 213; Lavau 2011).

Plastic occupies a central role in this context. The very presence of plastic, often readily recognizable as a quintessential commodity, can evoke how the circulation of capital renders social worlds porous, pervious (Weiss 1996, 176). As waste, too, plastic dwells in the afterlife of the commodity, threatening to pollute and annihilate life (Hawkins 2001). Its ability both to take on rigid, solid forms and to shape-shift may also resonate with new market tendencies to render identity at once immutable—the very stuff of DNA—and ever more malleable to shifting trends of speculation and consumption. But this does not tell us much of how plastic shapes—and is, in turn, shaped by—particular relations of belonging and citizenship.

Rather than posit a causal relationship between the global circulation of plastics and the politics of belonging, I prefer to approach their intersection as premised on "constitutive resonance." This concept, William Mazzarella (2017, 5) argues, "suggests a relation of mutual becoming rather than causal determination." Accordingly, plastic and belonging materialize in new ways in relation to one another. I understand materialization here as the processes through which subjects, objects, and relations gain thing-like qualities (Miller 2005).[6] I explore plastic's materiality by examining resonances entailed in its objectification: how desires, fears, and attachments come to echo and reverberate in plastic's material properties, how plastic's mutability becomes iconic of anxieties over value and durability, and how its polluting trajectories render immediate utopias of political order and belonging. As Daniel Miller (2005, 9) argues, here "the very act of creating form creates consciousness."

I first show how the simultaneous emergence of plastic boys and plastic objects in northern Kenya gave new material forms to the idea of nonbelonging. With the rise of Samburu nativist politics, plastic came to represent foreignness in many forms. The disavowal of various plastics in the region has allowed Samburu to sustain the idea of an autochthonous order with new means. Similar cultural grammars have played out in the national public as government officials have reassured citizens that the state is protecting them from plastic's myriad afflictions. I then return to the plastic boys to show how people displace prominent threats of social failure onto them in ways that make plastic resonate with dominant socioeconomic anxieties in the present.

Plastic Boys: Desire, Deception, and the Foreign

Plastic boys were invariably the first people to greet foreigners upon their arrival in Maralal (fig. 11). They sold "*curios*": old, traditional household objects and bodily decorations they collected from the region's pastoralists. They also offered travelers tours of nearby villages or treks into the northern desert. When I began my research in the region in 2005, I was fascinated with these men's vast knowledge about the customs of Samburu, the dominant ethnic group in the region, but also those of neighboring Turkana, Pokot, Rendille, and Borana. Despite their interest in local cultures, however, these men imagined themselves as cosmopolitan, urban youths who, although relatively poor, aspired to become middle class. Their style reflected these aspirations. They dressed in blue jeans, running shoes, shirts, or T-shirts, listened to reggae music, played soccer, entertained ideas of romantic love, and spoke English, Swahili, and two or more regional ethnic languages. Without formal employment and with few foreigners passing through Maralal, plastic boys also sold sunglasses, watches, and other plastics to the town's residents. As locals said, they traded old culture for foreign plastics.

FIGURE 11. "Plastic" boys in front of their curio shop, Maralal, Samburu County, Kenya, July 2011. Photo by George Paul Meiu.

But "plastic boys" is also a phrase for what Samburu living in and around Maralal despised as "useless paupers" who, not unlike plastic itself, had no capacity to grow, reproduce, thrive, or attach themselves in meaningful ways to a place or a people. Locals said they failed to marry, accumulate resources, or set up respectable households. During my fieldwork, I learned that plastic boys invested in numerous intimate attachments but that town-based Samburu elites and Samburu in nearby villages did not recognize these ties as legitimate kinship. Unable to prosper, these Samburu believed, plastic boys could contaminate others with their poverty. One woman explained that "these boys are bringing lots of problems to us. They never amount to anything. They are just inauspicious [M: *kotolo ake*]." Plastic boys, like plastic itself, were agents of pollution. Villagers sometimes paid plastic boys to bury young men who died unmarried and childless, a highly polluting ritual task. Perceptions of failure and pollution also worked to delegitimize these men's ability to access land, employment, and welfare in town.

When I asked plastic boys where their name came from, they all told me the same story: In the late 1970s, a group of poor young boys walked to a campsite outside Maralal where U.S. Marines were training. In the evening, the boys returned to town wearing dozens of glow-stick bracelets the Marines had given them in exchange for curios. "At that time, we did not yet have electricity in town," Adam, a thirty-six-year-old "plastic boy," told me in 2010. "And those bracelets were glowing so nicely." The boys told locals that the bracelets would glow for three months, so people bought them. "That was big business," Adam said. "But, after only a few hours, the bracelets stopped glowing. So, people came asking: 'Where are those stupid boys who sold us these plastics? Where are those plastic boys?' That's where our name comes from."

This story illustrates how people imagined plastic boys as sharing some of plastic's qualities. If plastic objects enticed consumers with their shiny, glowing surfaces while deceiving them with their inherently poor quality, plastic boys used trickery and persuasion to make customers desire low-quality goods. They made money by deceiving others, locals said. When used as an adjective, the Swahili and Maa *plastiki* can also mean "fake" or refer to inauthentic goods or cheap things "made in China." Desire and deception figured here as twin characteristics of both the substance and the men. But, despite the adjective's pejorative connotations, plastic boys were proud of their name. As one man put it, "the name 'plastic' was chosen [for plastic boys] because of [the substance's] flexibility and [its being] weatherproof," echoing the men's qualities of entrepreneurship and hard work.

Plastic boys emerged as a social category in the late 1970s, roughly around the same time that plastic became prevalent in northern Kenya. At first, plastic goods were useful and attractive. Jerry cans, basins, baskets, cups, thermoses, strainers, mirror frames, flashlights, slippers, sacks, and soccer balls became popular throughout the region. They came in a wide range of sizes and colors, were easy to wash, and were quite cheap (fig. 12). So much have some of these goods shaped local desires that their names became synonymous with plastic. In Maa, *plastiki* is partially interchangeable with *lkasuku*, a name derived from the national cooking-fat brand Kasuku, whose plastic containers women recycle; *lpiyrai*, "rubber" or "condom"; and *lgunia*, "gunny sack." Beads imported from the Czech Republic became the most popular plastic commodity (Nakamura 2005, 12; Straight 2002, 19n26). Samburu women, as we have already seen, used these beads to make elaborate necklaces and other jewelry that were now emblematic of their traditional dress, and young morans wore brightly colored plastic flowers and feathers in their hair. Plastic, in these forms, was beautiful and desirable.

But soon another side of plastic unraveled: waste—bags, bottles, and fragments of old artifacts—became suddenly overabundant. "It is tragic to see how much inroad plastic has made into Kenya," a Swiss traveler to the region observed (Hofmann 2005, 13):

PLASTICS 125

FIGURE 12. Stores selling plastic goods, Maralal, Samburu County, Kenya, July 2011. Photo by George Paul Meiu.

> Fifteen hundred feet before each village the first signs of it appear: starting with just pink, blue or clear plastic bags hanging on the shrubs, but then the nearer we get the worse it is. There are plastic bottles impaled on virtually every thorn on every bush. At first glance, it almost looks like they're in bloom, but a second later the tragic truth is all too painfully evident... [Plastics] hang on the bushes in their thousands.

Livestock often died ingesting plastic bags. "If you slaughter a goat or a cow," a Samburu man told a national newspaper, "you find bags that could fill a sack in its stomach."[7] Locals therefore embraced the government's ban on plastic bags, and in recent years, Samburu women have worked with NGOs to clean villages of plastic waste.

Over the past four decades, northern Kenyans have imagined plastic things and plastic boys in similar ways. If objects could generate desire through their appearance, men did so through their ability to persuade others to buy such objects. But both deceived with their essences. The essence of plastic objects revealed itself quickly because they broke easily; their life as useful things was temporary. But they did not decompose, so their presence as waste was everlasting. Something similar was at stake with "plastic boys." The category emerged when impoverished families who had lost their cattle to raiders across northern Kenya sought refuge in Maralal. Their young sons took to the streets in search of a living. At first, they worked as cultural entrepreneurs, which was fine, Maralal residents said. But then they started cheating, drinking, and wasting away their lives. For locals, both plastics and plastic boys were devoid of life force, a property they could impart to others. In both instances, then, plastic designated entities with foreign origins, deceitful essences, and polluting properties, but for plastic boys, it also connoted flexibility and malleability as, at times, desirable skills of a late capitalist market.

The Substance of Belonging in Northern Kenya

Images of cattle grazing on piles of plastic waste have become emblematic of northern Kenya's geopolitical marginality. National media, NGOs, and churches used such images to situate the region's pastoralists at what Paul Rigby (1992) calls "the periphery of capitalism." Let us recall that, since the advent of colonialism, Kenya's northern territories have occupied a marginal position within the state. Lacking natural resources and being unsuitable for agriculture, British colonials and later Kenyan leaders saw the region as unworthy of government investment. Moreover, for them, the apparent cultural conservatism of northern pastoralists, including Samburu, only offered further reason to defer building roads, schools, and health facilities (Waweru 2012). Since Kenya's independence in 1963, administrators who governed northern districts came from other parts of the country and were of Kikuyu, Luo, or Kalenjin ethnicities. This exacerbated northerners' sense of marginalization. Plastic's proliferation in the region only confirmed that powerful leaders had cheated them out of a good life and into consuming fake, toxic things; it was a bodily and environmental symptom of their longstanding marginalization.

Since the 1980s, a growing Samburu elite, mostly educated traders, teachers, and development workers residing in towns like Maralal, have pursued an ethnic politics claiming state resources and rights. They joined opposition parties and initiated NGOs to advocate on behalf of Samburu. With international funding, some built schools and boreholes, installed electricity, and replenished rural livestock. Others engaged in ecological projects on wildlife conservation, forest management, or waste control, seeing their environment as an asset for safari tourism (Lekembe 2010). Becoming "green citizens," some elites also demonstrated their strong attachment to the land. Following the 2010 constitutional reform that decentralized state administration, some of them took over, for the first time ever, the governance of their county.

In this context, Samburu have tried to decide who would be entitled to their region's share of national resources and foreign aid. Determining this was no easy task. People of various ethnic backgrounds have long lived in the region, some being adopted into Samburu lineages and clans (Hjort and Salzman 1981; Spencer 1973, 135–36). Since the 1960s, towns like Maralal have also attracted traders, migrant settlers, and people displaced by violent cattle raiding elsewhere. But, with the turn to autochthony, their presence became problematic. Rural Samburu worried that their urban kin would "mix" with foreigners and forget their origins. The previous chapter has shown how relations of descent and generation became uncertain and elders now sought ways to reify their importance for belonging (see also Holtzman 2006; Meiu 2017, 70–74). This has had uneven gendered implications. Women, for example, were easier to adopt into patrilineal clans because they eventually married into other clans. Men, however, had to "grow" their own clans. Hence, as one elder told me, "Raising another man's son can bring death into your homestead." Therefore, Samburu did not adopt plastic boys, many of whom were orphans. Referring to them as "plastic," then, also lent strength to arguments for their nonbelonging.

Material substance has long played an important role in imagining belonging. My interlocutors said, for example, that *lkunono* or blacksmith lineages were unpropitious because melting metal generated polluting forces, forces that, in turn, would not allow them to prosper. These forces could also contaminate those who lived close to them (Straight 2007, 20). Because few other Samburu generally agreed to marry *lkunono*, the latter have been mostly endogamous (Kasfir 2007, 135ff). Samburu, to be sure, have long depended on lkunono for knives, spears, machetes, and other metal objects (Larick 1987). But because these objects "belonged" to—and could act on behalf of—lkunono and kill others, their relation to such objects was ambivalent. Before circumcision rituals, for example, elders blessed the sharp metal objects of each household lest they would kill novices.

Consider another example: the Ilgira, a people of Turkana origin who, since the early days of colonialism, have been adopted, if ambiguously, into Samburu lineages (Hjort and Salzman 1981, 55). Samburu considered Turkana impure because they did not circumcise and because they ate foods that Samburu considered taboo. Although Ilgira long adopted Samburu customs, including circumcision and food prohibitions, their Turkana origin kept them in a somewhat marginal, polluting position. Like the lkunono, Ilgira have therefore been relatively endogamous, forming a group of their own. In Maa, their name derives from the verb *a-gira*, "to be quiet" (1981, 57), which suggests that they have no voice in Samburu affairs.

The examples of the lkunono and the Ilgira show how the material qualities of particular attachments, their substances, could affect, for better or worse, people's "life force" (M: *nkishon*), itself a condition for sustained belonging. Locals said that, like the lkunono and the Ilgira, plastic boys undermined others' life force. Yet plastic's entanglements in local belonging require further discussion.

Desiring Autochthony, Disavowing Plastic in Rural Samburu

As plastic became prevalent, rural Samburu objectified it in light of their own moral dilemmas. Since the 1990s, for example, they spoke of "plastic hair" (M: *lpapit le plastik*) and "warriors of plastic" (M: *lmurran le plastik*). Some morans—young men who have been circumcised but had to wait several years before marrying and becoming elders—have migrated to Kenya's coastal tourist resorts to make money (Meiu 2017). They devised an easier way to maintain their long, braided hair, dyed with ochre, which is emblematic of their age-grade status at home and an important part of how they appeal to tourists at the coast (Kasfir 2007, 228–35). Rather than keep their hair long, they wore extensions. Their choice was significant because, for Samburu, hair represented an important aspect of kinship. Those belonging to the same lineage and morans of the same age set were said to "share hair" (M: *keng'ar lpapit*): that is, the substance of their hair made them co-present in one another (Spencer 1965, 74; Straight 2007, 125–26). If, say, a lineage member died, the hair of all members of that group became polluting and had to be shaven, lest they too would die. Town-based Samburu sometimes postponed shaving in such situations, prompting conflicts with rural relatives. Male migrants, however, took the insult even further: they produced fake extensions and caricatured kinship with plastic hair.

With time, locals have extended this label to refer to the men themselves, calling them "plastic morans" (M: *lmurran le plastik*). Jackson told me in 2015 that girls from the village Lorosoro, where he lived, used this phrase to tease young men who migrated to coastal tourist resorts. "The girls are trying to provoke morans," he told me. "They call them plastic morans to say that they are not real morans, because they do not wear the real [traditional] clothes. They are wearing plastic hair—the kind that town ladies buy in hair salons." In a 1990s folksong, girls tease these men, saying: "They have gone to Mombasa with *sakana* [a traditional hairstyle] to braid it with plastic hair / Oh, [one man said proudly:] 'I join the long hair to the plastic hair.'"[8] Later, young women began using "plastic morans" to refer more generally to educated men who wore trousers, shirts, and other urban clothing styles. "But why plastic?" I asked Jackson. "It's because these men lacked discipline," he said, "that respect for culture." Plastic figures here in opposition to culture, and its attribution probes, as women do, migrants' devotion to their place of origin.

If mobility was here a men's purview, women used plastic to emasculate migrants whose styles threatened local customs.

As plastic hair shows, plastic is problematic because kinship is entangled in substance and things. In rural areas, *plastiki* referred to objects that could not embed themselves in families and homesteads, things that didn't belong. Plastic basins, jugs, jerry cans, and buckets did not take on the *latukuny* or bodily substance—dirt, sweat, or smell—of their owners, unlike calabashes, wooden containers, headrests, and stools, which did.[9] In 2011, one man told me:

> You know, a calabash, even when it breaks, you can never burn it or throw it outside [the compound]. If you burn it, it will affect you. You can even die. But plastic, even if it was used for milking, you can go ahead and burn it. Plastic is just something which came late and doesn't have any value for people, because it is not theirs. They don't own it. But if you let a calabash without milk in it for too long, and it begins to crack, that calabash will curse you and your whole family.

Note how, on the one hand, the inability of plastic objects to attach themselves to persons could be advantageous in that it does not expose its "owners" to sorcery, as did calabashes (fig. 13) and wooden objects when stolen. Ownership required persons and things to be part of one another, something plastic never achieved. On the other hand, for persons to prosper, they had to cultivate relations to propitious objects, like calabashes, which, if used correctly, blessed them. As Bilinda Straight (2007, 65) argues, "calabashes are thoroughly entangled in Samburu personhood." Plastic objects, by contrast, remained unattached, sterile, unable to generate growth.

At least three of plastic's properties appeared troublesome in this context. First was its impermeability, its inability to absorb other substances organically. Locals I interviewed illustrated this property by saying that calabashes, for example, were constantly being touched and thus took on their owner's sweat, while plastic, if washed with water, was always restored to its initial sterile state. Similarly, Brad Weiss (1996, 174) shows how, among Haya of Tanzania, gourds contained the owner's generative heat, while "the coldness of plastic ... [restricts] these warm, ongoing processes."

Second, plastic was invariably associated with objects that arrive in the region ready-made (see also Weiss 1996, 176). "It is those things that people make themselves that have *latukuny*," one Samburu man said, "but not those that are made in a factory. It's those people make themselves." Objects made in the household were entangled in its growth, while objects made elsewhere threatened it. Recall that the sharp metal objects made by *Ikunono* or the clay pots made by Dorobo groups, though necessary to any household, were seen

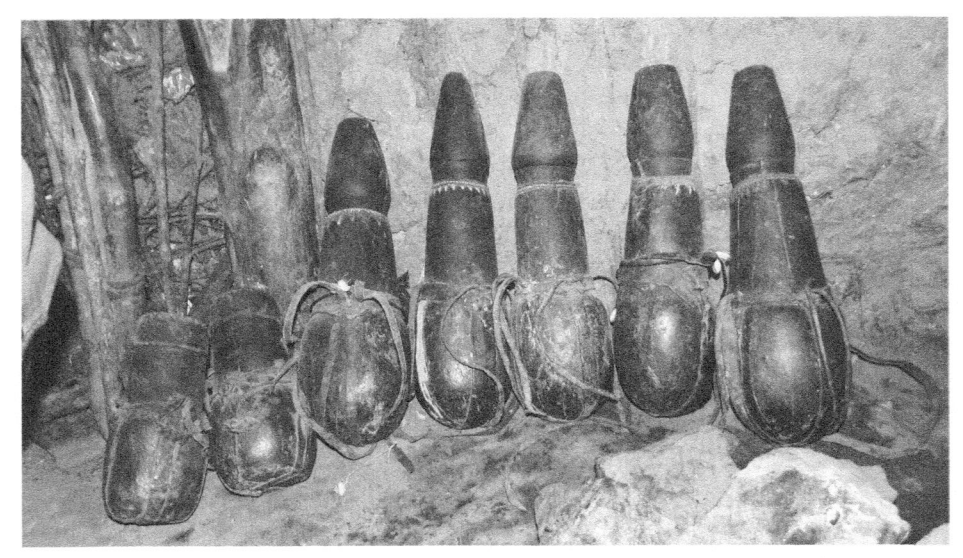

FIGURE 13. Wooden calabashes in a rural kitchen, Samburu County, Kenya, July 2015. Photo by George Paul Meiu.

as ambiguous objects, likely to curse or kill if not handled with care or, on occasion, blessed ritually. Objects, like people, had lineages. Samburu knew the lineages of metals or clay pottery. By contrast, plastic's origins remained obscure. Made in factories elsewhere, its intentions were vague, uncertain, and potentially dangerous.

Third, if plastic did not organically attach itself to bodies, it could nevertheless damage them. Some women, for instance, worried that sex with either condoms or plastic bags (used when condoms are not available) could "block the womb." An elderly woman told me that "plastic in the womb" (M: *plastik te kosheke*) was similar to AIDS in that it made bodies waste away. In Maa, *mbiita* (AIDS) is a noun derived from the verb *a-biita*, "to waste away" or become slim (Wanyoike 2011, 156). Similarly, in Malawi, becoming HIV-positive is known as "swallowing plastic," that is, eating "something inedible, undigestible . . . like a goat that becomes thin after swallowing plastic" (Uys et al. 2005, 16). In Tanzania, "plastic teeth," teeth that appear in toddlers and that can quickly lead to their death, manifested themselves like AIDS, through drastic slimming (Weiss 1996, 170). If sex and plastic goods enticed with the promise of pleasure but risked bringing depletion and death, then AIDS and plastic afflictions—their symptoms quite similar—expressed trouble with sexuality and reproduction. Plastic here brings sexuality right back into the picture.

It is no surprise then that *Nkai* (God), too, would ban plastics. Over the last two decades, in rural areas, several young girls who claim to have visited

Nkai returned home with messages for their communities (Straight 2007, 37ff). They urged women to abandon, among other things, plastic beads and containers. One elder told me, "These girls say women should stop wearing all these plastic beads. Nkai says that it is this plastic that is making women unable to give birth." Another man heard a girl say that "women should stop milking cows in plastic jerry cans or else cows will stop giving milk. To milk your cows in plastic is to curse them. It is to show them disrespect. So, Nkai will punish you for it." Writing about these messages, Straight (2007, 65) observes that "to approach a Samburu cow with a plastic container is to mix what cannot properly mix—outside and propitious inside." Albeit highly contested, girls' prophesies circulated widely in the region, solidifying a certain taxonomy of objects along the axes of culture versus foreign imports, life-giving versus polluting things. They also made plastic's arrival in the region a historical juncture when life-giving culture has begun being polluted. In some rituals, then, people had to "return" (M: *a-chukunye*) to using calabashes or wooden objects and refrain temporarily from using their plastic counterparts.

Two forces animate these diverse understandings and practices involving plastic. First, *desire*: a nostalgic longing to reconstitute a time before plastic—dangerous commodities and disease—arrived in the region, a time when life had not yet been threatened by the nefarious effects of foreign things. As part of this desire, plastic's coldness, ready-made forms, and impermeability resonated quite strongly with the idea of nonbelonging. Samburu desires for specific kinds of attachment deemed plastic a material impediment to propitious belonging. Invoking plastic, locals thus resisted attaching themselves to certain things, styles, and persons.

A second force is *disavowal*: an ongoing repudiation of plastic. The very idea of a world without it is, no doubt, aspirational. Nobody I spoke with believed it was possible to get rid of all plastics. "Isn't it Nkai who brought plastic to us in the first place?" one elder wondered. But neither was the disavowal of plastic a pointless act. Rather, it was through the plastic's repetitive repudiation that people called forth, rendered palpable the utopia of an unpolluted autochthonous community and made it inform the political projects of the present. Mary Douglas (2006, 139) argues that polluting substances "can distract from the social and moral aspects of a situation by focusing on a simple material matter." Such focus helps reinforce not the social order itself but rather the *idea* of an order. It consolidates the image of a political totality and thus produces in social life the effects of such an image, if only as an aspirational projection, a thing-yet-to-come. The resonance between plastic and nonattachment is thus constitutive of belonging; desiring what plastic forecloses and disavowing it as a condition for happiness, Samburu generated intimate ties while imagining themselves in a prosperous future.

The Nation's Foreign Contagions

The resonances between various instantiations of plastic and their wider social context have also represented an important symbolic resource for the Kenyan state and national public. In a satire published in the *Standard* in 2013, Mark Muthai suggests that the radical way Rwanda has implemented, since 2008, its ban on plastic bags—using police raids, drastic fines, and jail terms—reflects how it has been treating Kenyan migrants in recent years.[10] "The Rwandese government," Muthai writes, "has launched a crackdown on Kenyans living in Rwanda who have a record of wearing plastic smiles"— smiles that are fake, duplicitous. "This is in line," he suggests, "with the Rwandese government policy of eradicating all plastics in the country as an environmental conservation measure." Muthai quotes a Rwandese minister as saying, "We cannot tolerate plastics in this country and we will do everything in our power to root out any foreigner who goes about with a plastic smile." Though fictitious, Muthai's piece reveals a key premise shared by his Kenyan readership: that banning plastic bags is about the threat of multiple foreign contagions and the role the state must play to protect its citizens. Foreigners here take on the properties of plastic itself. "On a hot day," a police officer tells Muthai, "people with plastic smiles smell like, well, burning plastic."

When the Kenyan government passed its own—and, recall, by some accounts, "the world's toughest"—ban on plastic bags in 2017, there, too, more was at stake than environmental pollution. With a monthly use of twenty-four million plastic bags in Kenya and with plastic representing 80 percent of the country's solid waste, a major ecological crisis, to be sure, was underway.[11] But calls to rid Kenya of plastic bags have also resonated with popular desires to rehabilitate morality by eradicating foreign pollutants. In 2020, for example, President Uhuru Kenyatta promised to take strict measures against "foreign vessels" dumping plastic on the Kenyan ocean front, thus locating the agency of pollution with foreigners outside the country; and this, despite the fact that most of the plastic bags Kenyans consumed were produced domestically.[12]

In June 2017, the Kenyan Bureau of Standards pursued an investigation into allegations that plastic rice circulated in the country. "Watch Out! Plastic Rice Now on Sale in Kenya," warns an online article, claiming that "a leaked video reveals that producers of long grain rice in China are now making plastic rice ... then mix it with natural rice for commercial exportation to African countries."[13] The ensuing panic was part of a recurring set of nationwide scandals over counterfeit foodstuffs (see also Rahier 2022). On social media, a Maralal resident describes the situation thus:

> Poisonous sugar, fake honey, plastic rice, fake eggs, our meat is being injected with formalin . . . counterfeit cooking oil . . . Almost everything we eat is processed. . . . and everything else is made in China. In short EVERYTHING IS FAKE. There's nowhere to run.[14]

Pursuing an investigation into plastic rice, government authorities responded to such deep anxieties. In Nigeria, for example, similar panics over plastic rice led the government to temporarily ban rice imports and try to revitalize the local rice production. Kenyan authorities disclaimed the existence of plastic rice instead. But, as in the Nigerian case, their highly publicized investigation asserted a particular image of the state. If some Kenyans have long been skeptical about their country's new economic dependence on China, investigating the import of plastic rice, authorities reassured Kenyans the state would protect them from any foreign contagion.

At stake in such panics was, among other things, the future of citizens' very "nature," now undermined by the afflictions of globalization. "The most offensive part of being gay," writes Kwamchetsi Makokha in a homophobic rant in the *Daily Nation*, "is its unnaturalness on a continent of nature like Africa, which shuns aeroplanes [sic], plastic, spectacles, and other unnatural things like genetically modified organisms."[15] Makokha depicts Africa as unpolluted nature when global circulations of plastics, gay rights, or technology have corrupted humanity elsewhere. He was certainly not alone in depicting homosexuality as a Western contagion; many political and religious leaders across the continent have done so too (see Epprecht 2004). But in Makokha's statement, homosexuality also borrows plastic's substance as a contagious affliction, something conveyed strongly by the popular term *gayism*. Like plastic, but unlike "homosexuality," gayism connotes a trend that proliferates. In 2017, for example, a national scandal emerged over two male lions photographed copulating in Kenya's Maasai Mara National Reserve. Ezekiel Mutua, at that time head of the Kenya Film Classification Board, made headlines claiming that the lions "caught" gayism from Western gay tourists kissing in the park.[16] Like Makokha, Mutua depicted African nature—and a naturalized heteromasculinity—as being at risk of foreign contaminations. Accordingly, if plastic threatens nature, then gayism is plastic in that it undermines the heteronormative "nature" of normatively gendered bodies.

Fighting such contagions plays an important role in the making of what Paul Amar (2013) calls the human-security state, a form of rule based on moral securitization. This may involve the rescue of nature and heritage, the rehabilitation of traditional family and normative gender relations, or the capture and reform of dangerous masculinities, whether criminals or homosexuals. Here, as Adeline Masquelier (2005, 12) argues, "polluting and threatening things are thought to originate from the outside—whether outside the body, the household, the clan, the village, the suburb, or the nation." In this context, panics over plastics reorient citizen subjectivity by producing desire both for an authentic autochthonous nature and gendered order *and*—importantly—for the state as an ultimate guarantor of moral security in times of flux.

We might be tempted to understand regional politics of ethnicity as opposed to the politics of national belonging. Yet plastic sustains similar cultural grammars in publics of different scales. In northern Kenya, elites have been deeply invested in environmental conservation. They organized rallies, workshops, and seminars to teach rural residents about the dangers of trading timber, making charcoal, and littering plastic. They also debated ecological policies on Maa-language radio and social media. But because their environmental concerns focused almost exclusively on the ecology of Samburu County, their efforts anchored ethnicity in territory. The conservation of local nature was thus care for ethnic territory, a claim to ethno-regional belonging.

The ban on plastic bags drew so much support precisely because it resonated strongly with both regional *and* national concerns. Political leaders and the media have strengthened extant discursive grammars of plastic and banked on their powerful resonances to legitimize the state's authority as a source of moral security.

Displacing Failure, Disambiguating the Foreign

If plastic created strong semiotic and sentimental resonance between different foreign contagions, it was also because people could engage it as an object-cause of moral problems. Plastic boys as subject position—as a category of selfhood—reflected this well. "We call them 'plastic boys' because they hang around like that, with no families, with no purpose," Simon, a Samburu NGO worker in Maralal, told me in 2011. "They just run after the whites to sell things to them and then they drink that money. They are just like that plastic, that garbage, those thrown-away plastic bags that you see everywhere and that don't belong anywhere." Simon suggests that "plastic boys," like plastic waste, permeated the local landscape without a "purpose" or ability to attach themselves. They shared plastic's tendency to persist as waste. When northern Kenyans like Simon spoke of plastic boys disparagingly, they expressed collective anxieties over work, kinship, and respectability and imagined foreign afflictions as causes of social failure.

One day in June 2011, Mama Loleku, a Samburu woman who owned a business in Maralal, warned me not to hang out with plastic boys. Two had stopped by her store the previous day to ask where I lived. She told me she had given them the wrong directions. "I wanted to protect you," she said. "They are dangerous, these boys." Then, she explained, "they bring white people to my shop and quote them prices three times higher than the ones I want. They tell the whites, in English, that my shop is the cheapest in town. But then they tell me in Swahili that they will come later to collect their commission. They cheat people." Mama Loleku described plastic boys as "youths who make a living for themselves with their mouths" (S: *vijana wenye wanajitafutia na midomo yao*). "They are fake," she concluded. Traders, teachers, and development workers in town also saw plastic boys as lazy, unwilling to study and work, and looking instead for quick, easy money. By depicting schooling and work as conditions for success, elites' narratives occluded how recent political-economic transformations made education an uncertain asset, employment scarce, and speculative practices widespread modalities of value creation.

In this context, middle-class lifestyles were also fragile, uncertain, and unsustainable. Local elites depend on foreign donors, NGO funds, trade networks, or employment to sustain a good lifestyle. Such ties could dissolve easily, quickly. Some plastic boys, for example, come from previously well-to-do families. James joined the plastic boys in 1990 when he was seventeen. His parents, both high school graduates, had worked for tourist lodges. They rented a large house in Maralal and sent their children to the town's best schools. But in 1988, James's father lost his job suddenly and, a few months later, as James put it, "died of sorrow." His mother died shortly thereafter. Without an income, he and his siblings dropped out of school. "Before my parents died," he told me, "we had a lot of money for school and everything. Then, life changed. Nobody was helping us. I learned English in school and knew about tourists, so I joined the plastic boys."

Stories of sudden wealth loss, such as James's, echoed in the daily worries of elite men and women. When I visited Mama Loleku in June 2018, only seven years after I had met her, she had lost most of her savings. She had just campaigned for a councilor seat with the local government, a five-year position with a large salary. But she lost the election and now struggled to pay her children's school fees. In this sense, when Mama Loleku and others criticized plastic boys, they overlooked contexts and speculative modalities of livelihood that they shared with these men. They also displaced deep anxieties over uncertain livelihoods onto them: if educated people who worked hard to accumulate wealth could lose it so easily, they argued, it was because of socioeconomic trends that the plastic boys manifested most saliently. These trends included speculative pursuits of money, the depreciation of education and stable employment, and an inability to hold on to wealth. Though aware that elites disregarded plastic boys, James saw his ability to speculate on and persuade potential customers as skillful entrepreneurship. "This is our work," James said. "It is not stealing." Yet, for others, plastic boys embodied the dangers of perpetual plasticity—a speculative malleability—that threatened ideals of durability, continuity, and stable identity so central to ethno-nationalism.

Like Maralal's elites, Samburu living in nearby villages considered plastic boys troublesome. A few elders told me it was bad to make money by trading calabashes or old wooden objects. These, let us recall, were bodily extensions of those who made them. Elders said that plastic boys did not prosper because they "ate" life-giving objects, consuming thus—almost cannibalistically— other people's bodies and life force (cf. Straight 2002, 13). Not only did they benefit from such life-giving objects, but they also imported polluting plastics instead. Here, plastic ate away at culture, alienated its capacity for growth. It is important to note that many rural Samburu saw their own contemporary means of livelihood, including charcoal-making and alcohol brewing, as inauspicious (Meiu 2017, chapter 4). Therefore, when they spoke of plastic boys, they also reflected, indirectly, on wider conditions of precarity. But, like Maralal's elites, they also displaced prevalent social anxieties onto plastic boys.

In December 2010, I asked Mama Seiyina, a widow from a village near Maralal, what she thought of plastic boys. "Those thieves?" she replied.

> We call them street children of the whites. A child might decide to go and do that work. And nobody told him to go. His disobedience alone has taken him. He will just go and do that work. But he will not come home again. He will age and he will not marry. He will just be a pauper and you won't have any relationship to him. He can be just anybody. He will not be able to say: "This is my father and my brother." Nothing is there. They lost that respect that Samburu have.

Referring to plastic boys as "street children of the whites" (M: *lchokorani lomusunku*), Mama Seiyina suggested that the legacies of colonialism had shaped belonging and mobility. Plastic boys, for her, became dependent on white people in ways that uprooted them from kinship and left them uncontrollably mobile. The Swahili noun for "whites," *wazungu* (in M: *lmusunku*), derives from the verb *kuzunguka*, "to go around," "to move in circles," echoing here an older experience of white administrators and later African labor migrants in the colonial context as displaced, uprooted, unattached. Rural

Samburu, for example, teasingly called their urban kin "black whitemen" (M: *lmusunku orok*) to warn them, as it were, that pursuing modern, "white" values could render them non-Samburu, alien to local attachments. As "street children of the whites," plastic boys embodied most visibly this longstanding tendency of young men to be seduced by and subordinated to "white" values. "When people say: 'Ah, plastic boys,'" James explained, "it means they have degraded you. That is to say you are just of lower dignity. You are someone running, running [after whites] without purpose."

Belonging, Mama Seiyina implied, was less about an immutable identity and more about continuously demonstrating one's commitment to local kinship and custom. It was about sustaining ties to a rural home and growing one's lineage. As these customary relationships were decisive in assessing local belonging, the decline of cattle economies, land alienation, and rampant unemployment have left many impoverished rural families unable to pay bridewealth, fund weddings and funerals, and hold important ceremonies (Meiu 2017, 184–90). But if both town-based and rural Samburu at least appeared to invest in local custom, it was also obvious to them that plastic boys did not.

Indeed, plastic boys explicitly dissociated themselves from rural worlds. James, for example, told me that, had he wanted, he could have returned to his father's village. Over the years, his father, a Samburu, had supported his rural kin. But James preferred to live in town. "You know, those people are very primitive," he said. "They are uneducated, but they want you to do things their way." James's decision severed his relationship to them. "If you don't show up to participate in those ceremonies," he said, "people will ignore you . . . because you know nothing about their ways." Associated with an inauspicious livelihood and embedded in attachments that others devalued, plastic boys then figured as, by definition, non-Samburu. Most Samburu, in fact, saw plastic boys as Turkana, despite these men's otherwise diverse ethnic backgrounds.

Most plastic boys preferred to identify as Kenyan over any particular ethnicity. "As a Kenyan," Adam said, "this is my country. I can live any place I want." But the Kenya to which they belonged was, for them, one of a utopian future: an anticipatory projection in relation to which they were still "boys" waiting to become men. Tribalism and corruption, plastic boys said, held Kenya back. "I am Samburu," James said. "But for me, someone who helps me is more important than people of my own tribe . . . I don't like tribalism [S: *ukabila*]. I am happy to be like the other plastic boys, without a tribe." Adam, another plastic boy, said, "Now, if I get into an argument here, Samburu say [he switches from Swahili to Maa]: *Miyolo dei nkop ang itii?*—'Don't you know this is our land?' They will beat you in the street because they say: 'This is our land.'" Plastic boys' rejection of ethnicity can be read as a claim to a more legitimate kind of belonging, a form of belonging that transcends the corruption and tribalism of elites, rural Samburu, as well as national party politics. It is pursuing citizenship to a nation that is yet to be rescued from immorality and corruption.

Plastic boys' pursuit of good citizenship was clearly visible in their quests for respectability through the notions of rescue, work, and dignified manhood. For example, plastic boys saw their mode of livelihood as "work" (S: *kazi*) that should grant them the recognition and respect of an imagined national public. Seeking moral legitimacy for their work, since 1996, some plastic boys have registered with the government as the Plastic Boys' Self-Help Group, a cooperative society meant to attract funding from the governmental youth programs and NGOs. Kenya Wildlife Service, with money from USAID, built a shop for them in Maralal, "to keep them off the streets." The shop, in turn, made plastic boys more visible to reformist interventions. Soon thereafter, a Dutch NGO initiated a set of microfinance projects among them, disciplining them into becoming good entrepreneurs. By registering as a labor cooperative and fashioning themselves as entrepreneurs, plastic boys claimed respectability and national belonging.

Since 1997, however, insecurity related to cattle raids, carjacking, and road thieves prompted tourists to avoid traveling to northern Kenya. Since then, only one or two backpackers or NGO workers visited Maralal each week. In the absence of foreigners, some plastic boys repaired flat tires. Others made leather belts. And yet others sold household objects and secondhand clothes. The local government administration promised plastic boys access to state funds earmarked for youths. But, despite plastic boys having submitted numerous proposals for such funds, the money never arrived. "We see that all other youth organizations in Maralal get a lot of money from the government," Adam said. "So, we go to the offices all the time and ask where our money is. They say: 'The money that comes here is for Samburu. You are not Samburu. What do you want?' These people are very stupid." Despite the decline of tourism in the region and their exclusion by the local government administration, plastic boys have retained a sense of pride in being tourist guides and curio traders, work that defined, for them, who they were.

Although plastic boys shared dominant perspectives on plastic as a pollutant, they insisted, as James once told me, that "people dismiss us because they don't know who the plastic boys really are." To further cleanse their name—to recycle it, if you will, as a dignified masculine identity—plastic boys who were associated with the cooperative sought to distinguish themselves from others.

"There are those who spoil our name," James explained, "those *chang'aa* boys from *Soko Mjinga* [the Idiot's Market]," men, that is, who consume alcohol in roadside bars. "They go around and say they are plastic boys," he added. "They give us a bad reputation." Distancing themselves from those they dismissively see as the *chang'aa* boys or drunks, claiming respectability through entrepreneurship and "work," and distancing themselves from ethnic politics, plastic boys sought to counteract social forces that, drawing on imaginaries of plastic, marked them for detachability, exclusion.

*

Over the past decades, ethnicity, indigeneity, autochthony, and culture have played important roles in how postcolonial subjects have imagined, contested, and actualized attachments to territories and the state (e.g., Broch-Due 2005; Comaroff and Comaroff 2009; Geschiere 2009; Hodgson 2011). Less readily recognizable as constitutive of belonging are the politics of matter: how substances and surfaces resonate with and shape the politics of inclusion and exclusion; how things and textures echo, magnify, or deplete possibilities to belong; how polluting matter complicates, subverts, or reinforces identity and its attachments; and how matter itself is a product of such struggles.

What is fascinating about plastic is that its substance and its multiple, mutable forms lend themselves evocatively to postcolonial subjects' efforts to identify and diagnose—to "theorize with poor means" (Thiong'o 2012, 2ff)—dilemmas of belonging in the present. In Kenya, plastic is inextricably tied to belonging: its mutability appears to undermine identity; its impermeability to resist relationality, to annihilate life; its presence as ready-made commodities to render tangible globalization's neocolonial forces. Plastic can pass for culture (as with Samburu beads) or appear autochthonous (as with plastic rice), suggesting the very ambiguity of determining who belongs and who does not. In Kenya since the 1980s, people have been extensively preoccupied with the dissonance between the appearance and essence of various things, whether money, goods, or bodies (Blunt 2004; Smith 2008). Concerns with plastic extended this preoccupation: plastics mimicked the form of particular objects without also reproducing their essence, value, or durability. If plastic spoke so saliently in Kenya, it is because it efficiently congealed such wider anxieties over bodies, relations, and polities on both regional and national scales.

Plastics, then, can be seen as queer objects in several ways. As Davis (2016) states, in many regards, as substance, plastic seems queer in and of itself: it lacks interiority, it has the capacity to undermine identity, to render malleable things that otherwise need to be stable. "There is an uncanny resemblance," Davis says, "between the modalities of queerness and plastic's expression, even though one emerges from liberatory struggle and the other from advanced petrocapitalism." But the analogy between plastic and sex, Davis suggests, also has the queer potentiality to reveal that in both "there is no mystery, no identity, no ontology, only a carefully crafted seduction; a critical potentiality that Giddens does not pursue with his notion of 'plastic sexuality.'" In other words, sexuality is an empty signifier—a "negative ontology" (Zupančič 2017). In addition, I suggest, plastic's queer potentialities emerge from the concrete social and historical contexts of its deployment. In such contexts, plastic may help name subjects and things—plastic boys and plastic buckets, among others—that have the ability to pollute and thus subvert normative aspirations and attachments. It is this historical property of plastic that, as I show in chapter 7, also makes it centrally constitutive of the homosexual body.

I do not suggest that the different instantiations of plastic described in this chapter—boys, bags, rice, smiles, hair, and homosexuality, among others—form an integrated system of meaning. Instead, I have approached them as *coincidental* and *resonant* in ways that are generative. The intersection of plastic's different manifestations with a particular politics of belonging is coincidental in that it is not part of a unified, linear, progressive time, but an outcome of a "queer timing," "a temporality that produces truth through coincidence, through intersectionality" (Boellstorff 2007, 30). Plastic boys emerged in the late 1970s, ecological concerns with plastic pollution in the 1990s, and the rhetoric of a "war on plastic" in the 2000s. But their coincidental arrival in national and local publics generated new meanings and actualized belonging in new ways.

Key to their coincidental arrival in these publics is their ability to resonate with one another. Mazzarella (2017, 5) argues that resonance establishes a mimetic relation that is mutually transformative. Sustaining relations of mutual becoming, plastic boys, plastic objects, plastic trends, and their wider social and economic contexts come to share grammars that produce the foreign. Two processes, I have shown, drive their mutual becoming. First, there is the dialectics of desire and disavowal through which the repetitive repudiation of plastic sustains aspirations for the utopia of an unpolluted autochthonous order. In the national arena, this dialectic also produces desire for the state as the ultimate guarantor of moral protectionism. Second, there is the dialectics of displacement and disambiguation through which plastic comes to congeal common forms of social failure and to attribute these to foreign contagions. These dialectics demonstrate how plastic's historical objectification and efforts to define belonging are co-constitutive.

Barthes (1988, 92) argues that plastic prompts "a perpetual amazement, the reverie of man [sic] at the sight of the proliferating forms of matter." For

Barthes, "this amazement is a pleasurable one since the scope of the transformations gives man [*sic*] the measure of his power." Approached from the postcolony, however, plastic's mutability hardly appears as a pleasurable realization of the measure of one's power. Produced elsewhere, proliferating against collective will, and difficult to control, for postcolonial subjects, plastic is dubious at best—a reminder that globalization, like colonialism, works through multiple, nested forms of alienation and marginalization. It is, then, not as much *through* plastic, but *against* it—through its repudiation—that postcolonial subjects imagine order, autonomy, and autochthony. Plastic is, then, *pace* Barthes, an inherently cosmopolitan object, one that—not unlike the homosexual—generates and is transformed by different imaginaries of belonging.

6

Diapers:
Intimate Exposures and the Underlayers of Citizenship

> In pressing against an object, we arouse in ourselves the object's attitude of counterpressure.
> LEO BERSANI

In recent years in Kenya, some public figures have warned citizens of a new, less obvious sign of moral decay in the country: rising sales in adult diapers. In 2013, the *Star*, a national newspaper, announced that "those engaged in sodomy are said to be releasing waste uncontrollably, forcing them to use pampers whenever they walk."[1] On August 20, at a political rally in the coastal town of Malindi, Joshua Nkanatha, a police commissioner, explained: "A survey we conducted shows that boys engaging in sexual activities with male tourists are buying pampers because they can no longer hold their stool."[2] Worrying about the proliferation of anal sex, Nkanatha urges people "to take up the responsibility of enlightening the youths about the health risks of engaging in the vice." Or else, he warns, "prostitution . . . will lead to their death."[3] The *Star* blames this trend on "the booming tourism of pedophiles and perverts," including Europeans, Americans and, of late, "our so-called business partners who come all the way from China."[4] With similar urgency, in May 2018, Ezekiel Mutua, the director of the Kenya Films and Classification Board, stated in a public speech that "mature men end up in diapers because they have been 'destroyed' by their fellow men."[5] Infamous for his anti-homosexual rants and for banning any media featuring same-sex intimacies, Mutua warned Kenyans: "It is high time we stopped this Westernized and good-for-nothing practice, [lest] it will destroy . . . future generations." Like Nkanatha, Mutua blamed foreigners for the trend: "There are foreign NGOs in Kisumu and Kakamega, which move to the villages to manipulate our poor innocent youths with 'big money' of up to Ksh3 million [around US$30,000] . . . to engage in this wicked act." This, he claimed, was "a kind of neocolonialism that . . . will end up destroying the country."

Politicians, police, priests, and journalists, among others, have used diapers as what Rosalind C. Morris (2008, 201) calls an "inflationary discourse," a set of narratives that amplify the proportions of an act or affliction, rendering its cumulative effects catastrophic. Invoking a sharp rise in the prevalence of anal sex and, with it, adult diapers, Nkanatha and Mutua announced impending trouble for the nation. Foreign tourists, businessmen, and NGO workers, they warned, corrupt "innocent youths" from villages—idyllic loci of intimate purity in the Kenyan national imaginary (Macharia 2013, 283). In purchasing anal sex, these leaders said, foreigners destroyed not only the bodies of individual citizens but, exponentially, whole generations, the country itself. The inflationary quality of these discourses, in turn, prompted citizens to desire rescue from dangerous global afflictions, and thus protection by their leaders.

Discourses about men who end up in diapers because they engage in anal sex are not specific to Kenya. They circulate widely among evangelical Christians and radical-right activists in countries as far apart as the United States, Romania, and South Korea.[6] But since 2008, as American evangelicals and local political and religious leaders have exacerbated anti-homosexual campaigns in African countries, these otherwise cosmopolitan discourses also became widely deployed in places like Cameroon, Ghana, Kenya, Nigeria, and Uganda.[7] The strong capacity of diaper discourses to evoke a simultaneous destruction of bodies and polities made them appealing as a means to govern sexuality through moral panics.

Human rights and LGBT activists in African contexts have struggled to dismantle such discourses, seeing them—in the words of the Danish Institute for Human Rights—as "unsubstantiated rumors," "urban legends," or "outright lies," circulated because of "widespread popular ignorance."[8] For activists, rebutting such discourses is crucial when leaders strategically employ them to prosecute homosexual men. In 2014, Ugandan refugees in Kenya said that during arrests in Kampala, to confirm their homosexuality, "police stuck their hands down their pants to see if they were wearing diapers."[9] In 2016, similar assumptions about incontinent homosexual bodies led police in Kenya's coastal Kwale County to subject two men to anal medical exams before charging them under the penal code's anti-sodomy law. Ideas about diapers, then, played a critical role in violent imaginaries of the homosexual body. But dismissing them as mere instances of "widespread popular ignorance" means supporting ideologies of an "African homophobia"—a racist trope, as scholars have shown, commonly deployed in global LGBT liberalism (Hoad 2007; Awondo, Geschiere, and Reid 2012; Judge 2017). To better understand how homophobic sentiment emerges and how it produces the bodies it disavows, it is important to take diapers seriously as an idiom of politics.

During my fieldwork, I encountered diapers in a variety of settings. In the town of Mtwapa, on the coast, I heard rumors about adults in diapers that focused not only on homosexual men but also on women. Locals said that anal penetration destroyed women's bodies, leaving them incontinent, in need of diapers. I later encountered diapers in contexts unrelated to sexuality, in conversations about drug addicts, alcoholics, and youth involved in quick-money schemes, all said to end up ill, tragically spending the last days of their lives in diapers. I began to make sense of these disparate invocations of diapers in 2014, in Nairobi, where I encountered a photography exhibit provocatively entitled *Diaper Mentality: Something Needs to Change*. Curated by the activist Boniface Mwangi and the art group PAWA 254, the exhibit featured scenes in which Kenyans who commit various mundane wrongdoings—jaywalking, bribing, cheating—appear without trousers or skirts and wear, instead of undergarments, adult diapers. The project's Facebook page defines "diaper mentality" as "the primitive, backward behavior we wish to outgrow as a nation." Across these contexts, I learned, diapered adults appeared as products of their own everyday misdeeds and moral impediments to the nation's progress. To understand the role of diapers in anti-homosexual discourse, I realized, I had to explore this object's wider circulation as a symbol of moral affliction. To do so, my ethnographic archive became a bricolage of various deployments of diapers from across different sites and scales.

The resonances between different deployments of diapers—many unrelated to (homo)sexuality as such—helped constitute the homosexual body as a target of outrage. What made diaper discourses so evocative in the present? What collective desires, fears, and anxieties did people express when exposing others as wearing adult diapers? And what did the cultural logics of such revelations show about the relationship between intimacy and citizenship in contexts of growing anti-homosexual violence?

I make two related arguments. First, I suggest that diaper discourses are instances of what I call *intimate exposures*: performative attempts to unmask signs of social failure hidden beneath appearances of respectability, to peel off—in speech or deed—an outer, visible stratum (e.g., clothing) of bodies and relations and bring to light their troubled underlayers. Representing social reality as consisting of materially layered phenomena, intimate exposures involving diapers constitute an important "technology of citizenship" (Lorway 2014). That is, they work to realign desires with national fantasies of intimacy and propriety. Second, tracking diapers as technologies of citizenship across different social contexts, I show how logics and sentiments associated with homophobia do not emerge simply in relation to the reified category of the homosexual. Instead, references to diapers help displace and condense desires, fears, and anxieties associated with bodies, work, reproduction, and respectability across domains of social life. Rather than existing prior to homophobic discourse, then, the homosexual body emerges through the deployment of objects such as diapers. In this sense, diapers are then queer objects, marginal things whose repetitive disavowal sustains normative orientations and forecloses subversive possibilities.

The following section shows how exploring preoccupations with the hidden layers of social life can expand conceptualizations of intimate citizenship. Turning to the Kenyan coast, I then describe how sex workers and NGO workers use rumors involving adults in diapers to express anxieties over anal sex. Such rumors concern not only sexuality but also struggles over the body's (re)productive capacities, work, respectability, and progress. A quick detour through the exhibit *Diaper Mentality* will demonstrate how revealing hidden layers of ruptured intimate life offers an avenue to good citizenship. Returning then to anti-homosexual imaginaries, I describe how intimate exposures work to produce and secure national heterosexuality. If both men and women are said to end up in diapers, the male homosexual becomes the ultimate object of displaced and condensed social anxieties—the destructive force of noncitizenship.

Underlayers of Intimate Citizenship

What makes diaper discourses resonant is a broader context in which citizenship in Kenya is saliently debated in relation to bodily well-being, work, reproduction, and respectability. Debates about citizenship, as we have already seen, have intensified in the past four decades as the country grew dependent on international loans and foreign investments and as migration has been amplified both within and across its borders. Francis B. Nyamnjoh (2018, 61) argues that with rising migration and urbanization across Africa, "the logic of ever-diminishing circles of inclusion dictates that the next foreigner or stranger is always *one layer below* the obvious one" [my emphasis]. "In this bizarre nativity game of exclusionary violence," Nyamnjoh writes, "the next target is just *a layer below*" (61, my emphasis). To understand intimate exposures as technologies of citizenship requires attending closely to this fascination with the "layer below," that which lies beneath the visible surfaces of everyday life and which, while not fully knowable, undermines efforts to build futures.

Claiming that numerous adults now wore diapers, Kenyan politicians like Nkanatha and Mutua exposed afflictions otherwise hidden from public scrutiny. They warned that appearances of bodily integrity could prove deceptive and should be approached with vigilance and discreet inquisitiveness. Such intimate exposures are important in contexts in which both the citizen and its antitheses—the foreigner, the pervert, the national security threat—make for existentially unstable entities, their presence opaque, elusive, uncertain. Incitements to intimate exposures orient subjects toward such hidden layers to produce citizens who, suspicious of the objects and persons surrounding them, must desire the state as a guarantor of their truthful value. In an ironic twist, however, citizens may often turn such tactics against their leaders, using rumors or art to expose powerful politicians as corrupt—indeed, in diapers.

In Kenya, corruption, fiscal inflation, a rising gap between the rich and the poor, and private appropriation of public resources have also rendered the inclusionary promises of citizenship suspicious at best. Robert Blunt (2019, 7) argues that during the presidency of Daniel Arap Moi (1978–2002) and ever since, "the power to back everything from the stability of monetary value to political promises of development . . . was . . . fundamentally up for grabs." The fact that "the regime had resorted to counterfeiting everything from currency to title deeds" gave rise to a common perception of dissonance between the appearances and essences of persons, goods, money, and other media of value and authority. Under these circumstances, the visible itself became ambiguous. A sticker I spotted on a public minibus at the coast articulates this quite suggestively, stating that "The more u look, the less u c." Discourses and practices of intimate exposure and concerns with the hidden layers of the everyday became more common in this context.

Adults in diapers are examples of how such generalized suspicion comes to revolve around the less visible domains of intimacy and bodily private life. They cannot be seen or known simply by looking. Instead, like terrorists, devil worshippers, or *jini* spirits, all widely discussed in Mtwapa, they conceal their identity underneath unremarkable appearances. They are thus "innocent criminals," to use a phrase I read on another sticker on another minibus. Hidden in the underlayers of intimate life, the afflictions that diapers conceal expand. And so, people seek to reveal their presence through rumors, art, or violence.

Broken Bodies, Hidden Ruptures

"Many men nowadays ask for 'sex from behind' [S: *ngono ya nyuma*]," said Nabaro, a woman engaged in sex work in Mtwapa. "I refuse to do it. Other women also refuse. But, when you refuse, men go with those who agree to it and you are left without customers." She nodded, looking at me sternly, as if to assure me she was not joking. "Some women," she said, "have to wear Pampers because they have ruined themselves. Others need surgery worth 80,000 shillings [about US$800]."

When Nabaro and I spoke in April 2011, she was twenty-eight. A Samburu migrant settler from northern Kenya, she had moved to Mtwapa in search of a better livelihood. We had lunch often that month to talk about my research, Samburu customs, and life on the coast. She told me she enjoyed our conversations—mostly in a mixture of Swahili and Maa (Samburu) languages—because they reminded her of her childhood. Nabaro had not returned to the north in more than ten years. For the past two years, she had been in a relationship with an elderly man from Switzerland who had rented her a luxurious apartment in town and supported her financially. In February, however, their relationship had ended, and Nabaro "returned to the bars," as she put it, to meet men.

Because the number of tourist arrivals in Kenya declined following post-election violence in 2008, competition in sex work grew. Most nights during the following years, Mtwapa's clubs and bars hosted, by my estimates, as many as ten or more sex workers for every male patron. Fifteen female sex workers I interviewed between 2011 and 2017 said that with heightened competition, those offering "sex from behind" stood higher chances of finding customers. They blamed the prominence of anal sex not only on customers but also on the growing presence of gay male sex workers in the town's nightlife. "[Gays] are cheating us out of customers," said Ruth, a thirty-year-old sex worker, in 2017. "There are those customers who want [sex] from the behind. If you refuse them, they will just go with gays," Nabaro explained. Because some customers thought "sex from behind" was "sweeter" (S: *tamu*) and safer than "from the front," "they don't care if they go with women or men." "This is what is destroying our market these days," she said. Ruth and Nabaro appeared to echo a national public that blamed homosexuals for moral decay. But their statements evoked more complex logics and sentiments, which will become more apparent shortly.

Nabaro was firm in her indignation with demands for anal sex: "Me, I tell customers: 'You want to destroy me? Fine. Build me a house, buy me a car, put money in my bank account, and then I will agree.' At least that way I know my children will live well. Then, I can accept to wear Pampers for the rest of my life." What anal sex "destroys," she implied, was not the body alone. It was also one's autonomy, one's ability to act in and on the world, to build relations, and to generate value. To convey this state, Nabaro and other women used the Swahili *kuharibika*, "to be(come) spoilt," "broken," "destroyed." This verb, also referring to women who lost their virginity early or became pregnant in school, suggests that respectability, bodily integrity, and individual autonomy make for co-constitutive processes.

Bodies unable to control their flows are commonly seen as polluting (Douglas 2006; Masquelier 2005). Writing about Kenyan women with fistula, Kathomi Gatwiri (2018, 157) argues that "a leaking body is often constructed as being out of control, dirty, disgusting, and contaminable." Kenyans whom Gatwiri (2018, 128) interviewed saw fistula as the outcome of sexual transgression—promiscuity or adultery. My interlocutors did not speak of fistula as such, but, like Gatwiri's informants, they explained chronic incontinence in women as an outcome of sexual transgression. Vivian, a thirty-six-year-old sex worker I interviewed in 2017, illustrated the bodily damage anal sex can cause by telling me a horrific story about a local woman whose baby had died at birth. "It came out," she said, "with a leg through her ass and the other through her vagina," leaving her incontinent. If moral personhood requires contained bodies, then adults in diapers are persons only in appearance, spectral embodiments devoid of interiority and reproductive capacity.

Nabaro, Ruth, and Vivian did not so much condemn women for providing anal sex as worry about the Faustian bargain the act entailed: that anal penetration generated wealth quickly only in exchange for one's productive and reproductive bodily capacities, leaving women broken and helpless. Reflections on such bargains often entailed quite specific calculations: the enumeration of monetary gifts or the costs of reparative surgeries. These numbers underscored the sheer magnitude of the body's alienation through commodification. The house, car, and bank savings that Nabaro listed as conditions for participating in such bargains were widely recognized media of middle-class success. But, she implied, they represented also the commodity value of bodily integrity. After she lost her former partner's support, Nabaro found herself in a predicament in which such bargains could easily become appealing. She had two children: a ten-year-old daughter and an eight-year-old son. A single mother with no savings, she struggled to make a living. When I met her, she had just moved out of a luxurious, self-contained apartment into a rudimentary single-room home. She desired to regain the lifestyle she had lost, but worried that to make money, "nowadays, one must do all sorts of dangerous things."

Locals did not only share such rumors with me. When I visited sex workers at the offices of a local NGO, where many worked as peer educators, I often heard them tell such stories to each other. Sensationalist rumors about women in Pampers shocked their audiences. The very mention of diapers scandalized them. Though Pampers-branded baby diapers available in Kenyan supermarkets were expensive, cheaper versions—generically called "pampers"—were common. By the 1990s, single-use baby diapers had become so widespread that even poor mothers saw them—along with milk and soap—as essential to caring for their infants. Rumors about women in diapers redeployed this familiar mundane object to highlight the fragility of motherly care today: mothers who, trying desperately to feed their children, ended up in Pampers became themselves like their babies—helpless and dependent. Expressing anxieties over shifting contexts of livelihood, these rumors also allowed women to negotiate the limits of their participation in the sex economy. To understand why these rumors resonated so strongly with everyday struggles, it is important to understand first how, according to NGO workers, anal sex undermined "progress."

Ruptured Progress, Revelatory Rescue

Public health workers in Mtwapa spoke of how "sex from behind" was an expanding "fashion." "For quite a while now, there has been too much anal sex here," said Amos, a man in his early twenties, whom we met earlier, in chapter 3. He and I sat with five other young men and women on the veranda of their office in February 2017. Operating under the patronage of a regional NGO, with funds from the United Nations for Population Activity, since 2013 their community-based organization (CBO) has offered sex education through workshops, theater, and social media. "You will find that a girl is doing that," Amos said, "and, at the end of the day, she is wearing Pampers. For what reason? She got destroyed there in the back, at the seam [S: *mshono*]. She is no longer able to persevere [S: *kuvumilia*]. She lets out water all the time." I asked Amos how he knew that anal sex was on the rise. "We learn about these things from our peers in the community," he said. Other public health workers echoed Amos's claims. "If you hang out with youths, you will know that it [anal sex] has become widespread," said Fred, a forty-year-old working for another NGO. To emphasize this growth, Fred and Amos used Swahili verbs like *kuenea*, "to spread out" or "expand," and *kuzidi*, "to become overabundant."

Claiming novelty and expansion for the practice of anal sex occluded its longer history in sex economies and occult imaginaries along the Swahili coast (Shepherd 1987; Thompson 2017). Rather, what was new was the production of knowledge about the practice. Beginning in 2004, public health workers have published statistics showing that anal sex is a prevalent avenue for HIV transmission throughout Kenya. Both "men who have sex with men" (MSM) and heterosexual couples, these statistics revealed, engaged in it (e.g., Schwandt et al. 2006; Mannava et al. 2013, 4). A significant number of men, they also showed, moved between these two categories, expanding the possibilities of infection. A public health poster announces that "HIV doesn't care if you have sex with men or women" (see fig. 14). Depicting two men and one woman in an intimate grasp, the poster warns: "Anal sex without a condom is the highest risk sex for HIV infection." Amplifying anxieties over

FIGURE 14. Public health poster cautioning men against the health risks of anal sex with either men or women, Kenya, ca. 2014. Liverpool VCT Care and Treatment, Maisha National AIDS Control Council, Kenya Ministry of Health, Elton John AIDS Foundation.

heterosexual reproduction, these public health findings and the iconography of HIV prevention have informed, since 2009, a humanitarian rush to rescue "key populations," including sex workers and MSM (Moyer and Igonya 2018, 1013).

Amos and Fred participated regularly in training sessions that disseminated these findings. But, to better convey the magnitude of risk associated with anal sex to their "beneficiaries," they also shared local rumors about incontinence and diapered adults. To emphasize anal sex as the "highest-risk sex," Amos would tell the following story:

> There was a sheik here in Mtwapa. And his daughter was having sex from behind because Muslims protect their virginity. This girl had a *charli* [boyfriend], and she was having anal sex. . . . So, that child, she got complications and was brought to the hospital. The doctor told the father that this girl has a sexually transmitted disease, that she was getting laid there, in the back, until she got wounded. So, the father set her down and she told him: "I was having sex from behind because, if I have sex from the front, I might not get a husband and it won't be good."

Amos performed an act of intimate exposure: he revealed to his audience how anal sex, driven by the young woman's naiveté, eroded the body from beneath appearances of normality. A medium for respectable marital and filial relations, the body may appear intact (virgin). But its appearance is deceptive, its deceptiveness difficult to spot. Such revelations, in turn, cautioned people that the relations through which they built futures were fragile, easily rupturable.

Workers like Amos used intimate exposures to impart knowledge about sexual risks for the greater good of *maendeleo*, "progress" or "development." Since independence, *maendeleo* has referred broadly to national progress through modernization. With the neoliberal overinvestment in the self-reliant individual, the word later also came to designate *personal* growth, wealth, and well-being initiated, among other things, through private, domestic efforts (Smith 2008). Within this framework, anal sex undermined both private and national progress. "If people see someone else do something in a Western way," Fred explained, "curiosity is making them want to try, so they can also become 'modern' [S: *wa siku hizi*]." Youths, he said, watched porn on their smartphones and emulated its "foreign styles." They called those who did not know of anal sex, for example, *washamba*, "peasants" (i.e., backward). Thus, anal sex expanded by deceptively promising youths modernity and progress and delivering instead dependence and helplessness. "What is spoiling us here in Kenya," Fred said, "[is that] we are poured upon [S: *tumemwagiwa*], all at once, information that is otherwise to be swallowed [i.e., discerned] slowly. So, I take it all at once and start using it, thinking I will become Westernized. But [as a young person], I am not mature enough to handle it all at a go." For both Amos and Fred, maturity and moral discernment enabled genuine progress, while the rush to emulate foreigners—a temporal acceleration toward progress—ultimately short-circuited and undermined it.

For NGO workers, then, bodies in diapers signaled failed progress. To commence the pursuit of progress, Kenyans had to rescue bodily autonomy by cultivating moral discernment and respectable sexuality. To move forward in time and acquire autonomy, the nation and its citizens had to foreclose the expansion of anal sex in space. Rumors about diapers and incontinence were meant to shock audiences into pursuing collective well-being. But here is an interesting twist in my story: diaper discourses did not only pertain to sexuality. They were also commentaries on illegitimate moneymaking practices that required careful concealment.

Work, Concealment, and Respectability

What makes revelatory discourses about adults in diapers meaningful is partly a context in which people feel that, to make a living, they must engage in morally problematic "work" (S: *kazi*). As Nabaro suggested above, in Mtwapa, a strong sense prevails that the present is a time of exceptional deeds and tough bargains. "These are hard times," I often heard people say, "you do what you need to do to eat." The moneymaking strategies people found troublesome included, besides sex work, theft, drugs trafficking, and sorcery. Rumors circulated of various get-rich-fast schemes and their dire consequences. Such rumors typically involved protagonists from poor backgrounds who, using questionable means, became rich quickly, only to lose their wealth, turn HIV-positive, "go mad," and die. Many spent their final days in diapers. Such stories allowed people to negotiate what kinds of work, otherwise "immoral," were nevertheless becoming permissible, given the difficult economic circumstances. In these rumors, diapers did not always relate to sexuality, but expressed anxieties about how the redefinition of legitimate work affected people's bodies and ability to progress.

At a government meeting on drug trafficking in Nairobi in 2008, a woman said:

> In June 2006, I buried a childhood hero of mine. He had spent twenty-five years suffering of drug abuse. He went in and out of Mathari Mental Hospital. By the time he was dying, he was [in] diapers. As a mother of a small child, I know how happy a parent feels when their child stops using diapers. When you have a forty-year-old child who is addicted to drug[s] and is using diapers, it means that we, as a society, have failed our children . . . It is us adults who allow drug traffickers to pass our porous borders. We give minimal sentences to drug traffickers and thus increase the proliferation of drugs in our country.[10]

This statement depicts unregulated economic flows moving freely through the nation's "porous borders" as finding expression in uncontrollable bodily flows that render citizens similarly pervious. According to this logic, without national security and border regulation, citizens cannot grow out of infantile dependence, becoming instead "forty-year-old children." Problematic moneymaking practices thus put adults in diapers, making them regress to infantile dependence. "Forty-year-old children" reflect their society's failure to progress. Here, bodies constitute central means through which shifting political economic trends play out more generally. Exploring preoccupations with the "underneath of things" in Sierra Leone, Mariane C. Ferme (2001, 8) argues that "the individual's body [is] the site for locating hidden, potent forces of the underworld, as well as for contesting and reorganizing the sociopolitical order."

If illegitimate work ruptured bodies, diaper discourses also implied that much energy was invested in hiding those ruptures, along with the means of livelihood that caused them. Diapers could conceal incontinent bodies to preserve their respectability only if, at the same time, they were themselves concealed by outer clothing. The resulting image of layered concealments resonated strongly with people's everyday attempts to veil how they made money. Nabaro, for example, told her children and neighbors that she worked night shifts as a waitress in a restaurant. To avoid rumors of her sex work reaching her parents in the north, she also frequented bars located far from where Samburu migrants typically socialized. At night, when she walked from home to the bars, she covered her short skirts with long, traditional *kanga* fabrics that she later removed. "I make myself a bit more respectable," she once told me, laughing, "so that mamas in my neighborhood won't talk too much."

Seeking to acquire money through sex work while maintaining respectability, Nabaro had to cover—quite literally, at times—different aspects of her life. Like others, she engaged in a "politics of pretense," to use Julie Soleil Archambault's (2017, 43, 94) term, "juggl[ing] visibility and invisibility," "embellishing reality . . . through concealment." The careful management of the body in space and time, its strategic covering and uncovering, reflects how the preservation of respectability, over the long run, presupposed the concealment of one's more immediate means of livelihood. It also reflects how an imaginary of social life as layered proved important in this context.

In rumors that reveal the hidden layers of others' lives, people expressed and reflected on their shared anxieties. In May 2017, Vivian told me and two friends of hers how delighted she had been to discover recently that her neighbor, a woman who "pretends" (S: *anajifanya*) to be a respectable "mother of the community" (S: *mama wa mtaa*), was herself "just a prostitute" (S: *malaya tu*). As we all laughed, entertained by Vivian's narration, I remembered that she, too, had recently been outed as a "prostitute" on national television. A

Nairobi crew filming a reportage on Mtwapa's nightlife had promised to blur Vivian's face in the interview she offered. They didn't. And after the segment aired, her parents and kin upcountry called her to say that she was no longer welcome home. I do not mean to suggest that Vivian's laughter at exposing her neighbor constituted a form of Schadenfreude or abreaction. But, taken together, these experiences show how, in intimate exposures, anxieties, aspirations, and amusement are ambiguously intertwined. Rumors exposing others also expressed unease with a shared predicament in which people must work illicitly to build respectability amid suspicious appearances and uncertain attachments. Yet these rumors were more than expressions of fear and desire. They also represented, as I have suggested, technologies of citizenship. To show this, I take a brief detour in the following section, away from my ethnographic data, through the Nairobi exhibit *Diaper Mentality*.

Intimate Exposures, Queer Objects, and Good Citizenship

Diaper discourses, I have shown, help people express and negotiate aspirations and anxieties related to bodies, work, respectability, and progress even in circumstances unrelated to sex. This means that public revelations of diapered adults reflect a cultural logic independent of—though, at times, overlapping with—discourses of sexuality. *Diaper Mentality*, the photography exhibit curated by Mwangi and PAWA 254, illustrates how this cultural logic forms a technology of citizenship, a way to produce subjects within national frames of moral propriety.

Organized for the fiftieth anniversary of Kenya's independence from British colonial rule, *Diaper Mentality* showcased images of a wide range of troublesome behaviors. In all pictures, let us recall, those doing bad things appear in adult diapers. In one image, a group of people jaywalk on Nairobi's busy Kenyatta Avenue. In another, three youths sit behind the driver on a motorcycle cab, stretching its carrying capacity beyond the limit (see fig. 15). A painted inscription on the wall behind them reads *Uhuru*—Independence—suggesting satirically how some Kenyans misunderstand liberation from colonialism as liberty to misbehave. Also featured are unreasonable or offensive acts: a group of drivers wash their trucks in a lake, polluting the water; waiters in a restaurant serve light-skinned foreigners smilingly, ignoring fellow black Kenyans; and a group of coastal men drink beer, chew khat, and play board games, while their wives undertake the hard—traditionally male—work of climbing palm trees to harvest coconuts. Yet other pictures portray corrupt or abusive deeds: police demanding bribes from drivers or destroying informal alcohol joints; and men harassing a woman on the street for dressing

FIGURE 15. Three customers riding one *bodaboda* motorcycle cab. *Diaper Mentality* exhibit, Kenya, 2014. Photo by PAWA 254.

"scantily." All images capture evocative public affects Kenyans will likely recognize, including innocent smiles, angry demeanors, or panicked gazes.

The use of diapers is metaphoric. What renders bodies incontinent are not ruptures caused by sexual penetration or illness, but immorality broadly construed. Although a significant number of photographs focus on sexuality, they nevertheless dissociate bodily incontinence from actual sexual penetration. In a particularly evocative picture, three female high school pupils, all pregnant, point their index fingers at the male teacher who impregnated them. Another male teacher, who has already sired a baby with a schoolgirl, stands nearby, looking amused (see fig. 16). The phenomenon of teachers impregnating schoolgirls has seen widespread debate in recent decades. In this image, the accused appears on his knees, holding up a biology book, against the background of a blackboard with terms related to sexual reproduction. The image thus ridicules supposedly pedagogical circumstances that lead to such pregnancies and exposes male teachers as failed persons. Notably, the teachers wear diapers not because they have been penetrated, but because their irresponsible deeds have rendered them, senior men, subservient to their immoral desires. This logic subverts the causal relation between sexual penetration and diapers, rendering the latter a more generic symptom of ethical failure.

Diaper Mentality is an attempt to rescue norms of propriety, which the artist-activists think should have defined Kenyan national identity since

FIGURE 16. Schoolgirls point their fingers at the teacher responsible for their pregnancies, while another teacher has already fathered a child with his pupil. *Diaper Mentality* exhibit, Kenya, 2014. Photo by PAWA 254.

independence. The exhibit draws on popular understandings of diapers as tools of infantilization to announce the nation's ruptured progress. Political activists worldwide have used diapers in this way to satirize leaders. Consider, for example, Baby Trump in recent U.S. and U.K. protests, or the "red diaper" of the 1960s U.S. communist scares (in which homosexuals themselves were associated with the communist threat). Echoing colonial and developmental temporalities that have long infantilized non-Western racial Others (Fabian 1983), Mwangi and his team use diapers to underscore the urgency of moral rescue and to shame fellow citizens into good behavior. They condemn certain private practices to restore ideals of propriety, gender, and family that should define progress.

More important for my argument, the exhibit uses bodily incontinence to depict broken citizens and expose hidden layers of intimate life. Such uses of diapers have been common in the national public in recent decades. They started when, in 1985, in a public hygiene campaign on the island of Lamu, local politicians called on the island's residents to put diapers on the donkeys they used for transport. Kenyan artists, including the famous cartoonist Gado, found the idea so ludicrous that in their art, they put corrupt politicians in diapers instead. While *Diaper Mentality* also features former president Uhuru Kenyatta, former Nairobi senator Mike Sonko, and other politicians, the exhibit builds on this genealogy to focus primarily on ordinary citizens. The journalist Oyunga Pala explains that the main focus of the exhibit is "the ordinary *mwananchi* [citizen] behaving badly."[11] "Diaper mentality," he suggests, is another name for what has "evidently become an accepted culture of individualism in Kenya." Inspired by Mwangi, he claims, "whenever I spot bad behavior in public places, I think of Lamu donkeys and mutter under my breath: 'Stop being an ass and be a responsible citizen or we will dress you in diapers.'"

Diaper Mentality seeks to reform Kenyans. An op-ed described it as "a campaign on . . . general ethics in the country."[12] This approach continues Mwangi's previous work, a photography exhibit depicting the gruesome carnage of the 2008 postelection violence, which traveled across the country to educate citizens about the perils of interethnic hate (Githuku 2016, 438–46). Similarly, *Diaper Mentality* means to shock with its revelatory gesture: it invites citizens to contemplate the broken layers of their everyday. This gesture recognizes and redeploys the otherwise common tactic of intimate exposure to foreclose bad behavior and produce good citizens. It thus works as a technology of citizenship that confronts subjects with the tremendous impact of their actions for the nation's progress and pushes them to work on themselves.

As grammars of social action, intimate exposures are neither inherently oppressive nor merely empowering. To classify them thus would be to miss their quite complex and sometimes contradictory implications. In 2016, a quite fascinating instance of intimate exposures took place in the Kenyan public sphere. Using the hashtag *#ifikiewazazi*, which in Swahili means "let it reach the parents," a few people started posting on social media photographs of youth caught engaging in sexualized behavior in public spaces. Some were kissing, others danced with erotic postures, and yet others dressed "revealingly." The point was to use this hashtag not just to shame youth but also to make sure that images of them would literally "reach their parents," who would then supposedly discipline them. As more and more parents started scrolling through images tagged *#ifikiewazazi* in search of their teenage offspring, the hashtag went viral. It soon produced an immense archive of erotic public behavior that, instead of leading to the disciplining of youth, unexpectedly led—one can argue—to the sexualization of public space. Youth then also appropriated the hashtag to circulate imaginatively staged, witty images of such behavior to further scandalize the disciplining gazes of their elders. This is one example of how, as a grammar, intimate exposures can be mobilized for otherwise contradictory purposes. The use of diapers as a technology of citizenship can help us better understand the deployment of intimate exposures in rumors in Mtwapa. Like Mwangi's art, NGO workers and sex workers uncovered ruptured strata of bodies and social life, performatively exposing the magnitude of their sheer damage. Revealing how anal sex undermines bodies and society, they sought to restore national reproductive heterosexuality as a foundation of citizenship. They thus performed "exceptional citizenship" (Grewal 2017, 10), a mode of empowerment prompting subjects "to rescue, to save, to become humanitarians." We can interpret intimate exposures as technologies of citizenship because they aim to produce citizens who, doing the work of the state, surveil underlayers of social life and expose their ruptures to secure collective well-being. Their ability to shock fuels their inflationary quality: anal sex emerges as an excess, an expanding affliction that makes the act of exposing it a performance of exceptional citizenship.

I think of diapers as queer objects, things that one must repudiate, relegate to the margins, to acquire heteropatriarchal respectability (Ahmed 2006, 90–91; Davidson and Rooney 2018). Often deemed vulgar, repulsive, or shameful, such objects are "straightening devices," media that, in demanding disavowal, orient subjects away from subversive intimacies, toward normative ones (Ahmed 2006, 66): *If you don't want to end up in diapers*, so the argument goes, *don't engage in x behavior*. What makes such objects "queer" is not that they subvert heteropatriarchal intimacies. Rather, they prove central to producing them. Even so, within normative frameworks, such objects disturb and offend. Interlocutors often regarded me skeptically, for example, when hearing I was writing an essay on diapers, and colleagues have suggested more than once that I look at more "dignified" things. But this is precisely what, to me, makes such queer objects fascinating: the expectation that their seeming vulgarity or indecency should disqualify them from being serious objects of research. It is, in part, this expectation that sustains their efficiency as a means of disciplining desire. It is important to remember that the reification of any normative framework of intimate citizenship depends on and is constituted by the things it disavows as shameful, unserious, or perverse. Hence, the queerness of this object rests both with its marginality and with my analytical choice to focus on it; for, as Ahmed (2006, 166) argues, "bringing an object that is often in the background to the foreground ... can have a queer effect." In this case, diapers decenter the homosexual body as a hegemonic target of outrage and illustrate the forms of imagination through which it is produced.

Homophobia as Diapered Displacements

Having traced diaper discourses across different domains of social life and shown how they help normalize intimate exposures as technologies of citizenship, I now return to their role in homophobic imaginaries. At the beginning of this chapter, I showed how political leaders invoke diapers to highlight the threat of homosexuality to national integrity. In this sense, how diapers circulate in rumors about anal sex and illegitimate moneymaking or in activist art is also, if indirectly, constitutive of the homosexual body as an object of outrage, violence, and exclusion.

Nkanatha, Mutua, and other leaders' references to diapers may seem trivial in this context. They are not. Such references catalyze disparate affects and meanings associated elsewhere, as we have seen, with struggles over bodies, work, respectability, and a progressive futurity. Diapers thus enable a process of displacement and condensation through which different *elsewheres*—other scenes of social life in which people invest diapers with aspirations and anxieties—become constitutive of the homosexual body. The homosexual body not only takes on these displaced affects but, in so doing, also becomes the externalized object-cause of national intimate trouble more generally, and thus a ready target of repudiation.

Men who identified interchangeably as gay, *msenge*, *kuchu*, or—using public health parlance—MSM rebuked diaper discourses. In June 2017, I spoke to Kent, a twenty-four-year-old from Mtwapa, who had come of age during a time of amplified political homophobia in the country. "I think I was in fifth grade" (about eleven years old), he recalled, "when I thought about whether to continue or to stop [being gay] and the repercussions." He explained:

> It was about how people perceived you. They'd say that in the future you will be walking in Pampers. Those rumors. So, those myths, to me, were scary. I remember... my mom had been told I could be gay. So, that was the first time my mom told me about sexuality: "If you practice this, you will be in Pampers. You will not be able to hold your stool. Blah, blah, blah." So, I started believing that until I was older and joined high school. I told myself I have to stop this. But time was passing, and I was still practicing [anal sex], and I saw no difference, no nothing.

Diaper discourses, though false, Kent suggested, shaped gay men's subjectivities as they grow up. Linking anal penetration to incontinence, such rumors inculcated fear.

Diaper discourses also informed violent homophobic imaginaries. Kent recalled how, in 2010, while in high school, teachers and classmates caught him having sex with a roommate. They took them both into the schoolyard and beat them. Kent remembered receiving the harsher beating because he had been the receptive partner—"bottom," or "queen." As punishment, the headmaster expelled Kent, only giving his partner—the "top," or "king"—extra cleaning chores. "I think they perceive gayism to be in the bottom," Kent said. "So, if you are topping, you are a man who has been forced or socially corrupted . . . I was told I am the one who is influencing socially the rest of the boys."

On another occasion, a few years later, neighbors caught Kent having sex in his home. They dragged him and his partner out into the street and beat them. Once more, Kent received the worse beating. "Then again, the blame was on me being the bottom. They said, 'He is the one who went to boarding school and then brought us the habits [S: *tabia*] from there to the neighborhood.'"

In discourses about gayism, diapers conceal deeper anxieties over anal erotic pleasure. Receptive anal sex, queer theorists argue, has long threatened to dissolve the modern, rational, male subject of liberal discourse, to blur interiority and exteriority, leak gender distinctions, and diffuse sources of agency (Bersani 2009; Guss 2010). In Kenya, rather than appearing passive, men's anal receptiveness was often imagined as assertive, active, and agentive. Critiquing phallocentric understandings of agency, Nkiru Nzegwu (2011) shows how the idiom of the "devouring vagina," common in African imaginaries, captures the dangerously agentive power of feminine sexuality, its ability to engulf the penis, to make it disappear. One can expand this argument to what people perceive as a "devouring anus" that undermines worlds, enticing "normal" men to turn them into bottoms. Diaper discourses disavow anal erotic pleasure as unbearable, unthinkable. "When people say you end up in Pampers," Kent said, "they don't count the pleasure part of it . . . only the traumatizing part." According to this logic, if heterosexual anal sex is simply the outcome of poor moral judgment, men's desire for and pleasure in receptive penetration signal a quest to devour society, to turn men into *mashoga* or "fags," and reproductive sexuality and national progress into selfish self-gratification.

The notion of gayism common in Kenya (and elsewhere in anglophone Africa) is distinct from—if also coexistent with—liberal understandings of sexual orientation as immutable identity. It is akin to evangelical renderings of homosexuals as unable to reproduce and so needing to "recruit," a logic that Euro-American right-wing conservatives have long employed (Angelides 2019, 86). Gayism, like any *-ism*, is a trend, a current that proliferates through conversion, much like how Freemasonry is depicted in West Africa (Geschiere 2017; Geschiere and Orock n.d.). It posits men who desire receptive penetration as feeding off the bodies of others. In Mtwapa, interlocutors, including some gay men, told me that a man becomes gay by first being "ruined" (S: *kuharibiwa*) by another man (see also Amory 1998, 82), a logic that political leaders also employed when warning against foreigners who seduced Kenyans with money. Once ruined, a man spread the vice to quench his thirst for nonreproductive, antisocial pleasures, becoming the ultimate embodiment of not only intimate noncitizenship but something like *anti*-citizenship. Thus understood, gayism expanded one layer below what can be seen, afflicting, like a contagion, ever larger numbers of people. Pandemic anal sex and gayism were constructed as two only partially overlapping yet co-constitutive afflictions. And diapers enable this co-constitutive process as a point of resonance that alerts people to the rapid deterioration of their society from underneath.

Accordingly, leaders, police, and urban crowds also deployed violence as a form of intimate exposure to identify, reveal, and rectify the hidden layers of social life through which gayism secretly expanded. They drew on such popular perceptions of intimacy to expose homosexuals, "uncover" their "underground networks." Similarly, citizens could drag homosexual men—as they had done to Kent—into public spaces to reveal otherwise invisible, troubled strata in the town's intimate life. Crowds thus performed their own version of intimate exposure and good citizenship. As Tom Boellstorff (2004, 480) argues for Indonesia, so too in Kenya, leaders' homophobic rhetoric made "violence not only thinkable but sensible as an emotional 'gut reaction' to . . . an assault on the nation's manhood." Diapers, if anything, lend strength to such violence. Discursive conduits for the displacement and condensation of social anxieties, they help disambiguate the homosexual for exposure and exclusion.

*

What makes diaper discourses so evocative in the present is their ability to resonate with how people perceived political economic and social transformations. These discourses rehearsed cultural logics that some Kenyans already employed to make sense of how shifting definitions of licit work affected their bodies and respectability. Social anxieties over these matters have found new expression in diaper discourses. Neither merely the product of the political class nor simply a folk concept, these discourses brought leaders and the citizenry into a relationship of conviviality—a shared experience of a common predicament, a "community of affliction" (Turner 1968). This conviviality finds expression through a longstanding "aesthetics of vulgarity," as Achille Mbembe (2001, 104) calls it, discourses involving bodily orifices, genitalia, or feces and that maintain citizens and the state in the same discursive realm. Deployments of diapers in everyday rumor, political art, or leaders' rhetoric reflected a newly amplified concern with concealing, revealing, and suturing broken intimate underlayers as a condition of citizenship.

As technologies of citizenship, intimate exposures, including diaper discourses, promised exceptional citizenship to those who revealed ruptured underlayers of social life and helped reform them. Like Nyamnjoh (2018), I use *layers* as a descriptor for what my ethnographic material suggests as an implicit, emic topography of citizenship. In Kenya, as elsewhere, citizenship is experienced today, in part, as intimate, in that people understand their private lives as both symptomatic of and consequential for national progress. This implicit topography animated a wide array of practices, including strategic concealments and performative exposures, through which people imagined and negotiated attachments to each other and the polity.

As queer objects, diapers—like the other objects we have encountered throughout this book—also take us beyond the readily recognizable targets of state exclusion. To understand shifting forms of intimate citizenship, anthropologists must therefore also explore threats to the nation and its private lives that are less concrete, more fleeting, and ambivalent, and sometimes appear quite vulgar or ridiculous. Diapered bodies constitute such indeterminate threats, easy to miss if our analysis focuses only on the globalized repertoire of sexualized identities readily marked for exclusion. Understanding the homosexual body, for example, as a normative target of exclusionary violence requires that scholars explore how the signifiers producing this body in particular contexts—diapers, among others—carry traces of other "troublesome" bodies (e.g., sex workers, alcoholics, drug addicts). As key conduits for the displacement of anxieties and aspirations across social terrains, such signifiers lend strength to homophobic repudiations. Diapers' queerness, then, rests with this object's ability to trouble normative social types, even as its deployment enables their reproduction.

7

The Homosexual Body: Gayism and the Ambiguous Objects of Terror

> They told me that I was gay when they arrested me. They told me that I was paid to do my *chinkhoswe* [engagement ceremony] by LGBTs from overseas. But the first time that I heard the word gay was when . . . the policemen came and took me away.
> TIWONGE CHIMBALANGA

Instead of approaching the homosexual as a ready-made body that preexists the violence in which it is targeted, I see it as a set of processes that only become a *thing* as people express desires, fears, and anger toward it or attack it violently. Bosia and Weiss (2013) are right to suggest that to be effective, the deployment of "political homophobia" does not require, initially at least, any concrete bodies one can identify as homosexual. Rather, its deployment often entails digging up such bodies along the way, assembling them, and investing them with various fantasies of national doom and redemption. It is important, then, not to take for granted the homosexual body as imagined in such fantasies, not to confuse it with the actual bodies of people who desire sex with partners of their own gender. Instead, we should pay close attention to how the homosexual body is situationally objectified. For this globally circulating tactic of governance could not take off in any given place were it not to resonate meaningfully with local struggles and aspirations. Mundane rumors, mass-mediated scandals, or outright moral panics implicate leaders, elites, and commoners in an open-ended, asymmetrical dialogue. This dialogue generates, in turn, the homosexual body as a bricolage of all kinds of other, unanticipated objects. These are things people deploy to make sense of their changing life circumstances; things that have become part of the "social poetics" of their national public sphere (Herzfeld 1997, 27–32).

Sexuality is—globally—a salient domain of national politics. Similarly, the homosexual is an emblematic object in the politics of sexuality. To understand the historical centrality of sexuality, more generally, and of the homosexual body, more specifically, it is important to push our ethnographic imagination to first decenter both. We must attend to what, drawing on Freudian psychoanalysis, I call their "other scene"—a wider arena which, if central to the emergence of the sexual, is also disavowed, repressed, or erased so that (homo)sexuality can appear as a ready-made object. Undertaking a set of ethnographic detours, the previous chapters have pivoted around objects that were not always explicitly related to (homo)sexuality as such. Yet, in the public sphere, these objects appeared, at times, in an uncanny proximity to (homo)sexuality—in "slips of tongue," as it were, that associated them, metaphorically or metonymically, with the domain of the sexual. Saying, for example, that "gayism is a fatal plastic import" is such a slip of tongue that has determined me to take plastic seriously in understanding the politics of (homo)sexuality. Such objects can illustrate how gayism came to congeal destructive potential and how its ousting from body and polity became a way to rescue a "moral" national community. Exploring male-power, bead necklaces, plastics, and diapers, among other things, shows how the homosexual body emerges through the displacement and condensation of fantasies, perceptions, desires, and affects that originate *beyond* itself. Rather than being an exceptional object of politics, it is part of an arsenal of similarly constituted objects that sustain technologies of citizenship by making intimacy the basis of membership in the polity.

But, as with every detour, my analysis must eventually arrive at its (intentionally) postponed destination. As with every imagination that is "perverse" in the Freudian sense (i.e., lingering where it must not and deferring arrival to its normative aim), the ethnographic imagination I pursue in this book must show what this "other scene" of the (homo)sexual body may teach us about this object of politics. I return now to this body, to show how it figures in contemporary public imaginaries, and explore how the objects I introduced throughout this book's circuitous ethnographic journey may explain some of its political salience. The homosexual body represents, in the end, but another queer object. Like with the other objects I examined, its queerness has little to do with its presumed sexual identity or essentialized interiority. Rather, it names its capacity—if properly decentered by our imagination—to show the stakes of its obsessive foregrounding in the present.

What, then, is the homosexual body that is disavowed or excluded as part of various efforts to actualize a national community anchored in "moral" forms of intimacy? At the beginning of this book, I suggested that the homosexual is at once an "empty signifier" *and* an object that is overdetermined by particular discursive logics and grammars: that is, whatever *it* actually turns out to be, it is always already known to be foreign and polluting, dangerous to the integrity of persons and polities, a non-reproductive entity devoted to the anti-future. I will introduce other logics here, but I must mention that, beyond these, no concrete description of the homosexual body is really possible.

The reason for this obscurity is part of this chapter's main argument: that to be an efficient device of citizenship technologies, the homosexual body must be both concrete *and* abstract, visible *and* invisible, an object that promises *categorical certainty*, albeit hidden in its interiority, and therefore also an ambiguous object of knowledge, something not readily knowable. This body's ability to make people obsess about it rests with its imagined essence: a substance that vows to hold the true difference between citizens and noncitizens, "us" and "them," the good and the bad. Its spectrality and opaqueness conceal this substance, rendering it mysterious, and thus generate desire for its exposure, whether in rumor, violence, or deadly dismemberment.

I first explore two instances of how people encounter and "recognize" the homosexual body in the public sphere to lay out some of the logics constitutive of this body. Then, I examine this body's links to the more obscure notion of gayism, and its co-constitutive relation to another spectral object of contemporary Kenyan politics—the terrorist body. I return then to the two events with which this book began: the 2010 anti-homosexual protest in Mtwapa and the 2018 panic over the "boy with beads" in Samburu County. These events illustrate the role the homosexual body plays as people seek to disambiguate, displace, and disavow queer affordances of their lives, past and present, and to imagine a future that restores heteronormative respectability.

The Ambiguous Body and the Desire for Certainty

I have already suggested that for analytical purposes, it is important to distinguish between the homosexual body of homophobic imaginaries and the actual bodies of people who desire erotic intimacies with partners of the same gender. I make this distinction because it allows me to attend to how the homosexual body is a spectral image that same-sex-desiring—but also, as I will show, gender-nonconforming—people encounter, at first, as an object that is other than themselves. However, when others recognize the bodies of some gender-nonconforming people as homosexual, the spectral object of the homosexual body does not remain fully separate from them. Instead, images of their concrete bodies now dialectically constitute the iconography of this generic object; they generate what Brian Axel (2001, 230) calls a "real abstract formation" or "abstract forms that have become very real." Once recognized through the generic category of the homosexual, such concrete bodies became abstracted, hollowed of subjectivity and history. Focusing on the contradictions of this duality and its generative capacity demonstrates the central role of ambiguity in identifying bodies as homosexual. It demonstrates also how a desire to "know" the ambiguous bodies emerges.

One characteristic of the homosexual body is its presumed ambiguous gender appearance. A public art performance by Kenyan artist Neo Musangi captures well the moment of disorientation that comes *prior* to—and is often also a condition for—the recognition of a body as *shoga*, homosexual. Published on YouTube in June 2013, the performance, entitled "In Time and Space," takes place in Nairobi's busy city center. Neo dresses and undresses, alternating between outfits that can be read as masculine and feminine. "The performance," Christopher Ouma and Mphathi Mutloane (2014, 38, 40) note,

> begins with Neo, whose hair is styled in a gender neutral and currently popular hairstyle . . . with a heap of clothes at her feet. Neo's hairstyle consists of short dreadlocks on the top of her head, and a "fade" haircut (short back and sides/German cut). Neo is dressed in a white t-shirt and black pants, and rummages through the heap of clothes, with an expression of exasperation and annoyance, and selects a striped orange and white tight-fitting dress. Neo proceeds to change into the dress in a way that avoids showing more than arms and legs. Once the dress is on and the t-shirt and pants are off, Neo puts on a pair of black high heels. As a curious crowd gathers around, Neo proceeds to change clothes several times, alternating between clothes that can be read as masculine and/or feminine respectively. In the end, Neo changes into black pants, a black and white striped shirt, a waistcoat, sneakers, a tie and a hat. Neo packs the rest of the clothes on the floor into a rucksack, puts on a pair of spectacles and walks out of the camera frame . . .

Neo's performance, one can argue, works like a social experiment. Denaturalizing the normative relation between the body and the clothes meant to reflect its presumed gendered interiority, it suggests that no hidden truth is to be revealed beneath one's bodily surface. If anything, the opposite is the case: rather than a stable source of identity, the body's presumed interiority is but an effect of its outer surface, its clothing.

For onlookers, this generates confusion. Over video footage of Neo's performance, members of the crowd comment in Swahili: "This is certainly a lady," someone says, "but [the breasts] are small." "If s/he wears a young man's clothes, it is a young man," remarks another. "But where did the breasts come from?" Others add: "S/he needs to be checked, that one"; or "This is to show how alcoholism creates confusion [S: *vile ulevi zimechanganikiwa*]." After the performance ends, the film crew invites audience members to comment on camera. "I don't know if it was he or she," a man confesses in English. "I was very much confused. I don't know . . . We didn't know why. We didn't know the intention, really." Reversing the indexical relation between the body's underlayer and outer layer, the performance generates ambiguity and disorientation.

But, rather than abandon the idea of a deeper bodily interiority, the crowd pursues it even more explicitly. "Help me out," a young man demands boldly, in English:

> and I explore the kind of person that you are. 'Cause we saw on the TV . . . I think there are some . . . some of people of your type who are here . . . who are just here to source. So, I'm asking about the cause. 'Cause I was seeing she [sic] dressed [unclear] to male and female. And I also need to get some confirmation of that. Now, which part, on the genital side, eh . . . Are you active on the men or are you active on the female? 'Cause you should be active on one side. I don't understand.

Note the move from confusion to suspicion ("I think there are . . . people of your type . . . who are just here to source") and, finally, to a desire for certainty ("I . . . need to get some confirmation"). This is a desire to expose "the kind of person that you are" by revealing who one is active with "on the genital side." "The crowd's inability to assign Neo a gender role," Ouma and Mutloane (2014, 40) aptly note, "leads to questions about Neo's sexuality." In a moment of ambiguity and disorientation, sexuality promises the ultimate truth about the subject, the *certainty* of their identity, the possibility for its viewers to reorient themselves morally—to take a stance—in relation to Neo's body. Sexuality is here the hidden link between the ambiguous body and the generic category of the homosexual; it is what makes this body recognizable as such.

Ouma and Mutloane (2014, 38) draw particular attention to the symbolic value of the performance's location: the capital city's center, a busy area hosting both a thriving informal economy and key national monuments (e.g., the statue of Tom Mboya, a politician assassinated in 1969; the imposing building of the Kenya National Archives). Neo's performance is thus well positioned to question normative spatial alignments of the body with objects meant to "set it straight" (Ahmed 2006) in a world of extant normative possibilities. Indeed, the crowd is left wondering how Neo might fit into what I have called the "circles of encompassment" that engender bodies by enclosing them in the metaphoric nested compounds of the family, the lineage, and the nation (chapter 4). "Since you are now both male and female," says one audience member, "you dream of one day, one time, you will marry a lady, or you will get married [to a man]?" In other words, this man asks how Neo's body fits into the national "homestead" (S: *boma*) and its organization of heteropatriarchal reproduction. I should add that in the early 2010s, in the city area where Neo held this performance, crowds had on several occasions assaulted individual young women whom they considered "scantily dressed."[1] These were conservative attempts to realign women's bodies with patriarchal ideals of national respectability. But this was also a liminal location where citizens have long performed comedy skits and political satires or engaged in spontaneous acts of political oratory, an experimental place for crafting citizenship.

Rapidly alternating between styles of clothing associated with seemingly stable gender identities, Neo's performance also plays imaginatively with the relation between body and time. It enacts and exacerbates a key epochal feature of late capitalism, what Mbembe (in Shipley 2010, 659) calls "the generalization and radicalization of a condition of temporariness." As things become inherently transitory, binary gender difference—otherwise imagined as durable, immutable—also turns dangerously fluid. "Male-power," let us recall, flew now in unprecedented ways (chapter 3): it vitalized women's over men's bodies; turned men alcoholic, impotent, and unable to work, while women "became men"—that is, strong, hardworking providers. In this perception, the homosexual body was, in part, responsible for the liquification of normative gender roles: engaging in receptive anal sex, it not only lost its ability to have erections or ejaculate but also "seduced" other men to the pleasures of gayism. Gayism was accordingly an affliction of "male-power." Neo's performance engages and plays with this historical common sense, highlighting the fragility of male-power, an object expected to be solid, durable, a signifier of the nation's wholeness, its phallus.

Raising questions about Neo's sexuality, this performance illustrates the fleeting moment that precedes the recognition of concrete bodies as homosexual. It is important to specify that nowhere in the video recording of this performance does this recognition fully occur.[2] However, gay men I spoke with described having experienced abuse and assault in public settings, in situations that started off, just like Neo's performance, with moments in which the crowd's gazes turned from confusion to suspicion, and, finally, to a desire for certainty. Ali, a twenty-nine-year-old Mtwapa resident I interviewed in July 2017, described himself to me as "girlish" (using the English word). He wore outfits that combined masculine and feminine items, kept his hair long, straightened, and tied in a ponytail, and walked and gestured in ways he himself deemed feminine. I once asked Ali why he only agreed to meet me in places that were so far from the town's center. "There were incidents," he explained. "I was almost beaten there at the market." People insulted Ali: "They call me *shoga, msenge, fago, homo*." Crowds thus recognized in Ali's body the "real abstract formation" of the homosexual. It is safe to assume, then, that Neo's performance generates a kind of ambiguity that has a double potentiality: on the one hand, it can interrogate normative gender roles and, on the other, as in Ali's experience, it can lead to the body's violent recognition as homosexual.

But why, one might ask, am I talking here of the homosexual body as opposed to the transgender body? Kenyan transgender activists have long complained that people *mis*recognized their bodies as homosexual. Maureen Muia Munyaka, a transgender woman who became famous after, in 2001, Nairobi police stripped her naked in public to establish her "true" gender, made this point precisely. In 2020, in an interview for the *Daily Nation*, Munyaka decried how Kenyans associate being transgender with "sexual immorality[,] even mistaking it for homosexuality." "The society is yet to understand," she said, "there's a difference between homosexuality and transgenderism."[3] Grasping this enfolding of the transgender body in the body of the homosexual, that Munyaka so clearly names, is important, then, when figuring out how anti-homosexual imaginaries work. For, when suspicions over gender nonconformity generate a desire for certainty, sexuality becomes the body's ultimate essence.

Disambiguation: Plastic and the Essence of Gayism

If Neo's performance illustrates how the ambiguous appearance of the homosexual body generates desire for certainty, the next example shows how this body's interiority may promise such certainty; how people can expose its inner affliction with gayism in material, visible, and palpable form. On February 16, 2021, *Shared Moments with Justus*, a YouTube channel featuring hour-long confessions by Kenyans who underwent various life-transforming experiences, premiered an episode entitled "My Uncle Introduced Me to Gayism." In it, Henry Karanja, a twenty-one-year-old, recounts in detail his life as a gay man, prior to his becoming an ex-gay, "born-again" Christian.

He was fifteen when his father's cousin, then twenty-five, raped him. "I knew this was a sin," he said, referring to sex between men, "because I had been to church since I was young." Henry feared telling his parents about this incident and did not know that "that thing will affect me in any way after that." But "after one week, I just said, 'No. I need to run away from [home]. Maybe I go out there and look for another man.' So, that's what I did." Henry looked up gay men on Facebook and, hiding his age, met them for sex. Note here two logics widely associated with gayism in Kenya: first, that a man is "introduced" or "recruited" to gayism by another man who seduces or forces him into having sex; and second, that this experience, in turn, activates in the victim an ongoing desire for sex with men.

Wealth, Henry says, also makes gayism seductive for many young men. The first time he went to a gay bar in Nairobi, he remembers, "I gave more than twenty people my number . . . From that day, my life changed, because I used to get money now. And now, I started comparing my life in [gayism] and [my life back] home. I said, 'Let me just stay here because I am getting my own money.'" Interestingly, the seduction of wealth required Henry to make himself seductive in turn, to commodify his body to make it desirable *as* homosexual. He now wore facial piercings and dressed distinctly. "I am so exposed to a lot of people and a lot of people have started knowing me. They are knowing me . . . that I am a new person into gay life. So, I'm in demand. Everybody wants to be with me." An interior transformation generated by Henry's introduction to gayism facilitated then a transformation in his body's exterior.

And then again, this exterior transformation further changed his interior life. For no sooner did Henry experience material success than he also began to spiral. He became depressed, attempted to commit suicide, and eventually grew dependent on alcohol and drugs. Henry represents his downfall as metonymically reflected in his alienation from Pentecostal Christianity. After running away from his parents' home, he became friends with a gay *mokorino*, a man of the Holy Ghost Church of East Africa, who Pentecostals regard as devilish, unsaved pagans. If this friendship marked the advent of Henry's self-alienation, its zenith arrived with his trip to Zanzibar, Tanzania, sponsored by an older, gay Muslim man who wanted to "introduce" him into an "Islamic cult." When read against politicians and clergy's recent representations of Kenya as a "born-again nation" (Deacon 2015), this cartography of religious self-alienation is also metonymic of one's estrangement from national citizenship. Indeed, in the context of Kenya's "war on terror," the reference to the "Islamic cult" resonates with anxieties over terrorist recruitment in the country, a parallel to which I will return shortly.

When Henry fled Zanzibar and returned to his parents' home in Kenya, he wore a white *kanzu*, a long fabric coat typically associated with Muslim men. He also wore a ring he had bought on his journey. Intrigued by these strange objects, Henry's mother called the bishop at her Pentecostal church. The bishop advised her to take these items, place them outside the house and, after fasting for six days, bring them to church. Although Henry had returned to Nairobi and was unaware of this initiative, the bishop hoped to use these objects to exorcise—remotely—gayism from Henry's body. Henry's mother later told him that the ritual took place one night at 3AM in the church's yard. People poured paraffin over these items, covered them with dry leaves, and set them on fire. The details of the ritual, as Henry describes it, are intriguing:

> The cloth did not burn . . . They didn't know what was happening. They said, "Let's pray again maybe it will burn." So, they prayed, they prayed, and the

cloth finally burned. So, when it was burning, the ring jumped up and it disappeared. Until today, they don't know where it went. So, that cloth, instead of burning like any other cloth... it was rolling like a snake. And, after it finished burning, instead of turning to ashes, it became a plastic. That plastic stayed there for two years [before it disappeared].

This ritual illustrates fascinating assumptions about the homosexual body. In Henry's absence, his kanzu is a mimetic representation of his bodily presence. Turned into a snake-*cum*-plastic, the kanzu is the body turned inside out: in the fire, its interiority, its concealed underlayers emerge onto its outer stratum. In Kenya, the kanzu was surely an ambivalent object. A sartorial marker of respectable, pious Muslim masculinity, the Islamophobic rhetoric surrounding the state's "war on terror" has also rendered it suspicious. When I once asked Musa, a gay man from Mtwapa, why many gay men chose to marry women, he compared marriage to a kanzu: "Many marry to hide... It's like wearing a kanzu. You wear it and when you are outside [the home] you go fishing [for men, without being suspected of anything foul]." The kanzu is thus emblematic of attempts to conceal troublesome underlayers of intimate life and therefore also a persuasive target for public acts of intimate exposure. It was this underlayer of the kanzu-covered homosexual body that the Pentecostal ritual exposed for its participants.

The plastic that refused to turn to ashes is a resonant metaphor of gayism's substance, the essence of its manifestation as bodily interiority. As I have shown in chapter 5, historical experiences with plastic in Kenya linked it to bodily contagions, infertility, nonbelonging, nonreliability, and polluting persistence. In the form of colorful commodities, plastic seduced people into consuming it, only to deceive them with its poor quality, ephemeral usefulness, and toxicity. So too gayism appeared to seduce with promises of wealth and enjoyment, only to deliver misery, depression, death. Here, the idea that "gayism is a fatal plastic import," to which I have returned throughout this book, is particularly salient. Expanding through seduction (or recruitment), gayism was like plastic in that it could contaminate people, fool them into intoxicating their bodies, all while they blindly pursued lust or wealth.

As an intermediary form between the body's outer layer (the kanzu) and its hidden essence (the gayism-*cum*-plastic), the snake is an important demonic symbol: it stands for the devil, who, coiled around one's body, encompasses it in his own circles of belonging, estranging it, as Henry's body has been, from the family's homestead and the compounds of the church and the nation. Like the snake, the ring Henry wore—a circle appended to his body (similar to the bead necklaces discussed in chapter 4)—tied him into a "cult" imagined to be not only external to the Christian nation, but also its very antithesis. For Pentecostals, such forces manifested themselves in the body, possessing it and leading it into sexual sin (Hackman 2018, 98–107; Parsitau and Van Klinken 2018, 593–95; Van Klinken 2019, 48–50).

Henry was in Nairobi at the time of the ritual. He said that as the bishop prayed that "the evil things that are inside me burn like that cloth," he felt a sudden change. "I don't know what happened. I got . . . let's call it rejection from the fellow gays." Friends stopped calling or inviting him to parties, and he lost all his sex-work clients. In 2017, he returned to his parents' home where, to his mother's and her bishop's joy, he decided to become "born again."

Henry's story is part of a popular genre of confessional accounts by Kenyans on social media, radio, and television. In the last five years, these have included filmed personal disclosures pertaining to homosexuality. On YouTube, confessions by Kenyans had titles such as "Gayism in Prison"; "Our Househelp Introduced Me to Lesbianism"; "I Am Tired of Using Men" (a man's confession); and "My Gay Husband Ruined Our Marriage" (a woman's confession). Assumed to generate the ultimate truth about the speaking subject, confessions about sexuality are important disciplinary means of self-making (Foucault 1978). Writing about "ex-gay" Pentecostals in South Africa, Melissa Hackman (2018, 4, 57) argues that confessions are an important element of "desire work," "a process of emotional, bodily, and religious discipline," which "trained men to be new kinds of selves, teaching them a new frame with which to view and discuss themselves." Such desire work is, to be sure, not specific to Pentecostals. If anything, it has become emblematic of a generalized technology of citizenship, in which rescue ideologies and narratives of self-transformation play a critical role. "I started another journey," Henry said by way of concluding his story. "I waited for six months or so and then I said, 'I can feel that I'm healed.' Maybe I can help someone out there. Maybe they are also in that situation in which I was and want to change. So, I decided, 'Let me just come out in public.'" For this purpose, in 2017, he launched the Inspire and Transpire Youth Organization, an FBO that rehabilitates men from gayism. Here, once more, the rescued turns into a rescuer, pursuing good citizenship by rehabilitating intimacy.

But the desire to consume such confessions—to listen to them—is also a desire to "know" the homosexual body, to reveal the certainty of its essence. Rather than an immutable identity of the body, gayism figures in the public imaginary as a contagion, an affliction. Bodies may be "introduced" *to* it through seduction or coercion, and it is this act also that introduces gayism *into* the body. Gayism is thus also an inner bodily substance that drives the body into seducing others. The snake-turned-plastic is here a resonant material manifestation of gayism as bodily affliction. Plastic disambiguates the homosexual as a body that, being infertile and toxic, does not—indeed, *must* not—belong. Objects such as plastic make the homosexual body concrete, visible, palpable.

Gayism, Terrorism, and the Spectral Body

To further elucidate the role of the homosexual body's spectral nature, I now turn to a set of striking similarities between this body and another major object of national suspicion and fear, the body of the terrorist. Over the last decade or so, both have gained prominence as emblematic dangers to Kenyan citizens. Both have also figured in public discourse as ambiguous, obscure, yet also highly sexualized objects that haunted the nation's intimate domains of life. Their spectral presence has cultivated alertness to the unseen threats lurking in and around the nation's intimate domains and underscored securitization and rescue as important conditions of good citizenship.

In March 2014, Aden Duale, a member of Parliament and the majority leader of the Jubilee Coalition (President Uhuru Kenyatta's ruling party), famously claimed that gayism is "as serious as terrorism": "We need to go on," he said, "to address this issue the way we want to address terrorism. It's as serious as terrorism. It's as serious as any other social evil."[4] Similarly, charismatic Pentecostal prophet David Owuor—infamous, among other things, for delivering men from homosexuality—also compared gayism to terrorism (Van Klinken 2019, 42). So common has this analogy become that by July 2015, when Kenya hosted U.S. president Barack Obama on an official visit, the danger of his promoting LGBT rights and gay marriage seemed, for many, to supersede the threats of terrorist violence. A cartoon published in the *Daily Nation* that month satirizes this exaggeration (fig. 17). It suggests that at the border with Somalia, terrorists are now allowed to cross into Kenya as long as they don't enter the country, like Obama, "to lecture us on gay marriage." Interestingly, this cartoon depicts the terrorist body as obscure. Wrapped in many layers of cloth, its face invisible, it is not unlike that of the *kanzu*-covered homosexual: ambiguous, not fully knowable, yet potentially recognizable (by its weapons), and certainly dangerous.

Scholars of sexuality have already explored the unexpected connections between the terrorist and the homosexual in the global "war on terror" (Jakobsen 2007; Mack 2017; Puar 2007; Weber 2016). Since 9/11, in the Global North, leaders, activists, humanitarians, and citizens celebrating their state's liberal protections of LGBT rights have invoked the terrorist as the antithesis of the homosexual and a threat to LGBT liberalism. The terrorist appears here

FIGURE 17. At the border with Somalia, terrorists are let into Kenya, lest they come—like President Barack Obama in July 2015—"to lecture us on gay marriage." Cartoon by Patrick Gathara, *Daily Nation*, July 7, 2015.

as a racialized, sexually repressed, illiberal, and oppressive Other, a spectral body that risks undoing historical achievements in human rights, feminism, and LGBT rights. Through this spectral body, scholars show, governments, police, and citizens have surveilled and disciplined refugees, immigrants, Muslims, and people of color. In Kenya, the link between the homosexual and the terrorist has played out somewhat differently. Here—but also in Uganda, Tanzania, and Nigeria—the homosexual body and the terrorist body have named *together* various, and at times overlapping, dangers to national intimacy; they *both* have been objects of terror.

Since the early 2000s, because of its strategic location, Kenya has been pivotal to U.S. and U.N. attempts to stabilize Somalia's government and launch counterterrorism initiatives. Its position in the global "war on terror," Jan Bachmann (2012) suggests, may appear contradictory. On the one hand, Kenya accepted U.S. funding to initiate anti-radicalization campaigns and expand its security institutions. On the other hand, it has used its new security strategies to violate the rights of some Kenyans, particularly Kenyan Somalis and other Muslims (see also Carrier 2016, 215–41; Weitzberg 2017, 157–74). But, Bachmann argues, rather than contradictory, these strategies have been part of "the regime's continuing efforts at consolidating stateness" (2012, 125). Militarized campaigns responding to major attacks by Al-Shabaab Islamist militia—for example, at Nairobi's Westgate Mall (2013), in the town of Mpeketoni (2014), at Garissa University (2015), and in Nairobi's DusitD2 Complex (2019)—have allowed Kenyan political leaders to perform "stateness" as a source of national security. The fact that "according to U.N. reports, almost half of the foreign fighters of . . . Al-Shabaab are Kenyans" has only heightened alertness among Kenyans who have worried that their sons, many of them unemployed, could become radicalized (Bachmann 2012, 134).

Throughout the last decade, this growing alertness to terrorism has coincided with the obsessive preoccupation with gayism. Damaris S. Parsitau (2021) argues that since 2010, anti-homosexual rhetoric has permeated the Kenyan public sphere. A few key moments, Parsitau suggests, have enabled this amplification. First, debates over the promulgation of a new Constitution in 2010 made the potential decriminalization of homosexuality a main issue of contention. Opponents of the new Constitution saw its anti-discrimination clauses as opening the door for LGBT rights, while its supporters merely dismissed this possibility (Parsitau 2021, 120; Mwangi 2014, 107). Second, in June 2011, Willy Mutunga was proposed for appointment as Chief Justice to the High Court of Kenya, when rumors that he was gay brought homosexuality back into the public sphere. Mutunga's longstanding support for human and LGBT rights but also a seemingly trivial object, the stud earring that he wore (i.e., a sign of the homosexual body), generated—albeit unsuccessfully—fierce opposition to his nomination (Parsitau 2021, 121–23). Third, Obama's visit in July 2015, only one month after the U.S. Supreme Court declared same-sex marriage legal in all fifty states, raised suspicion that he was intending to "promote gayism" in Kenya. Protests ensued (Parsitau 2021, 106; see also Van Klinken 2019, 1–2). Finally, in May 2019, the High Court of Kenya prepared to rule on a petition brought by three LGBT organizations, claiming that Sections 162 and 165 of the Penal Code (criminalizing "carnal knowledge against the order of nature") contravened the new Constitution's nondiscrimination clauses. Although in the end the High Court ruled to uphold the two Penal Code sections, this moment opened the door for further public condemnations of homosexuality. In all these cases, Parsitau (2021, 109) shows, "the language and rhetoric of politicians and clergy concretely shape not just political and public discourse, but also public policy and public opinion."

The homosexual body and the terrorist body have more in common than their coincidental arrival in the national public imaginary. They also share constitutive logics and grammars. To begin with, both bodies emerged through both recruitment *and* seduction, a seeming contradictory statement that further underscores their ambiguity. People imagined prisons, boarding schools, public health NGOs, tourist sites, and even some churches as key spaces where figures of authority recruited young Kenyans into gayism.[5] The idea of homosexual "recruitment" originates among 1980s U.S. Christian conservatives. For example, Anita Bryant, an American anti-gay-rights activist who spearheaded the campaign "Save Our Children" in the 1970s, famously stated that "Homosexuals can't reproduce, so they have to recruit" (Angelides 2019, 86). For Christians, "recruitment" also had demonological connotations pertaining to devil worship, illicit religious sects, and terrorist organizations, all said to reproduce their membership by enrolling innocent individuals. During my research in Mtwapa, town residents were also convinced that certain mosques and *madrasa* schools were "hotspots" for terrorist recruitment, where sheiks, imams, and teachers persuaded younger men—and, to a lesser extent, women—to join the Al-Shabaab in Somalia.

In both gayism and terrorism, seduction—and specifically the seduction of wealth—played an important role. Whereas "recruitment" involves an intentional, agentive act, a calculated pursuit to enroll others to a cause, "seduction" presupposes a more passive co-optation, one that is not fully rationalized. In seduction, one falls for or gets hooked to something against their better judgment. Money and fantasies of conspicuous consumption, people said, "lured" youths into both gayism and terrorism. In June 2017, Kent, the young gay man we met in chapter 6, told me of a former friend who had recently joined Al-Shabaab and had quickly become wealthy. "He was a Christian," Kent said, "but the recruiter told him to convert to Islam and to say he does this for his belief. He went for training near Lamu. It's because he saw others go and, when they came back, they bought cars, houses ... Everything. Now, he also returned with a lot of money." Kent's story resonates with Henry Karanja's confession. Henry also invokes riches as a main reason for his decision to "stay in" gayism. In Cameroon and the Gabon, Peter Geschiere and Rogers Orock (n.d.) argue, many imagine the seduction of riches as intrinsic to "recruitment" into homosexuality, a tendency also attributed to the Freemasons. Like with gayism and terrorism in East Africa, in this case too, the boundary between homosexuality and the terror of the seemingly demonic cults becomes blurry. Sheer devotion to wealth—commodity addiction—contrasts here sharply with the normative ideal of a nation devoted to social reproduction, where consumption is, instead of an end, merely a means for lineage continuity.

I should mention a few other similarities. First, in both gayism and terrorism, what is at stake is the interplay between an interpersonal, intersubjective force or current—their -*ism*—and the agentive body that is then sought out, exposed, blamed, and punished for furthering this force or current. Second, both the homosexual body and the terrorist body are spectral, opaque: they lurk in only partial visibility and can appear where one least expects them. Newspaper, television, and radio reports on both homosexuals and terrorists rehearse a discursive frame that goes something like this: at first sight, they "appear normal," "like everyone else," they "have children and spouses," and are "respectable citizens" of their community. Then, the shocking revelation follows: that underneath this deceitful layer of normality, evil forces have already been at work. Third, both bodies constitute what Katherine Verdery (2018) calls "target functions." "Targets," Verdery argues, "are ultimately not people with qualities and behaviors . . . They embody the enemy that power fears, and they occupy the site of danger that must be contained. The target function congeals those fears and dangers in a way that justifies an apparatus of repression" (292). Fourth, everyday rumor, religious sermons, political rallies, and the media depict both gayism and terrorism as being "on the rise," expanding unnoticed and entering the intimate spaces of the *mtaa* (domestic community) and the family.[6] This inflationary discourse amplifies alertness but also generates desire among citizens to rescue and securitize intimate domains of their lives and therefore to know and prevent dangers. Finally, in the case of both the homosexual and the terrorist, people's desire for certainty turns to sexuality as the ultimate truth of the body's nonbelonging. I have already shown this for the homosexual body, with the example of Neo's performance above. In the case of the terrorist body, I should mention that newspaper and TV accounts of terrorists' lives produce highly eroticized narratives of sexual orgies, the abduction and rape of women, and more.

The shared grammars of the homosexual and terrorist bodies suggest that these bodies are pivotal objects for the performative production of state legitimacy through rescue and securitization. They also suggest that, as objects cultivating fear and alertness as well as desire for knowing and expelling these ambiguous Others, these bodies are both central elements of contemporary technologies of citizenship.

Displacement and Disavowal: "Operation Gays Out"

Let us return now to the 2010 anti-homosexual protest in Mtwapa to tease out more concretely what is at stake in the desire to disambiguate the homosexual body. On February 12 that year, some two to three hundred protesters gathered in front of KEMRI's building, shouting angrily "No to homosexuals" and "Let them be burned to death." They then broke the metal gate of the organization's compound, entered its offices, and dragged out to the street two male health workers. They also caught a third man, KEMRI's watchman. Having identified all three as homosexual, young men in the crowd prepared to set them on fire. The police arrived in time to stop this from happening. But instead of arresting the violent protesters, they arrested "the homosexuals." A deep panic over the alleged spread of gayism had already ensued in Mtwapa and across the country. At the beginning of this book, I described these events in some detail and discussed the context of their occurrence (pp. 19–24). Having distilled key logics of intimate citizenship through ethnographic detours focused on other objects, I now return to how the Mtwapa protesters objectified the homosexual body.

In 2016, researchers with the Initiative for Equality and Non-Discrimination (INEND), an NGO supporting LGBT Kenyans at the coast, published a research article identifying "root causes" for violence against "gender and sexual minorities" (Adhiambo, Muraguri, and Kobayashi 2016). Revisiting the 2010 Mtwapa protest, the article claims that *bodaboda*, motorcycle taxi operators, were its "main perpetrators" (2016, 32). Drawing on questionnaire responses from 120 bodaboda in Mtwapa and other urban areas north of Mombasa, the researchers conclude that these men's "traditional African beliefs," "religious beliefs," and "political instigation" (by leaders) have caused anti-homosexual violence. "Sexual and gender minorities," Adhiambo, Muraguri, and Kobayashi argue, "have suffered physical violence, psychological torture and loss of property at the hand of motorcycle taxi operators" (32). When I first read this article, I found the "root causes" of anti-homosexual violence it identified abstract and vague. As an anthropologist, I wanted to know more about the kinds of imagination—the objects, logics, and grammars—that the authors generically describe, in their quantitative approach, as "African traditional beliefs" or "religious beliefs." I also found the exclusive focus on the bodaboda problematic at a time when government officials and police had already singled out these men as suspect and problematic. Unemployed, prone to violence, and with nothing to lose, so the argument went, they were the likeliest recruits to Al-Shabaab terrorism. For this reason, government- and NGO-driven anti-radicalization campaigns at the coast commonly targeted bodaboda.

In 2017, when discussing the 2010 protests with gay men in Mtwapa, I learned that they too saw the bodaboda as primarily responsible for the violence that had occurred then. For this reason, I decided to set some time aside and research how bodaboda imagined themselves, their livelihoods, and futures, and what stakes they might have had in attacking gay men (for a more detailed discussion of the bodaboda, see pp. 76–82). But what I learned from them only amplified the paradox I wanted to solve. On the one hand, bodaboda used their distinct ability to navigate urban space speedily and efficiently to generate not only money but also social value in the broadest sense. They prevented crime, offered free security services to the urban poor and, as they put it, undertook "the work of community rescue." As part of this work, their desire to "save" Mtwapa from gayism and punish homosexuals seemed less surprising. For them, as for many urban residents, rescue work entailed, in part, the moral rehabilitation of the imagined "lost" or "stolen" promises of the country's independence: access to the conditions of heteropatriarchal respectability. On the other hand, most of them also lived lives one could easily describe as non-normative. They had dropped out of school, could not afford to marry, and made money in ways that middle-class Kenyans devalued as dangerous or demeaning. In the Kenyan public sphere, bodaboda were not only suspect—easy targets for terrorist recruitment—but also negatively sexualized as promiscuous seducers of schoolgirls and wives.

As I then tried to listen more closely to what my gay interlocutors told me about the bodaboda, a more complex picture emerged. "I am telling you," Ali said,

> bodaboda are really hypocritical. Sometimes, bodaboda can give you deals [i.e., refer people they transport to gay male sex workers, as clients]. Because they transport lots of whites [i.e., tourists], they know people and they tell you. And the same bodaboda can also be a destruction. He can bring people and then they beat you and snatch your things. Sometimes, when you pass, they make noise [S: *wanapiga kelele*]. They swear at you.

I asked Musa why bodaboda had problems with gay men. He explained:

> Some of them are themselves clients [of gay male sex workers], though you can say they have their own devils [S: *mashetani yao*] erupting inside them. When he is with you at night, he is your client. Tomorrow, when it comes to people beating [gays], he will be one of them; he will be the first to beat you.

Rashidi, a twenty-nine-year-old, made a similar point:

> I have a friend who told me: "Those people of the boda, it is true they bring problems. And some, I have slept with them." It's like they pretend to be good [S: *wanajifanya wazuri*] in front of other people, but they are not good. That is, my other friends who live here in Mtwapa have already slept with them. Now, me, I don't like to go [have sex] with them because I believe that the day I need to go to KEMRI [and they see me], they'll show others: "Look, that one is such-and-such."

If Ali, Musa, and Rashidi also invoked common stereotypes of bodaboda as prone to "destruction," possessed by "devils," or, just generally, as "problems," they also suggested a subtler explanation for these men's duplicitous behavior. Rather than bigoted defenders of some anachronistic values (e.g., "African traditional beliefs"), they were, as Ali put it bluntly, "hypocritical." Bodaboda were active participants in Mtwapa's fluid urban sexual economies. As Thomas Hendriks (2016, 230) shows for urban life in the Democratic Republic of Congo, so too in Kenya, "despite pervasive homophobia . . . everyday life . . . is full of queer affordances," homoerotic and other non-normative possibilities of pleasure and attachment. Such affordances were not merely a matter of people employing "exceptional," illicit means to make livelihoods in hard times (2016, 233). Rather, new social and economic circumstances had also opened new possibilities for erotic enjoyment, or, as Hendriks put it, for "subject positions that are libidinally invested and entangled in the usually unspoken homoerotic affordances of everyday urban life" (233). I understand what my interlocutors saw as bodaboda's "hypocrisy" as acts of displacement and disavowal: gestures through which bodaboda condense anxieties over widely shared queer affordances in contemporary social life on the homosexual body, thus dissociating themselves from these affordances. The homosexual body then objectifies these queer affordances as *external* to these men, as something other than themselves, something that is easily refutable. Thus, the homosexual body is not only the objectification of that which the bodaboda repudiate in their own lives, but also an object-cause of gayism, an agentive body responsible for gayism's expansion.

To be sure, for many gay men in Mtwapa, bodaboda appeared threatening mainly because they were the "face" of a wider community that disregarded or even despised them. The sheer visibility of bodaboda across the urban landscape made their views and actions the best known and possibly the most impactful. I asked Ali why bodaboda attacked gay men, claiming to "rescue" the community. "It's just to make their presence matter in society," he responded. If cynical, Ali had a point. Demonstrating commitment to a future of normative respectability was indeed central to the ideologies of rescue precisely as people, like the bodaboda, lived their lives and made a living in circumstances they themselves described as unusual, non-normative. Kent, a twenty-four-year-old gay sex worker and public health worker I interviewed in 2017, made this point to me by way of a riddle-like question: "Do you know why there will always be gays in Mtwapa?" He paused. "Because here, politicians, businessmen, priests, imams, married men, all these men . . . they are our clients"—that is, men who purchase sex from male sex workers. "Hypocrisy is part of the community we come from," he said. "Like, I am backstabbing you during the day and, during the night, I am your sex partner. This is the community we are. Daytime, he will call me names—*shoga, msenge wewe.*

And the same people will call me at night and be [my] sex partners. So that is how it happens."

Gay men were not the only ones aware of these queer affordances of everyday life. In July 2017, I discussed the 2010 Mtwapa protests with Amos and Mosi, two young straight men who were development workers and whom we met in chapter 3 (pp. 82–84). Mosi was quite outspoken against homosexuality and had participated in the 2010 protests. Amos, overall, shared his friend's anti-homosexual stance. But he had not participated in the protests and was, in retrospect, critical of them. Amos said:

> People forget one thing. To be *shoga* is not [just] for you "to be placed" [S: *uwe unaitwe*; i.e., to be penetrated]. Gayism has the top and the bottom. Top is that man and bottom is that woman; the one who "places" [i.e., penetrates] and the one who is "placed" [i.e., penetrated]. You can be the husband of a person, you have a wife [at home], and outside you are the wife of another [male] person, without your wife knowing . . . In this community, people are wrong when they say "a person is not a man, he is a shoga." They should ask themselves a question: Who is the one who is penetrating this [shoga]? If you throw a stone at your partner, you should look where that stone came from [S: *ukirushia mwenzako jiwe, wewe angalia lile jiwe limetoka wapi*].

As a gay man, I found Amos's assumptions about bottoms as "wives" and tops as "husbands" unpleasant. But having anticipated their views, I had chosen not to share my being gay with him and Mosi and, instead of feeling offended, tried to better understand how they thought about these issues. And what Amos said turned out to be quite interesting. Sex between men, he explained, implicated not only those readily recognizable as "shoga" but a whole other set of men rendered invisible by their heterosexual marriages. Amos seemed to suggest that blaming those known as shoga for gayism was unfair, as in the biblical moment of the casting of the stone. But if Amos questioned the exclusive stigmatization of the visible shoga, his words also highlighted the importance of staying alert to the hidden layers of intimate life. For, there, respectable husbands might turn out to be other men's "wives."

Mosi explained that what compelled him and other protesters to break into KEMRI's offices was not that, as some said, the organization "brought gayism to Mtwapa." Sex between men, he knew, had been around, even if pursued "in secrecy" (S: *ya kisiri*). But KEMRI, he said, "brought all these people under one roof. They started walking around [openly] and doing lots of things, until people got fed up." He recalled:

> KEMRI, they do medical research. They have those projects that are continuing there, including that project with the *mashoga* [homosexuals]. When

KEMRI started, people failed to understand them. "Those ones, they came with the plan to support mashoga here in Mtwapa, to develop *ushoga* [homosexuality]." So, the community came together and went there. The gate was broken and they wanted to burn it down. [People shouted:] "What did you bring us here? You want to make it so that our sons will be mashoga?" So, that meant that ushoga here is not wanted.

According to Mosi, protesters blamed KEMRI for the *institutionalization* of gayism, what seemed to them a deliberate attempt "to *make* it so that our sons will be mashoga" (my emphasis). Hence, intimacies previously tolerated as "exceptional" or "secret" became dangerous when institutions appeared suddenly invested in securing and reproducing them. Rather than queer affordances unfolding accidentally or exceptionally as people pursued heteropatriarchal respectability, sex between men now appeared as the institutionalized pursuit of an openly queer futurity. Mufida, the head of a leading local women's group, mobilized thirty women, both Christian and Muslim, to join the 2010 anti-homosexuality protest. In a TV report later that year, she explained her worry over the future thus: "I am already married and have kids. Eh? But what about my girls? Are they going to get married if all men are becoming gays?"[7]

The homosexual body was, then, not only a situational objectification of the more abstract force of gayism, but also a means to externalize—to make visible, palpable, and repugnant—troublesome elements of social life that were otherwise widely shared. Mufida's daughters were more likely not to marry for a whole set of other reasons than "all men . . . becoming gays." Many Mtwapa residents postponed bridewealth payments and weddings, finding them unaffordable. Many lived in so-called "come-we-stay" domestic arrangements which, if less legitimate, had become quite common. And for the vast majority, acquiring tokens of marital respectability—houses, land, businesses, cars—were dreams indefinitely deferred. Was then insulting and beating the homosexual body not a way to also disavow this shared queer element of social life, to render it external to oneself, and thus to call forth the utopia of a "moral" future?

Like the *mbusa* clay figurines in the Bemba initiation rituals described by Richards (1982), the homosexual body does not need to be iconic of that which it represents. Indeed, it cannot fully instantiate the ambiguous category of "gayism," much less the queer affordances of contemporary social life. But like the *mbusa*, this object inculcates specific sensorial, affective, and mnemonic dispositions. In this case, the homosexual body must be an object that is easy to repudiate so that the social and material conditions for good citizenship may emerge. In other words, this cannot be a someone "just like us"; rather, its alterity must be magnified. It is thus that, as Musa explained to me, "in Mombasa, gay is that person that is a bottom. [People] don't take it that all who are in the gay community are gay. That top is not a thing. Every time there is violence against gays in Mtwapa or Mombasa, it's those bottoms who are beaten because [people] think they are at fault." If, as Musa put it, the top is not a *thing*, not worth objectifying, the homosexual becomes synonymous with bottoms, and bottoms, he explained, were gender-nonconforming men. When asked by a journalist what made her angry about homosexuals, Mufida described precisely such bodies: "They change their behavior as a woman. The way they walk, the way they dress up . . . talk. Everything. You can just notice this man is not correct. He is not a total man."

Three key processes are at play here in the objectification of the homosexual body: disambiguation, displacement, and disavowal. Faced with the uncertainties of social life but also with discourses about gayism and terrorism lurking in the underlayers of this life, people seek to disambiguate the sexual Other: they desire to know the body that is responsible for destruction, fear, and terror, to pin it down, to publicly reveal the essence of its alterity. Arjun Appadurai (1998) makes this argument brilliantly with regard to ethnic violence. He argues that uncertainties related, in late capitalism, to large-scale movements of people, colliding identities, and eroding networks of social knowledge have prompted violence against ethnic Others. "Violence," Appadurai says, "can create a macabre form of certainty and can become a brutal technique (or folk-discovery procedure) about 'them' and, therefore, about 'us'" (909). Violence "literally turns a body inside out and finds proof of its betrayal, its deceptions, its definitive otherness, in a sort of premortem autopsy" (911). Similarly, revealing the essence of the homosexual body—the snake-*cum*-plastic at its core—was a way to disambiguate this body as Other, to displace shared predicaments and pleasures of life on this object and thus make it available for collective repudiation.

Mtwapa protesters sought to identify, expose, and expel the homosexual body from the body social of their town and nation. In so doing, they took hold of their future. Bonhomme (2016, 57) shows how, across Central and West African cities, "mob justice" against so-called "penis thieves"—men who alienate other men's virility through a simple look or handshake—generates "a community of affects . . . out of what before had simply been individuals going about their business." "Reappropriating the power to act," Bonhomme argues, lynching "allows for a transformation of a passive affect (powerless fear) into an active one (the aggressive discharge against the suspected thief)" (55). Yet, Bonhomme also notes a peculiarity in the emergence of this community of affect: "*Identification with the victim* lies at the heart of this congregation; outraged by the thefts, the passer-by rally together into a hostile crowd against the suspect *all the more quickly for the fact that they themselves feel similarly at risk*" (my emphasis, 57). I could not help but think here again of the bodaboda, of Mosi and Mufida, and their disavowal of the continuities between their lives and those of the men whom they identified as shoga or homosexual.

As a *thing* extrapolated from the body social, as the objectification of an otherwise epochal collective mode of social being, the homosexual body became then an object of sacrifice. "Sacrifice," Henri Hubert and Marcel Mauss (1964, 13) argue, "is a religious act which, through the consecration of a victim, modifies the condition of the moral person who accomplishes it . . ." Like in the Pentecostal exorcism of the snake-turned-plastic from Henry Karanja's body, Mtwapa protesters engaged in something of a "curative and expiatory sacrifice" (1964, 14): they sought to objectify and oust the queer affordances of their own social lives through the sacrifice of the homosexual body.

The sacrifice that protesters pursued may be understood, in part, as an effort to produce respectability. Mary Porter (1995) argues that coastal Kenyan Muslims have long associated questions of homosexuality with anxieties over the coast's political marginalization by mainland national leaders. Because national leaders continued to invoke an old colonial stereotype that associated coastal Muslims with a proclivity for homosexuality, coastal leaders have sought to distance themselves from it explicitly. But the Mtwapa protesters were not all Muslim or coastal natives. Christians of different denominations, migrants, and migrant-settlers were also present and numerous among them. As residents of Mtwapa, Kenya's notorious "sin city," for many of them, a sense that their lives and livelihoods were exceptional, unusual, non-normative might have informed a desire for respectability, a desire to rescue intimacies. The pursuit of rescue, to be sure, promised to put Mtwapa on the nation's map of respectable citizenship. But, as I have shown, more than respectability was at stake in their protests. These were also ways to secure vitality, the capacity for labor and social reproduction, for the crafting of a future.

Ousted from the Past: The "Boy with Beads"

So far, I have shown how the production of the homosexual body entails the disavowal of everyday life's queer affordances. This, one might say, is a synchronic argument. But my final example also shows its diachronic implications. Producing the homosexual body as an object of violence also entails disavowing the queer affordances of the past, ousting them from ethnic custom and collective memory.

In June 2018, in the village of Lorosoro, in northern Kenya, I interviewed Lemyinton, a Samburu man in his seventies. Jackson, my friend and research assistant, whom we also met in previous chapters, accompanied me to the interview. In the previous days, he and I had discussed at length the "boy with the bead necklace" who, in February that year, had generated controversy among Samburu on social media. A local politician had uploaded on her Facebook page photos of a rural Samburu girl wearing a large bead necklace only to reveal, in her post, that this was, in fact, a boy. In response, the MP's followers posted comments that they had already "recognized" the gender-nonconforming body of this teen as homosexual. "Homosexuality is un-African," someone wrote. "The world is turning slowly to Sodom and Gomorrah," wrote another.

In the opening of this book, I suggested that the appearance of this "boy with beads" in village life was particularly troublesome for Samburu leaders, elites, and town-dwellers (see pp. 1–7). For them, villages were repositories of ethnic culture, key loci of historical continuity, custom, and identity. Samburu had struggled, in recent years, to play a more central role in the administration of a state that had long marginalized them politically and economically. Claiming a heteropatriarchal sexuality as customary was a way, for them, to seek respectability and recognition in the national arena. Yet in Samburu rural life, a "boy with beads"—a body they recognized as homosexual—risked undermining precisely these efforts.

In our interview, Lemyinton brought up this controversy. But unlike Jackson and I, who owned smartphones and social media accounts, Lemyinton had neither. Instead, his knowledge of the controversy came from having recently attended an elders' meeting near Mount Nyiro, the sacred mountain of Samburu, in the far north of their county. There, he had represented the elders of his region's Lorokushu clan in preparations for the ritual initiation of a new age set. This was a significant event for Samburu. It occurred only once every fourteen years. One of the main topics elders discussed at that meeting, Lemyinton said, was what to do about the *sunkulaate*. Neither Jackson nor I had ever heard this Maa word before, so we asked Lemyinton what it meant. "A *sunkulaate*," he said, "is a boy. But if you look at him, he is just like a girl, like a 'girl of the beads' [S: *ntito e saen*]." Sunkulaate, he said, have existed for as long as he could remember.

As an anthropologist researching sexuality and gender, I was thrilled to have come across an indigenous category that appeared to name a nonnormative form of social being. Having worked in the region for nearly thirteen years by then, I was also surprised and embarrassed not to have heard anything about it until then. Had I bought into the heteronormative and cis-genderist assumptions of some of my interlocutors and of much of the ethnographic literature on East African pastoralists? Or was sunkulaate one of those categories that existed latently in the collective memory of a group only to resurface when contemporary events demanded it?[8] So, in the following weeks, I set out to explore as much as possible about it.

The term's meanings varied and people's memories of actual sunkulaate were fragmentary. Sempele, another elder from Lorosoro, told me that in the past, "sunkulaate" had referred to both humans and animals. Cattle, for example, could be sunkulaate if their genital morphology mixed male and female genitalia. This reminded me of the category *serrerr* described by anthropologist Robert B. Edgerton (1964) for Pokot people, Samburu's southwestern neighbors. Edgerton defines *serrerr* as a form of "intersexuality" emerging in livestock and humans and considered, at times, an unfortunate occurrence, at other times, "God's wish" (1964, 1291). Unlike sunkulaate livestock, Sempele said that for humans, criteria other than "the looks of one's genitals" could make one sunkulaate. He recalled, for example, that a sunkulaate elder had lived, until recently, in a neighboring village, among the Longeli clan:

> They[9] had a penis, but stayed just like a woman, with beads, the head shaven. They had been circumcised [with men, in 1948, as part of the Lkimaniki age set]. But, after that, went back to living like a woman. I don't think they were able to sleep with women. I don't know. But their family had arranged a marriage for them [as a "son"], so the wife would give birth to children in their name.

I asked Sempele if he remembered whether people laughed at or mocked the sunkulaate. "No, no," he said. "People would not laugh at them. They wouldn't dare. A sunkulaate can fight and even kill you if you insult them." In other words, a sunkulaate could be respected.

Furthermore, a few elderly men and women also told me that in the past, sunkulaate had been occasionally also seen as propitious for the homesteads in which they lived. Sunkulaate cattle made their herd grow and prosper; sunkulaate children brought wealth and "life force" (M: *nkishon*) in their fathers' lineage. Others said sunkulaate were a "bad omen" (M: *kotolo*). Like with most "unusual" bodily signs (e.g., disability), however, I imagine that elders and prophets (M: *laibon*) assessed contextually the potentiality of any one sunkulaate, whether human or animal. Even so, what some interlocutors said about the "propitiousness" of sunkulaate resonated, for me, with what I already knew about the logics of ritual among Samburu. The propitiousness of the sunkulaate could have been an instance of the common logic that, under some circumstances, *the inverse produces its inverse.* For each age set, for example, elders appointed one of its members as its "chief" (M: *launoni*) who, for the rest of his life, had to remain poor so that his age mates could prosper; if he became rich, the whole age set would, inversely, become impoverished. Similarly, perhaps, sunkulaate, in blurring gender categories, rejuvenated their normative instantiations, thus playing an important role of counterbalancing the normative. The situational blurring of gender categories was also a ritual source of life force, whether in initiation or fertility rites.[10] Propitious or not, it appears that the sunkulaate had been much more than a simple object of disavowal or exclusion. How, then, could someone elders described as sunkulaate become a homosexual object of repudiation?

Preoccupied with this question, I went to see my longtime friend and research collaborator Simon, with whom I shared a passion for both anthropology and Samburu history and culture. Having recently become an important political figure in the Samburu County government, Simon traveled widely across the district to hold political rallies. So, he too was familiar with the "boy with beads." But because I now kept referring to the "boy with beads" as sunkulaate, Simon corrected me. He said he was not sure that the "boy" was sunkulaate. "To me, sunkulaate translates as intersex," he said in English, using a term that was growingly common in Kenyan public debates. Simon explained:

> Sunkulaate is a person who has both kinds of genitals, somehow. This boy is not intersex. I heard elders say he has a penis. But he took to wearing girls' beads. He prefers to dress as a girl, with skirts and beads, and he even has that high-pitched voice and behaves like a girl. I heard elders complain that he now started to seduce morans [young male "warriors"] who actually do not know he is a boy.

Distinguishing the "boy with beads" from "intersex" people—a category that, because highly medicalized in Kenya, was perhaps less problematic than "homosexual"—Simon emphasized that the essence of this difference was this "boy's" seducing other men—in other words, sexuality.

To understand what made the sunkulaate problematic now, why the name came up, and why mostly school-educated elites insisted that it had not been an umbrella term for both intersex and homosexual, I had to pay attention to what had prompted contestations of the "boy with beads." Elders had brought up the sunkulaate because this young person lived near Mount Nyiro, by the sacred ceremonial site where age sets are ritually opened. The teen was also of the age of the boys who would be initiated in this new age set. Much was at stake in this initiation. Age sets, as I said, are groups of men initiated every fourteen or fifteen years who spend the rest of their lives as part of a named generational cohort. The actions and mishaps occurring at the opening of an age set on Mount Nyiro were said to replicate themselves in the lives of its members (e.g., if someone who killed went on the mountain, the age set would kill, and so on) (see also Meiu 2017, 7–8). The symbolic significance of the ceremonies' location then drew sudden attention to what some called the "boy with beads" and others sunkulaate.

Furthermore, elders had high stakes in this particular initiation cycle. They explained to me that three age sets formed a *ntalipa* or "era" (of some forty to forty-five years each) and such eras alternated between times of propitiousness and times of "disaster" (M: *emutai*). The ending ntalipa (which had begun in 1975) had been an era of hardship. Numerous droughts coupled with land alienation, increasing violence, and cattle rustling further marginalized Samburu in the post-independence state. It is no surprise, then, that the name of the new age set was to be Lkisieku, or "the ones hurrying up"— the ones rushing their community out of an era of depletion. But, if the new era was to indeed be a time of abundance, it also had to be aided ritually in becoming so. Elders had to cautiously survey the deeds, characters, and ritual objects involved in these ceremonies. As a boy who qualified for initiation into this new age set and who lived near Mount Nyiro, the sunkulaate became suddenly problematic. Indeed, I learned, elders asked that the sunkulaate be dead before the initiation's commencement.

How did the elders decide that the sunkulaate was, in this instance, unpropitious? And why have they disavowed the propitious potentialities sunkulaate could have had in the past? I suspect here that elites' insistence that the "boy with beads" was a homosexual shaped elders' assessment of the meanings of this novice, even as they continued calling them "sunkulaate." Here, then, a discursive encounter between the homosexual body of a national antihomosexual imaginary overdetermined the meanings of "boy with beads" and shaped how the past was remembered. Because for elites, "there is no homosexuality in Samburu culture," sunkulaate, an indigenous category, could, in retrospect, never have had anything to do with homoerotic desire. Instead, it became translatable with the medicalized category of the intersexed, thus referring strictly to bodily biology rather than sexual desire. Ironically perhaps, as this dialectic of meaning unfolded, it was elders who now called for the death of the sunkulaate (as a possible inauspicious presence in an epochal ritual) and elites who, invoking human rights, sought to "rescue" the teen. In the end, Simon and his friend, another politician (who was otherwise outspoken against homosexuality), succeeded in rescuing the "boy" and placing "him" in an orphanage. But from the point of view of rural elders, theirs was an act equivalent to the child's social death. The homosexual body had thus been ousted from the temporal work elders pursued in aligning the past and the future, through age sets and the initiation of a new epoch or *ntalipa*.

The homosexual's ousting was, however, not a totalizing move. Indeed, in this example, the homosexual body overdetermined the meanings of a gender-nonconforming teen's body. But at the same time, older meanings of sunkulaate resurfaced and pushed against the neat separation of the homosexual from the intersex person, further heightening the ambivalence and uncertainty of bodies identified as homosexual. The bead necklaces that I discussed in chapter 4 worked here, if anything, as objects of disambiguation: as "sex objects," let us recall, they were indisputable signs of sexual intimacies between morans and girls that further underscored, in this case, the boy's desire to seduce young men—the homosexual's sexual essence.

*

Unlike the liberal identitarian "gay," "gayism" has figured in Kenyan public discourse as less of an inborn, immutable identity and more of a current or contagion that amplifies at given moments and that works in somewhat hidden, mysterious ways. The homosexual body is, in turn, less a body defined by a stable "sexual orientation" and more a corporeal leftover of gayism's expansion, a body consumed by it. Indeed, gayism is said to swallow up healthy, fertile bodies and leave behind bodies hollowed of moral personhood, leaky bodies in diapers, non-persons dedicated to excess pleasure and the anti-future. As in vampirism, in gayism, so the logic goes, the homosexual body is born as victim of seduction or predation but turns eventually into an agentive predatory body to recruit others to it. The homosexual body is then a material conduit for gayism's expansion, a body afflicted with gayism and contaminating others with it. But this body is also a signifier of the obscure, impersonal force of gayism, even as this force remains irreducible to any one body as such. Like the plastic to which it is commonly compared, gayism is a substance that circulates between bodies and, at times, also takes corporeal form. If plastic becomes body as "plastic boys" or "plastic-in-the-womb," gayism gains material expression through the homosexual body.[11]

The objectification of the homosexual body is hardly a straightforward process. Key here, I suggest, are a set of dialectical processes that implicate ambiguity centrally. First, we encountered a dialectic between the ambiguities of bodies and the desire to know such bodies as *certainly* Other, to draw out and publicly reveal their essence, the snake-turned-plastic at their core. A second dialectic is that between displacement and disavowal, wherein people represent widely shared queer affordances of life in the present and the past as external to themselves, as properties of an objectified Other. The homosexual body thus takes on the disavowed epochal features of collective existence and, like in a sacrificial ritual of purification, carries them outside society and the nation.

Conclusion

> Beyond their practical functions, objects give body to the image of what one wishes to be.
> JEAN-PIERRE WARNIER

This book set out to situate recent anti-homosexual imaginaries in relation to the wider transformations of intimate citizenship in Kenya. To do so, I took queer objects as alternative points of departure for understanding these transformations. I wanted to avoid reproducing tropes of exceptionalism associated with homosexuality in current nationalist politics and with "African homophobia" in global LGBT liberalism. My goal has been to decenter homosexuality. Rather than study the people, practices, and domains of life that it purports to describe, I pursued a set of ethnographic detours focused on objects only tangentially related to it. A striking observation at the beginning of this project determined me to choose this approach: that despite the global proliferation of political homophobia as a tactic of governance, the "homosexual threat" that it invokes is often very difficult to pin down or identify in everyday life. To make the homosexual body a more stable target of outrage in the collective imagination, leaders, media, civil society groups, and citizens often deploy a vast set of unexpected objects. These objects might appear trivial to the violent politics of homophobia. But, as this book has suggested, quite the opposite is the case: their poetic deployment in rumor and political rhetoric centrally informs the construction of the homosexual body as a target of repudiation, exclusion, violence.

I call these "queer objects"—an analytic I borrow from Ahmed (2006)—because they help me decenter homosexuality and show how its salience rests upon struggles in domains of social life that have otherwise nothing to do with it. As I have shown, objects such as male-power, bead necklaces, diapers, and plastics can displace and condense on the homosexual body desires, fears, and anxieties from elsewhere. Such sentiments and aspirations may emerge in struggles over the changing meanings of work, wealth, the body, gender, and kinship. But through displacement and condensation, metonymy and metaphor, they come to constitute various targets of repudiation, including—but certainly not limited to—the homosexual body. What is fascinating about these queer objects is their ambiguity, their murky visibility, the ease with which they can be ignored, either because they are not sufficiently "serious" or "dignified" to merit scholarly attention (e.g., diapers) or because their ties to belonging, citizenship, or sexuality are not readily observable and, therefore, empirically provable (e.g., plastics).

Here, then, is one of this ethnography's central takeaway points: thinking that sexuality revolves merely around bodily pleasures, practices, and orientations can too easily reify it—fetishize it—as a distinct domain of life. This would be a major loss for understanding emerging dynamics of citizenship because the politics of such attachments themselves require the fetishistic reification of sexuality; they require us to think that there *is* something called *sexuality*—whether as bodily interiority, subjective orientation, or essence—that can make or break worlds. If we are to understand the political centrality of sexuality, it is essential that we decenter it first. Attending ethnographically to objects that come to constitute various kinds of sexualized, but also racialized and ethnicized subjects helped me do precisely that. I am inspired here by a psychoanalytic emphasis on sexuality's different *elsewheres*, its social unconscious—what Freud (1913) calls "the other scene"—its constitutive outsides that centrally inform its historical salience and political fetishization.

The queerness in "queer objects" is then a relational potentiality and not an intrinsic property of things. In the case of this study, this queerness becomes most evident when, in pursuing a set of objects to decenter sexuality, sexuality's explanatory power itself begins to dim down, fade away, melt into elements of a context that had initially deemed it so salient. All we are left with is a desire for its certainty, tireless attempts to pin it down, to disambiguate it, to render it material, to expose it for all to see. A queer approach to sexuality should not only decenter it (or offer better concepts to capture its fluidity, ambiguity, and so on). It must also understand and explain why *it* has become historically so central. In this book, the ethnographic detours that have sought to decenter sexuality have also suggested that *it* had not been there in the first place—at least, not as we commonly understand it. Inspired by Lacan's psychoanalysis, queer theorists and anthropologists have shown that sexuality is a signifier premised on an absent signified—an ontological negativity—and that the repressed knowledge of this absence continuously informs our desire to know it, to get hold of it (through science, commodity consumption, law, violence, and other means) (Dean 2000; Zupančič 2017). Building on this insight, I proposed a form of ethnographic imagination—one

CONCLUSION

premised on detours through objects—that would help us better understand and critique the contemporary political salience of sexuality.

If pursued through this kind of ethnographic imagination, a *political economy of homophobia*—a term I borrow from Rao (2020)—shows that, in the end, the homosexual body of anti-homosexual imaginaries is itself best understood as an absence, albeit a highly generative one. Ambiguous, opaque, and spectral, this body enables what Rao calls "the tendency of queerness to mutate in different configurations and fields of power to become a metonym for other categories such as nationality, religiosity, race, class, and caste" (2020, 9). Being at once a vector of global, national, and local anxieties over various other categories, the homosexual body of anti-homosexual panics is indeed a dialectical product of symbolic and emotional resonances across sites and scales. Might then the queer liberal notion of "African homophobia" not attempt to name precisely the cultural inflections associated with local histories and experiences, such as those described in this book? If indeed the homosexual body must remain open to contingency to become meaningful, then no doubt it is inflected with historically particular grammars and logics in African contexts, such as the ones described here. Alas, queer liberal invocations of homophobia in different parts of the world seek less to understand how imaginaries of violence emerge and work and more to demonize them—to render them irrational.

My approach suggests that addressing homophobia—foreclosing some of the semiotic and sentimental possibilities that lead to its violence—requires more than demonizing it. It might mean understanding the conditions of its reproduction in its social and political economic unconscious. Kenyan LGBT activists, artists, and public health workers have done precisely this (Amory 2019). Since 2014, KEMRI staff, for example, have launched "sensitization" programs teaching the wider urban community how stereotypes of homosexuality are detrimental to everyone. And artists like Neo Musangi (see chapter 7) or Kawira Mwirichia (Meiu 2022) have deployed all kinds of seemingly oppressive objects in their work to performatively dissociate them from normative assumptions and activate their queer potentialities. My ethnography has found inspiration in their work to imagine just how the queer object may indeed come to our rescue in contexts of anti-homosexual animus.

*

A methodological focus on queer objects also has important conceptual implications for intimate citizenship. First, as I said, it suggests that the semiotics and sentiments of homophobia are not always constituted in relation to a body readily recognizable as homosexual, emerging instead across vast domains of social life. Second, queer objects illustrate pervasive technologies of citizenship that work through everyday conviviality, and not merely through the manipulative efforts of political leaders or elites. And third, to reiterate, this approach suggests that sexuality is never a distinct, fixed domain, but if anything, an upper, outer layer—an appearance—of citizenship discourses. Just one layer below—to pursue metaphors related to the diapers analyzed in chapter 6—things look much messier: the sexual subject, the citizen, and its myriad threats are all unstable, ambiguous, shifting, always emerging anew.

Each object discussed in this book is part of technologies of citizenship, ways of producing good citizens by orienting desire toward some things and not others. Objects such as male-power and plastics, for example, can respectively orient desire toward the normative distributions of gendered vitality or the utopia of a morally, ethnically, and sexually unpolluted body politic. It is important to remember, though, that even as the discourses of political and religious leaders are central in shaping their logics, technologies of citizenship remain highly contested. Not only can leaders not monopolize them, but citizens can also turn these technologies against leaders. As part of their *Diaper Mentality* photographic project, for example, PAWA 254 activists have also depicted President Uhuru Kenyatta and Nairobi County Governor Mike Sonko as adults in diapers. Key here was not a top-down integration of citizens in the state, but the contestation of the very terms of membership to a utopian moral nation that corrupt leaders have long betrayed. The nation was thus a "community of affliction," of myriad rescue efforts driven by and oriented toward concerns with intimacy.

Indeed, a key overarching grammar of intimate citizenship in Kenya is that of what I called the *subject of intimate rescue*. This may be a leader, development worker, or the common citizen involved in preventing men's vital depletion, the beading and early sexualization of Samburu girls, the toxic pollution of the environment, the breaking of bodies under unusual, illicit conditions of work, the recruitment of youths to terrorism and gayism, and so on. It can be about a woman taking the neglected child of her neighbor to the police, a group of bodaboda drivers pursuing a thief, or an angry crowd trying to burn a homosexual man. The extent to which this grammar of intimate citizenship recurs across all these contexts and involves a wide variety of objects attests to its prominence in the local common sense. It also attests to the fact that rescue is meaningful in that, through the restoration of a moral nation, it promises to bring about a good life. I do not mean to suggest that the subject of rescue overrides other grammars of subjecthood in the present. If rescue presupposes the redress of—a return to—a *status quo*, there is

CONCLUSION

ample evidence also of desire to break off with the past, to produce radically new futures (Piot 2010); consider, for example, the desire to become a "born-again" Pentecostal; to cut off ties to families among gay and lesbians who have been chased away from home; or, as many young Kenyans do, to move permanently to Europe or North America. Rather than describing individual people, the subject of rescue is then a subjective orientation that coexists— sometimes in the same people—with other such orientations. Both gays and Pentecostals can imagine themselves to produce radically new communities even as they also engage in myriad practices of rescue and their intimacies replicate and elaborate on older ideals of respectability.

*

I began this book trying to make sense of how the homosexual body has come to congeal so much danger and doom to make its violent exclusion both necessary and urgent. Why has rescuing national intimacies and producing the utopia of a moral nation come to revolve so strongly around this exclusion? Pursuing this question via different queer objects has introduced a whole new set of themes and problematics. Among these, five are perhaps the most important.

First, one of the most recurring themes throughout the chapters of this book was a deep concern with *the body*. As I have shown, anxieties over gayism as a bodily affliction were not exceptional. Rather, the body has been at the forefront of all kinds of struggles with intimacy and citizenship, manifesting their emerging contradictions as corporeal afflictions. People's preoccupations with the body's health, integrity, and energy, its capacity to do productive work, to reproduce, and to extend into the future have permeated rumors and rescue, scandals and salvation. Bodily afflictions such as depleting "male-power," "plastic in the womb," or rectal incontinence (i.e., bodies in diapers) were symptoms of their time, ways for the body to incorporate and manifest the effects of social and political economic transformations. But the body has figured here as more than just a fragile object of affliction and anxiety. It also appeared as utopian, whether an imaginary object of a restored good life (e.g., the properly vitalized body of fantasies of middle-class lifestyle) or one of impending doom (e.g., the homosexual body, the terrorist body, etc.).

A second overarching theme is *gender*. If much of my ethnography has suggested continuous preoccupations with the fragility of the body in time and space, these preoccupations also revolved around the body's ability to "hold" gender. Concerns with the "leaking" of male-power involved both male and female bodies and implicated people in rescuing normative forms of both masculinity and femininity. But why, the reader might wonder, has this ethnography focused so heavily on *male* homosexuality? To some extent, this focus has been a function of the term's own connotations in the Kenyan context. Here, a longstanding masculinization of categories such as youth, ethnicity, or the nation—in what I have shown has been a "phallic" struggle over state power since independence—has made male homosexuality (and especially anal sex) particularly threatening to power. To the extent that the male body became emblematic of the power to rule—the nation's phallus—it is this body's breaking, its penetration, incontinence, loss of vitality and, therewith, its feminization that have become most feared. But the politics of anti-homosexuality, no doubt, implicates both men and women and also has drastic implications for lesbians. Lesbians—like the Nyeri wives or the female bodaboda described in chapter 3—now appeared deviously masculine, epitomes of women's appropriation of both "male-power" (vitality) and men's power (authority).

Third, so much of the anxiety surrounding bodies is also about the changing contexts of *economic livelihood*, especially the uncertain means and modes of value production in the present. In a context in which formal employment is scarce yet remains a central element in fantasies of good life and middle-class respectability, extant forms of work appear illicit, disreputable, exceptional. Stories about sex workers, bodaboda, or youths who join cults, gayism, or terrorism emphasize the predicaments of people who, in the pursuit of wealth, put their very bodies on the line. Rather than a Protestant ethic of work, the pursuit of wealth appears here more like a Faustian bargain, more like gambling with one's life than a commodified sale of one's labor power. Bodies broken, in diapers, killed in accidents or war, or dying with AIDS are thus symptoms of a speculative economy. But they also inform the emergence of a different, more dignified, if often unpaid, kind of labor—rescue. As the experiences of Besi (chapter 2), Mosi, Amos, or the bodaboda (chapter 3) suggest, people also pursued this kind of work when nobody employed them to do so. This work was speculative in the sense that it made its protagonists visible for future employment with NGOs. But it was also entrepreneurial in the sense that it made them into good citizens.

Fourth, *ethnicity* has been a recurrent theme introduced by the objects of my ethnography. Ethnicity, to be sure, has been central to the imaginaries of Kenyan nationalism: to be a good Kenyan citizen, as Kenyatta's (1938) early work suggests, is to be well anchored in ethnic custom. Indeed, the grammars of Kenyan nationalism and those of its ethno-regional nationalisms have worked themselves out dialectically. My discussion of plastics and bead necklaces among Samburu has revealed deep anxieties over the ongoing loss of indigenous land to elites and historically more dominant ethnic groups and over the pollution of native bodies and kinship by foreign substances. In different contexts, Samburu "girls of the beads," "plastic boys," Somali Kenyans, or the "boy with beads" or *sunkulaate* sparked anxieties and contestations over the very criteria through which to distinguish between ethnic bodies that can be encompassed in the nation and those that constituted unassimilable ontological difference. Not surprisingly, then, in some instances, the ethnic body, the homosexual body, and even the terrorist body come to overlap, share constitutive grammars, and render each other meaningful.

Finally, so much of this book has been based on what I called *imaginaries* of intimate citizenship. According to Lacan (1977), the concept of the Imaginary foregrounds the domain of the visual, if in less straightforward ways. It revolves around images (e.g., the body's image in the mirror) that are constitutive of subjects. But these images can be mere mental pictures, ideas, without being, at the same time, photographic. They can be visions of otherwise ambiguous, opaque bodies, such as those of the homosexual and the terrorist, that everyday talk, social media posts, or the national media continuously described. In this sense, the imaginaries described here are hardly just visual. Quite the contrary. To the extent the homosexuals, terrorists, ethnic Others, and other kinds of threats to national intimacies remain ambiguous, opaque, not clearly visible, rumors about them cultivate a certain sensorial astuteness: citizens who are hyperaware of their surroundings, proximities, intimacies. And it is in this imaginary and the sensorial astuteness it generates that the logics of leakage, layering, pollution, and encompassment offer a cartography of the body in space and time, a key orientative mechanism for intimate citizenship. For, as Jean-Pierre Warnier (1993, 169) argues, "Beyond their practical functions, objects give body to the image of what one wishes to be."

Acknowledgments

Queer Objects to the Rescue is the product of numerous *ethnographic detours* I took over the years with the help of friends, mentors, collaborators, and relatives. My foremost debt is to my research interlocutors in Kenya, who have welcomed me and thought with me about many, sometimes difficult, issues in their lives. While I cannot name them to protect their confidentiality, I remain deeply thankful to all of them. In Kenya, I have also found immense inspiration in conversations with Mohamed Abdilahi, Lelei Cheruto, Lorna Diaz, Evanson Gichuru, Eric Gitari, Maurice Lematunya, William Leparkiras, Elly Loldepe, Mary Mnazi Mwagona, Tom Odhiambo, Immah Reid, Lacrima Scholze, and Michael Soi. Linah Lelemoyog Lesiitu and Mirielle Dysseleer, two longtime friends and research collaborators from Maralal, passed away during the time I was writing this book; I will miss them dearly.

Research grants from the Weatherhead Center for International Affairs at Harvard University and the Harvard Academy for International and Area Studies helped me carry out field research for this book. In Kenya, the British Institute in Eastern Africa hosted me as a research affiliate and the National Commission for Science, Technology, and Innovation granted me permission to do research in the country. The High Commission of Canada in Kenya offered me immense help during moments of personal difficulty in the summer of 2015. This book was written in part during a sabbatical I spent as a fellow at the W. E. B. DuBois Institute of the Hutchins Center for African and African American Studies at Harvard University. I wish to thank Henry Louis Gates Jr., Krishna Lewis, and Abby Wolf for their warm support during this time. A small grant from Harvard University's Division of the Social Sciences financed a book manuscript workshop in April 2020.

Peter Geschiere, Don Kulick, Sanyu A. Mojola, David A. B. Murray, Kenda Mutongi, Charles Piot, and Adriaan Van Klinken have read closely earlier drafts of this book and offered eye-opening critiques and suggestions. I also discussed different parts of this book with Julie Archambault, Kelly Askew, Sam Balaton-Chrimes, Vigdis Broch-Due, Filipe Calvao, Kerry Chance, Jennifer Cole, Jean Comaroff, John Comaroff, Deborah Durham, Clemens Greiner, Thomas Hendriks, Michael Herzfeld, Sheila Jasanoff, Larisa Jasarevic, Ieva Jusionyte, Moises Lino e Silva, Sarah Luna, Daniel Mains, Adeline Masquelier, Angelika Mietzner, Durba Mitra, Erin Moore, Besi Brillian Muhonja, Nancy D. Munn, Pauline Peters, Derek Peterson, Robert Reid-Pharr, Dorothea E. Schulz, Kay Kaufman Shelemay, Parker Shipton, Deborah A. Thomas, and Brad Weiss. Anna Lea Aebischer, Sebastian Jackson, Eunice Mwangi, Cristina Paul, Renugan Raidoo, and Armanc Yildiz offered valuable research assistance at different stages in this project. Zainabu Jallo and Mary Mbewe helped me locate an important image for this book. To all, I am most thankful.

I have presented the material in this book in lectures at the British Institute in Eastern Africa in Nairobi, University of Basel, University of Bergen, Boston University, University of Cologne, Concordia University, University of Connecticut, University of Copenhagen, Graduate Institute of Development and International Studies in Geneva, Harvard University, James Madison University, Kenya Medical Research Institute, University of Michigan, University of Oklahoma, University of Oslo, and University of Vienna. I am grateful to my audiences for helping me think through my arguments.

At the University of Chicago Press, I have benefited from the support of Mary Al-Sayed, Fabiola Enriquez Flores, Dylan Montanari, Priya Nelson, and Alan Thomas, who at different stages have shepherded this book through reviews, revisions, and production. I am also thankful to my anonymous reviewers for the valuable feedback. Chapters 4 and 6 appeared previously in the *American Anthropologist* (Meiu 2020a) and *Cultural Anthropology* (Meiu 2020b). I wish to thank these journals for permission to reproduce this material as part of the current book.

Raphaël Schröter, my partner, has been a source of immense inspiration and warm support. In 2017, he joined me for long-term fieldwork in Kenya and, throughout the entire process of researching and writing this book, he has given me strength and confidence.

My mother, Liliana Meiu, has visited me in Kenya and the United States many times, offering help when I most needed it, and my grandmother, Rodica Drăghia, has always cheered me on and encouraged me to keep writing. Other family members, including Doina Dănescu, George Meiu, and Dan Tudor Meiu, have been by my side.

Notes

Chapter 1

1. This trend, common across East and Southern Africa, is very well captured in John Trengove's movie *Inxeba / The Wound* (2017).

2. Eddy Mwanza, "Tribe Where Same-Sex Marriage Is Allowed in Kenya," *Kenyans*, May 14, 2019, https://www.kenyans.co.ke/news/39634-tribe-where-same-sex-marriage-allowed-kenya (accessed May 15, 2019).

3. Kenya National Bureau of Statistics, "Economic Survey 2017" (Nairobi: Kenya National Bureau of Statistics, 2017).

4. Ibrahim Khamis, "State Selling Residency Permits and Citizenship to Shore Up Revenue," *Daily Nation*, November 18, 2019, https://nation.africa/kenya/news/state-selling-residency-permits-and-citizenship-to-shore-up-revenue-224272 (accessed November 20, 2019).

5. Drawing on Sara Ahmed (2006), my understanding of "queer objects" resembles that of some of the authors featured in the edited collection by Guy Davidson and Monique Rooney (2018). But it is substantially different from the approach of Chris Brickell and Judith Collard (2019), who use the term to mean, more literally, objects associated with the history of LGBT people.

6. A rich and fascinating scholarly literature on object ontologies has problematized the Marxian division between subject and object, attending, for example, to how objects act upon the world or to how this world may look from the point of view of objects (e.g., Holbraad and Pedersen 2017). While I do draw on some insights from this literature at times, my main goal is to understand what we can learn about the production of the subject-citizen from objects, as perceived and understood by humans in a particular social and historical context.

7. For a discussion of these dolls and other androgynous objects among Turkana, see Broch-Due (1990).

8. Embracing queerness as potentiality means also being caught up in one of the term's central paradoxes. "Queer," Margot Weiss (2022, 15) argues, has been "caught by its on formative conditions: a *queer* that simultaneously enjoins us to reach 'beyond' the sexed body, gendered subject, and same-sex desires *and* insists on the centrality of those objects (and subjects)." A queer critical engagement with sexuality in the contemporary global order must acknowledge then that the more one pushes it away, decenters it, and refuses its totalizing claims, the more

one becomes aware of its comeback, as it takes central stage in our politics, economy, and imagination.

9. In this and the following paragraphs, I describe the events in Mtwapa based on narratives I collected from locals and from the following public sources: Dan Smith, "Five Gay Men Arrested in Kenya," OpEdNews, February 22, 2010; *Daily Nation*, "Mob Attacks Gay 'Wedding' Party," February 12, 2010, https://nation.africa/kenya/news/mob-attacks-gay-wedding-party--623768 (accessed January 28, 2020); Nina Robinson, "Gay Pride and Prejudice in Kenya," BBC News, June 16, 2010, https://www.bbc.com/news/10320057 (accessed January 28, 2020); Human Rights Watch, "Kenya: Halt Anti-Gay Campaigns," February 17, 2010, https://www.hrw.org/news/2010/02/17/kenya-halt-anti-gay-campaign (accessed January 28, 2020); John Blevins and Peter Irungu, "Different Ways of Doing Violence: Sexuality, Religion, and Public Health in the Lives of Same Gender-Loving Men in Kenya," paper presented at the Annual Meeting of the American Academy of Religion, 2013.

10. Quoted in *Daily Nation*, "Mob Attacks Gay 'Wedding' Party."

11. I draw here on video footage showing Sheik Hussein make this statement during the demonstrations. This footage appears in the BBC documentary *Africa's Last Taboo: Homosexuality* (produced by Robin Branwell and Sorious Samura, 2010).

12. Blevins and Irungu, "Different Ways of Doing Violence."

13. *Daily Nation*, "Mob Attacks Gay 'Wedding' Party."

14. Quoted in Robinson, "Gay Pride and Prejudice in Kenya."

15. Kenya National Bureau of Statistics, 2014, "Marital Status by County and District," https://www.knbs.or.ke/marital-status-by-county-and-district/ (accessed November 7, 2022).

16. Quoted in *Daily Nation*, "Mob Attacks Gay 'Wedding' Party."

17. Kamau Ngotho, "The Making of a Casino Nation," *Daily Nation*, September 8, 2010, https://nation.africa/kenya/news/politics/the-making-of-a-casino-nation-85472.

18. Carole Maina, "Court Extends Order against Gambling Machines Clapdown," *The Star*, July 2, 2018, https://www.the-star.co.ke/news/2018-07-02-court-extends-order-against-gambling-machines-clampdown/.

19. Isaac Akeyo, "Nairobi Security Chiefs Destroy over 300 Illegal Gaming Machines," *The Star*, October 5, 2018, https://www.the-star.co.ke/news/2018-10-05-nairobi-security-chiefs-destroy-over-300-illegal-gaming-machines/.

20. For example, in the absence of employment, young men who engage in creating ways of waiting, of spending their surplus time, whether by brewing tea, chewing khat, or consuming conspicuously, are often scolded by leaders and elders for "wasting time," being lazy or idle (Honwana 2012; Mains 2011; Masquelier 2019; Newell 2012; Ralph 2008).

21. Quoted in Blevins and Irungu, "Different Ways of Doing Violence."

Chapter 2

1. National AIDS Control Council, 2016, "Kenya HIV County Profiles 2016," p. 68 (Nairobi: NACC).

2. Kiundi Waweru, "Vivacious Life at Kenya's Sin Spot," *Daily Nation*, December 27, 2010.

3. Carol Musyoka, "Mtwapa a Buzzing Town with Striking Contrasts," *Business Daily*, March 24, 2019, https://www.businessdailyafrica.com/bd/opinion-analysis/ideas-debate/mtwapa-a-buzzing-town-with-striking-contrasts-2243682 (accessed January 28, 2020).

Chapter 3

1. Kimani wa Njuguna, "Empower the Boy-Child by Inspiring Him," *Daily Nation*, June 4, 2015, p. 13.
2. Martin Muthai, "Nakuru Wife Storms Pub, Attacks Husband for Secretly Selling Family Land," *Standard*, January 30, 2017, https://www.standardmedia.co.ke/entertainment/counties/article/2001227670/nakuru-wife-storms-pub-attacks-husband-for-secretly-selling-family-land (accessed January 28, 2020).
3. The Central Province, like Kenya's other provinces, ceased serving as an administrative unit of government in 2013, following the implementation of a new Constitution and the devolution of government. However, Kenyans have continued to speak of these older regional categories in no small part because of their association with ethnicity and electoral support.
4. Demas Kiprono, "The Crackdown on Illicit Brews Should be Objective," *The Star*, July 11, 2015, https://www.the-star.co.ke/siasa/2015-07-11-the-crackdown-on-illicit-brews-should-be-objective/ (accessed January 28, 2020).
5. Benjamin Wafula, "President Kenyatta Bans Second Generation Drinks in Kenya," *Citizen*, July 1, 2015, https://www.citizen.digital/news/president-kenyatta-bans-second-generation-drinks-in-central-kenya-90820 (accessed January 28, 2020).
6. Wafula, "President Kenyatta Bans Second Generation Drinks in Kenya."
7. Wafula, "President Kenyatta Bans Second Generation Drinks in Kenya."
8. *Capital News*, "Uhuru Disbands NACADA, Orders Crackdown in Central," July 1, 2015, https://www.capitalfm.co.ke/news/2015/07/uhuru-disbands-nacada-orders-crackdown-in-central/ (accessed January 28, 2020).
9. Some journalists suggest that poverty, lack of employment, the scarcity of agricultural land, and growing social inequalities may better explain the predicaments of young men in the region, their desire to consume alcohol.
10. Since 2010, a government measure implemented in response to the 2008 postelection violence prevents statistical research from using ethnicity as a variable. Nonetheless, some Kenyans often read regional statistics with ethnicity in mind.
11. Women's protests represent modes of collective action that have been long common in East African societies. Generally, such protests sought to intervene, transform, or reverse social trends that affected access to resources, possibilities of reproduction, or women's role therein (Hodgson 2017, 133–56).
12. George Mugo, "Kiambu Women Rain Kicks, Blows on Men Found Having Early Morning Drink," *Star*, November 24, 2015, https://www.the-star.co.ke/news/2016-11-24-kiambu-women-rain-kicks-blows-on-men-found-having-early-morning-drink/ (accessed January 28, 2020).
13. Mugo, "Kiambu Women Rain Kicks, Blows."
14. On June 4, 2015, Daniel King'ori returned home in the morning, after a night of drinking in the village pub. His wife confronted him angrily. They fought. In the ensuing hassle, she found condoms in his pocket. She accused her husband of adultery. Then, she grabbed a knife and cut off his penis. On June 10, only six days later, a twenty-seven-year-old woman in Nyeri did the same, this time driven by a conflict over money. The man came home and went to shower, leaving money on the table. The woman took the money, seeing it as a contribution to the household. In the ensuing fight, in which he demanded she return his money, she took a knife and cut off his penis.

15. Rose Nyambura Maina, "Why Women of Nyeri County Chop Off Their Men's Genitals," *Art Matters*, July 27, 2015, https://artmatters.info/2015/06/why-kenyas-nyeri-county-women-have-taken-to-chopping-off-their-mens-genitals/ (accessed January 28, 2020).

16. Maina, "Why Women of Nyeri County Chop Off Their Men's Genitals."

17. Fridah Mochama, "Sex for Boda Boda Rises in Kisumu," *Kenyans*, December 19, 2015, https://www.kenyans.co.ke/news/sex-boda-boda-rises-kisumu.

Chapter 4

1. Tabitha Nderitu, "Kenya: Samburu Women See Red in Their Beads," *Women's Feature Service*, New Delhi, November 15, 2010.

2. Coexist Initiative, 2015, "Male Engagement for the Elimination of the Beading Practice in Samburu Community," Community Mobilization Report, p. 16.

3. Coexist Initiative, "Male Engagement," p. 17.

4. Coexist Initiative, "Male Engagement," p. 17.

5. Government of Kenya, Kenya Vision 2030 website, https://vision2030.go.ke (accessed March 1, 2020).

6. In 2016, UNESCO estimated that the rate of teenage pregnancies and motherhood in Kenya was at 18 percent, stating that "1 in every 5 teenage girls between the ages of 15–19 years, have either had a live birth or are pregnant with their first child." UNESCO Health and Education Resource Center, https://healtheducationresources.unesco.org/library/documents/teenage-pregnancy-and-motherhood-situation-kenya-county-burden-and-driving (accessed December 20, 2022).

7. This comment can be found at the bottom of the online article by Njeri Mbugua, "Samburu Morans Give Beads to Bed Little Girls," *Star*, April 23, 2019, https://www.the-star.co.ke/news/big-read/2019-04-23-samburu-morans-give-beads-to-bed-little-girls/ (accessed March 1, 2020).

8. For example, the Samburu Women Trust's 2016 Report, "Unspoken Vice in Samburu Community," invokes Article 21(3) of the Constitution, protecting vulnerable persons, and Article 27, preventing discrimination by gender, color, or origin.

9. H. B. Sharpe, 1936, Annual Report, Laikipia-Samburu District, Kenya National Archives, Nairobi, DC/SAM/1/2.

10. With a ban on a particular kind of bead strings known as *somi*, in the 1930s, argues Kasfir (2007, 108), "girl ornaments were made to conform more closely to those worn by married women, thereby effacing one of the visual boundaries that distinguished girls from women." "Needless to say," Kasfir says, "warriors did not give up presenting beads to girls; they just stopped presenting *those* particular beads..."

11. Dumont (1980, 239–45) defines "encompassment" thus: two things that, at a lower level of distinction, appear complementary may appear, at a higher order of unity, in a relation of domination, as one of the two terms comes to stand in for both (e.g., "man" and "woman" become encapsulated in "Man," as human).

12. Following Kenyatta's discussion of *ngweko*, numerous Kikuyu ethno-nationalists called for the revival of the practice.

13. For example, *Maarifa Ya Uzazi* ("Knowledge of Parenthood"), a Swahili language guide published in 1946 to instruct literate Kenyans on how to approach the sexuality of their children, presents an interesting case. Calling for the importance of Christian sex education, the book

NOTES TO CHAPTER 5   205

details the different phases of a child's growth into adolescence, including discussions of masturbation, menstruation, sexual attraction, wet dreams, sex in marriage, and more. It encourages parents not to deny or punish or to be ashamed of the sexual desires of their children, but to acknowledge them as "natural." Instead, parents should "distract" children from the desire for sexual pleasure and impress on them that sex belongs in monogamous marriage and its real pleasure—"sanctity of sex"—realizes itself through prayer and premarital abstinence.

Chapter 5

1. Jonathan Watts, "Eight Months On, Is the World's Most Drastic Plastic Bag Ban Working?," *Guardian*, April 25, 2018, https://www.theguardian.com/world/2018/apr/25/nairobi-clean-up-highs-lows-kenyas-plastic-bag-ban (accessed June 1, 2019).

2. George Omondi, "Retailers Risk NEMA Raid for Plastic Bag Stock After August 28," *Business Daily*, June 7, 2017, https://www.businessdailyafrica.com/news/Retailers-risk-Nema-raid-for-plastic-bag-stock-after-August-28/539546-3960204-13oq6d/index.html (accessed June 1, 2019).

3. Philip Etemesi, "Foreigners Are Now Being Stripped of Plastic Bags Before Entering Kenya," *OMG Voice*, September 26, 2017, omgvoice.com/news/foreigners-stripped-plastic-bags?country=KE (accessed June 1, 2019; link no longer active).

4. Pauline Kairu, "Will We Triumph in the War on Plastics?," *Daily Nation*, September 17, 2017, https://nation.africa/kenya/life-and-style/dn2/will-we-triumph-in-the-war-on-plastics--451908 (accessed June 1, 2019).

5. BuzzKenya, "Watch Out! Plastic Rice Now on Sale in Kenya," 2017, buzzkenya.com (link no longer active).

6. Scholars have recently questioned materiality's simplistic equation with artifacts or material culture (Miller 2005; Hodder 2012) and problematized clear-cut divides between matter and immateriality, substance, and its signifying regimes (Coole and Frost 2010; Ingold 2007). Although I am inspired by work demonstrating how objects exert "agency" to shape concepts and ideas (e.g., Holbraad and Pedersen 2017), the present chapter foregrounds the dialectical dynamics of materialization and objectification to demonstrate the co-constitutive process through which plastic and belonging materialize.

7. Martin Fundi, "Our Livestock Now Safer, Samburu Pastoralists Say on Plastic Bags Ban," *Star*, August 26, 2017, https://www.the-star.co.ke/news/2017/08/26/our-livestock-now-safer-samburupastoralists-say-on-plastic-bags-ban_c1623865 (accessed June 1, 2019; link no longer active).

8. The Maa version is: *Kiwata sakana Mombasa meturubi o te nkaniki / Oh, karubi ltoika nkaniki o lpapit le plastik.*

9. For a detailed discussion of *latukuny*, see Straight (2007, 69–93).

10. Mark Muthai, "Rwanda to Deport all Kenyans with Plastic Smiles," *Standard*, September 20, 2013, https://www.standardmedia.co.ke/article/2000094562/rwanda-to-deport-all-kenyans-with-plastic-smiles (accessed June 1, 2019).

11. Report by the National Environmental Complaints Committee, cited in Kairu, "Will We Triumph in the War on Plastics?"

12. Aggrey Mutamo, "Uhuru Kenyatta Tells G7 Countries to Lead Plastic Pollution Fight," *Daily Nation*, June 9, 2018, https://nation.africa/kenya/news/uhuru-kenyatta-tells-g7-countries-to-lead-plastic-pollution-fight-52738 (accessed June 10, 2020).

13. BuzzKenya, "Watch Out!"

14. Alois Leadekei, "Contraband Sugar Nabbed by Security Agents at Maralal," Facebook post, June 26, 2008.

15. Kwamchetsi Makokha, "How to Invite Public Odium and Make Your Life Difficult," *Daily Nation*, May 10, 2010, https://nation.africa/kenya/blogs-opinion/opinion/how-to-invite-public-odium-and-make-your-life-difficult--634800 (accessed June 1, 2019).

16. Sarah Malm, "Gay Lions Seen in Kenya Anger County's Moral Policemen," *Daily Mail*, November 3, 2017, https://www.dailymail.co.uk/news/article-5046653/Gay-lions-seen-Kenya-angers-country-s-moral-policeman.html (accessed June 1, 2019).

Chapter 6

1. Alphonce Gari, "Gay Sex Rampant in Malindi Resorts," *Star*, August 21, 2013, https://www.the-star.co.ke/news/2013-08-20-gay-sex-rampant-in-malindi-resorts/ (accessed June 1, 2019).

2. Gari, "Gay Sex Rampant in Malindi Resorts."

3. Quoted in "Commercial Sex Tourism in Africa: Kenya," *Africa Now*, https://www.africaw.com/commercial-sex-tourism-in-africa-kenya (accessed July 1, 2018).

4. "Commercial Sex Tourism in Africa: Kenya."

5. Stephen Mburu, "I'd Rather Lose My Job Than Promote Homosexuality, Says Ezekiel Mutua," *Standard*, May 5, 2018, https://www.standardmedia.co.ke/entertainment/news/article/2001279323/id-rather-lose-my-job-than-promote-homosexuality-dr-ezekiel-mutua (accessed June 1, 2019).

6. Personal communications with LGBT activists from these countries.

7. For Cameroon, see Peter Geschiere (2017, 11); for Ghana, see Nathanael Homewood (2019, 114–17); for Nigeria, see Benedict Hart, "Protecting Children from the Scourge of Homosexuality," *Vanguard*, March 22, 2014, https://www.vanguardngr.com/2014/03/protecting-children-scourge-homosexuality/ (accessed June 1, 2019); for Uganda, see J. Lester Feder, "Kenya Might as Well Be Uganda for Many LGBT Refugees," *BuzzFeed News*, April 29, 2014, https://www.buzzfeednews.com/article/lesterfeder/kenya-might-as-well-be-uganda-for-many-lgbt-refugees (accessed June 1, 2019).

8. Danish Institute for Human Rights, 2014, "Getting to Rights: The Rights of Lesbian, Gay, Transgender and Intersex Persons in Africa," p. 50.

9. Feder, "Kenya Might as Well Be Uganda for Many LGBT Refugees."

10. *Kenya National Assembly Official Record*, November 12, 2008, p. 3407.

11. Oyunga Pala, "Of Donkeys and Citizens Who Need Diapers," October 8, 2014, http://oyungapala.com/of-donkeys-and-citizens-who-need-diapers/ (accessed June 1, 2019).

12. Mkenya Mzalendo, "Kenyan Refers to Politicians as the Real Homosexuals," *Kenya Monitor*, July 23, 2015, http://www.monitor.co.ke/2015/07/23/kenyan-refers-politicians-real-homosexuals/ (accessed July 6, 2018).

Chapter 7

1. Jessica Hatcher, "Nairobi 'Miniskirt' March Exposes Sexual Violence in Kenya," November 18, 2014, https://www.theguardian.com/global-development/2014/nov/18/nairobis-miniskirt-march-exposes-sexual-violence-in-kenya (accessed December 20, 2021).

2. One can hear members of the crowd refer to Neo as "Semenya" (a reference to Caster Semenya, a South African athlete subjected to gender testing), as "Audrey-Andrew" (a reference

NOTES TO CHAPTER 7

to the transgender Kenyan activist Audrey Mbugua) (Ouma and Mutloane 2014, 40n1–2), or as an "aphrodite" (a likely mispronunciation of "hermaphrodite").

3. Pauline Kairu, "The Untold Horror Story of Being Transgender in Kenya," *Saturday Nation Magazine*, October 10, 2020, https://nation.africa/kenya/life-and-style/saturday-magazine/the-untold-horror-story-of-being-transgender-in-kenya-2461696 (accessed October 10, 2020).

4. Aljazeera, "Top Kenyan MP: Homosexuality Like Terrorism," March 27, 2014, https://www.aljazeera.com/news/2014/3/27/top-kenyan-mp-homosexuality-like-terrorism (accessed January 5, 2021).

5. Recently, Maseno Boys School and Moi Girls School, for example, have been among the very prestigious boarding schools in Kenya that have made national news for "outbreaks" of gayism and lesbianism among their pupils.

6. In 2018, in Kisumu, the county government announced that gayism was on the rise. Early that year, a local public health NGO—Men against AIDS Youth Organisation (MAAYGO)—had enrolled as many as 2,113 beneficiaries. By March, the number was up to 3,500. In response, the county government took it upon itself to recall the licenses of organizations like MAAYGO, to curb homosexuality.

7. BBC documentary *Africa's Last Taboo: Homosexuality* (produced by Robin Branwell and Sorious Samura, 2010).

8. I am thinking here of Robert Borofsky's (1987) discussion of how Pukapukan Pacific islanders suddenly "remembered" an indigenous category of political organization that had appeared long forgotten and that two generations of anthropologists had overlooked. Current political struggles that made that category necessary prompted it back into collective remembrance.

9. I use the pronoun "they" because it is a better translation of the Maa gender-neutral third-person pronoun *ninye* and better reflects my inability to know what gender assumptions my interlocutor might have held, had he told me this story in English.

10. We see this logic in Samburu ceremonies such as *lopiro*, which I have described elsewhere (Meiu 2016).

11. Further parallels can be drawn here between gayism and other contagions, including AIDS and COVID-19, both of which have figured in public discourse as impersonal and intersubjective and as afflicted bodies. Considering the history of pandemics in East Africa, throughout which new contagions have incorporated logics associated with previous ones (Geissler and Prince 2020), it is no surprise that in 2020, in Kenya, Uganda, and Burundi, political leaders and police have blamed homosexuals as responsible for the COVID-19 pandemic.

References

Adhiambo, Esther, Michael Muraguri, and Akiko Kobayashi. 2016. "Motorcycle Taxi Operators' Perceptions of Sexual and Gender Minorities in Coastal Region, Kenya." *International Journal of Humanities & Social Studies* 4 (12): 31–38.
Adorno, Theodor W. 1998. *Critical Models: Interventions and Catchwords*. New York: Columbia University Press.
Agbiboa, Daniel E., ed. 2018. *Transport, Transgression and Politics in African Cities: The Rhythm of Chaos*. New York: Routledge.
Agustin, Maria Laura. 2007. *Sex at the Margins: Migration, Labor Markets and the Rescue Industry*. London: Zed.
Ahmed, Sara. 2006. *Queer Phenomenology: Orientations, Objects, Others*. Durham, NC: Duke University Press.
Alexander, M. Jacqui. 1994. "Not Just (Any) Body Can Be a Citizen: The Politics of Law, Sexuality and Postcoloniality in Trinidad and Tobago and the Bahamas." *Feminist Review* 48 (1): 5–23.
———. 2005. *Pedagogies of Crossing: Meditations on Feminism, Sexual Politics, Memory, and the Sacred*. Durham, NC: Duke University Press.
Amadiume, Ifi. 1987. *Male Daughters, Female Husbands: Gender and Sex in an African Society*. London: Zed Books.
Amar, Paul. 2013. *The Security Archipelago: Human-Security States, Sexuality Politics, and the End of Neoliberalism*. Durham, NC: Duke University Press.
Amory, Deborah P. 1987. "Mashoga, Mabasha, and Magai: 'Homosexuality' on the East African Coast." In *Boy-Wives and Female Husbands: Studies in African Homosexualities*, edited by Stephen O. Murray and Will Roscoe, 67–87. New York: Palgrave.
———. 2019. "LGBTIQ Rights in Kenya: On Activism and Social Change." *Georgetown Journal of International Affairs*, May 14. https://gjia.georgetown.edu/2019/05/14/lgbtiq-rights-in-kenya/.
Amuyunzu-Nyamongo, Mary, and Paul Francis. 2006. "Collapsing Livelihoods and the Crisis of Masculinities in Rural Kenya." In *The Other Side of Gender: Men's Issues in Development*, edited by Ian Bannon and Maria C. Correia, 219–44. Washington, DC: World Bank.
Anderson, Benedict. 1991. *Imagined Communities: Reflections on the Origin and Spread of Nationalism*. London: Verso.

Angelides, Steven. 2019. *The Fear of Child Sexuality: Young People, Sex, and Agency*. Chicago: University of Chicago Press.

Appadurai, Arjun. 1998. "Dead Certainty: Ethnic Violence in the Era of Globalization." *Development and Change* 29: 905–25.

Archambault, Julie Soleil. 2017. *Mobile Secrets: Youth, Intimacy, and the Politics of Pretense in Mozambique*. Chicago: University of Chicago Press.

Awondo, Patrick, Peter Geschiere, and Graeme Reid. 2012. "Homophobic Africa? Toward A More Nuanced View." *African Studies Review* 55 (3): 145–68.

Axel, Brian Keith. 2001. *The Nation's Tortured Body: Violence, Representation, and the Formation of a Sikh "Diaspora."* Durham, NC: Duke University Press.

Bachmann, Jan. 2012. "Kenya and International Security: Enabling Globalisation, Stabilising 'Stateness,' and Deploying Enforcement." *Globalizations* 9 (1): 125–43.

Balaton-Chrimes, Samantha. 2016. *Ethnicity, Democracy and Citizenship in Africa: Political Marginalisation of Kenya's Nubians*. New York: Routledge.

Barthes, Roland. 1988. "Plastic." *Perspecta* 24: 92–93.

Beck, Rose Marie. 2005. "Texts on Textiles: Proverbiality as Characteristic of Equivocal Communication at the East African Coast (Swahili)." *Journal of African Cultural Studies* 17 (2): 131–60.

Bedford, Kate. 2009. *Developing Partnerships: Gender, Sexuality, and the Reformed World Bank*. Minneapolis: University of Minnesota Press.

Benjamin, Walter. 1999. *The Arcades Project*. Cambridge, MA: Harvard University Press.

Berlant, Lauren. 1997. *The Queen of America Goes to Washington City: Essays on Sex and Citizenship*. Durham, NC: Duke University Press.

———. 2011. *Cruel Optimism*. Durham, NC: Duke University Press.

Berman, Bruce, and John Lonsdale. 2007. "Custom, Modernity, and the Search for Kihooto: Kenyatta, Malinowski, and the Making of Facing Mount Kenya." In *Ordering Africa: Anthropology, European Imperialism, and the Politics of Knowledge*, edited by H. Tilley and R. Gordon, 173–98. Manchester: Manchester University Press.

Bernstein, Robin. 2011. *Racial Innocence: Performing American Childhood and Race from Slavery to Civil Rights*. New York: New York University Press.

Bersani, Leo. 2009. *Is the Rectum a Grave? And Other Essays*. Chicago: University of Chicago Press.

Biruk, Crystal. 2015. "'Aid for Gays': The Moral and the Material in 'African Homophobia' in Post-2009 Malawi." *Journal of Modern African Studies* 52 (3): 447–73.

Blunt, Robert W. 2004. "'Satan Is an Imitator': Kenya's Recent Cosmology of Corruption." In *Producing African Futures: Ritual and Reproduction in a Neoliberal Age*, edited by Brad Weiss, 294–328. Leiden: Brill.

———. 2019. *For Money and Elders: Ritual, Sovereignty, and the Sacred in Kenya*. Chicago: University of Chicago Press.

Boellstorff, Tom. 2004. "The Emergence of Political Homophobia in Indonesia: Masculinity and National Belonging." *Ethnos* 69 (4): 465–86.

———. 2007. *A Coincidence of Desires: Anthropology, Queer Studies, Indonesia*. Durham, NC: Duke University Press.

Bompani, Barbara, and Caroline Valois. 2018. "Introduction: Christian Citizens and the Moral Regeneration of the African State." In *Christian Citizens and the Moral Regeneration of the African State*, edited by Barbara Bompani and Caroline Valois, 3–18. London: Routledge.

Bonhomme, Julien. 2016. *The Sex Thieves: The Anthropology of a Rumor*. Chicago: Hau Books.

REFERENCES

Borofsky, Robert. 1987. *Making History: Pukapukan and Anthropological Constructions of Knowledge*. Cambridge: Cambridge University Press.

Bosia, Michael J., and Meredith L. Weiss. 2013. "Political Homophobia in Comparative Perspective." In *Global Homophobia: States, Movements, and the Politics of Oppression*, edited by Meredith L. Weiss and Michael J. Bosia, 1–29. Urbana: University of Illinois Press.

Boswell, Rosabelle. 2006. "Say What You Like: Dress, Identity and Heritage in Zanzibar." *International Journal of Heritage Studies* 12 (5): 440–57.

Boyd, Lydia. 2013. "The Problem with Freedom: Homosexuality and Human Rights in Uganda." *Anthropological Quarterly* 86 (3): 697–724.

———. 2015. *Preaching Prevention: Born-Again Christianity and the Moral Politics of AIDS in Uganda*. Ohio: Ohio University Press.

Brandzel, Amy L. 2016. *Against Citizenship: The Violence of the Normative*. Champaign: University of Illinois Press.

Braun, Yvonne, and Assitan Sylla Traore. 2015. "Plastic Bags, Pollution, and Identity: Women and the Gendering of Globalization and Environmental Responsibility in Mali." *Gender and Society* 29 (6): 863–87.

Brickell, Chris, and Judith Collard, eds. 2019. *Queer Objects*. New Brunswick, NJ: Rutgers University Press.

Broch-Due, Vigdis. 1990. "The Bodies Within the Body: Journeys in Turkana Thought and Practice." Bergen: University of Bergen.

———. 2005. "Violence and Belonging: Analytical Reflections." In *Violence and Belonging: The Quest for Identity in Postcolonial Africa*, edited by Vigdis Broch-Due, 1–40. London: Routledge.

Bryce, Jane. 2011. "The Anxious Phallus: The Iconography of Impotence in Quartier Mozart and Clando." In *Men in African Film & Fiction*, edited by Lahoucine Ouzgane, 11–27. Woodbridge: Boydell & Brewer Ltd.

Burchardt, Marian. 2018a. "Saved from Hegemonic Masculinity? Charismatic Christianity and Men's Responsibilization in South Africa." *Current Sociology* 66 (1): 110–27.

———. 2018b. "Citizenship Beyond the State: Pentecostal Ethics and Political Subjectivity in South African Modernity." In *Citizenship and the Moral Regeneration of the African State*, edited by Barbara Bompani and Caroline Valois, 163–76. London: Routledge.

Burke, Timothy. 1996. *Lifebuoy Men, Lux Women: Commodification, Consumption, and Cleanliness in Modern Zimbabwe*. Durham, NC: Duke University Press.

Butler, Judith. 1990. *Gender Trouble: Feminism and the Subversion of Identity*. New York: Routledge.

———. 2002. "Is Kinship Always Already Heterosexual?" *Differences: A Journal of Feminist Cultural Studies* 13 (1): 14–44.

Campbell, Jan. 2000. *Arguing with the Phallus: Feminist, Queer, and Postcolonial Theory: A Psychoanalytic Contribution*. New York: Zed Books.

Carrier, Neil C. M. 2016. *Little Mogadishu: Eastleigh, Nairobi's Global Somali Hub*. London: C. Hurst & Co. Publishers Ltd.

Česnulytė, Eglė. 2020. *Selling Sex in Kenya: Gendered Agency under Neoliberalism*. Cambridge: Cambridge University Press.

Chanock, Martin Leon. 2000. "'Culture' and Human Rights Orientalising, Occidentalising and Authenticity." In *Beyond Rights Talk and Culture Talk: Comparative Essays on the Politics of Rights and Culture*, edited by Mahmood Mamdani, 15–36. New York: Saint Martin's Press.

Cloward, Karisa. 2016. *When Norms Collide: Local Responses to Activism against Female Genital Mutilation and Early Marriage.* New York: Oxford University Press.

Cohen, Stanley. 1973. *Folk Devils and Moral Panics: The Creation of the Mods and Rockers.* St. Albans: Paladin.

Cole, Jennifer, and Erin V. Moore. 2020. "Introduction: Gender Panics in the Global South." *Anthropological Quarterly* 93 (3): 275–88.

Coly, Ayo. 2019. "The Invention of the Homosexual: The Politics of Homophobia in Senegal." In *Gender and Sexuality in Senegalese Societies: Critical Perspective and Methods*, edited by Babacar M'Baye and Besi Brillian Muhoja, 27–51. Lanham: Lexington Books.

Comaroff, Jean, and John Comaroff. 2001. "Naturing the Nation: Aliens, Apocalypse, and the Postcolonial State." *Social Identities* 7 (2): 233–65.

Comaroff, John L., and Jean Comaroff. 2009. *Ethnicity, Inc.* Chicago: University of Chicago Press.

Coole, Diana, and Samantha Frost. 2010. "Introducing the New Materialisms." In *New Materialisms: Ontology, Agency, and Politics*, edited by Diana Coole and Samantha Frost, 1–43. Durham, NC: Duke University Press.

Currier, Ashley. 2012. *Out in Africa: LGBT Organizing in Namibia and South Africa.* Minneapolis: University of Minnesota Press.

———. 2018. *Politicizing Sex in Contemporary Africa: Homophobia in Malawi.* Cambridge: Cambridge University Press.

Cynn, Christine. 2018. *Prevention: Gender, Sexuality, HIV, and the Media in Côte D'Ivoire.* Columbus: Ohio State University Press.

Darian-Smith, Eve. 2020. "Cultural Commodification in Global Contexts: Australian Indigeneity, Inequality, and Militarization in the Twenty-First Century." In *Ethnicity, Commodity, In/Corporation*, edited by George Paul Meiu, Jean Comaroff, and John L. Comaroff, 224–49. Bloomington: Indiana University Press.

Davidson, Guy, and Monique Rooney. 2018. "Queer Objects." *Angelaki* 23 (1): 3–4.

Davis, Heather. 2016. "Imperceptibility and Accumulation: Political Strategies of Plastic." *Camera Obscura* 31 (2): 187–93.

———. 2022. *Plastic Matter.* Durham, NC: Duke University Press.

Deacon, Gregory. 2015. "Kenya: A Nation Born Again." *PentecoStudies* 14 (2): 219–40.

Dean, Tim. 2000. *Beyond Sexuality.* Chicago: University of Chicago Press.

Death, Carl. 2017. "Bodies, Populations, Citizens: The Biopolitics of African Environmentalism." In *The Routledge Handbook of Biopolitics*, edited by S. Prozorov and S. Rentea, 204–22. New York: Routledge.

Donham, Donald L. 2018. *The Erotics of History: An Atlantic African Example.* Berkeley: University of California Press.

Dorman, Sara, Daniel Hammett, and Paul Nugent. 2007. "Introduction: Citizenship and Its Casualties in Africa." In *Making Nations, Creating Strangers: States and Citizenship in Africa*, edited by Sara Dorman, Daniel Hammett, and Paul Nugent, 1–26. Leiden: Brill.

Douglas, Mary. 2006. *Purity and Danger: An Analysis of Concepts of Pollution and Taboo.* London: Routledge.

Dumont, Louis. 1980. *Homo Hierarchicus: The Caste System and Its Implications.* Chicago: University of Chicago Press.

Edelman, Lee. 2004. *No Future: Queer Theory and the Death Drive.* Durham, NC: Duke University Press.

REFERENCES

Edgerton, Robert B. 1964. "Pokot Intersexuality: An East African Example of the Resolution of Sexual Incongruity." *American Anthropologist* 66 (6): 1288–99.

Epprecht, Marc. 2004. *Hungochani: The History of a Dissident Sexuality in Southern Africa*. Montreal: McGill-Queen's University Press.

———. 2008. *Heterosexual Africa? The History of an Idea from the Age of Exploration to the Age of AIDS*. Athens: Ohio University Press.

Fabian, Johannes. 1983. *Time and the Other: How Anthropology Makes Its Object*. New York: Columbia University Press.

Fahs, B., M. Dudy, and S. Stage. 2013. *The Moral Panics of Sexuality*. London: Palgrave Macmillan UK.

Fanon, Frantz. 2008. *Black Skin, White Masks*. New York: Grove Press.

Farris, Sara R. 2017. *In the Name of Women's Rights: The Rise of Femonationalism*. Durham, NC: Duke University Press.

Ferguson, James, and Akhil Gupta. 2005. "Spatializing States: Toward and Ethnography of Neoliberal Governmentality." In *Anthropologies of Modernity: Foucault, Governmentality, and Life Politics*, edited by Jonathan Xavier Inda, 105–31. Malden: Blackwell.

Ferme, Mariane. 2001. *The Underneath of Things: Violence, History, and the Everyday in Sierra Leone*. Berkeley: University of California Press.

Fiereck, Kirk, Neville Hoad, and Danai S. Mupotsa. 2020. "A Queer-to-Come." *GLQ* 26 (3): 363–76.

Foucault, Michel. 1978. *The History of Sexuality*. Vol. 1. New York: Pantheon Books.

Freud, Sigmund. 1905. *Three Essays on the Theory of Sexuality*. London: Verso.

———. 1913. *The Interpretation of Dreams*. New York: Macmillan.

Gabrys, Jennifer, Gay Hawkins, and Mike Michael, eds. 2013. *Accumulation: The Material Politics of Plastic*. Florence: Taylor & Francis.

Gal, Susan, Julia Kowalski, and Erin Moore. 2015. "Rethinking Translation in Feminist NGOs: Rights and Empowerment Across Borders." *Social Politics* 22 (4): 610–35.

Gatwiri, Kathomi. 2018. *African Womanhood and Incontinent Bodies: Kenyan Women with Vaginal Fistulas*. Singapore: Springer.

Gaudio, Rudolf Pell. 2009. *Allah Made Us: Sexual Outlaws in an Islamic African City*. Chichester: John Wiley & Sons.

Geissler, Wenzel P., and Ruth J. Prince. 2020. "Layers of Epidemy: Present Pasts During the First Weeks of COVID-19 in Western Kenya." *Centaurus* 62: 248–56.

Geschiere, Peter. 2009. *The Perils of Belonging: Autochthony, Citizenship, and Exclusion in Africa and Europe*. Chicago: University of Chicago Press.

———. 2017. "A 'Vortex of Identities': Freemasonry, Witchcraft, and Postcolonial Homophobia." *African Studies Review* 60 (2): 7–35.

Geschiere, Peter, and Birgit Meyer. 1998. "Globalization and Identity: Dialectics of Flow and Closure." *Development and Change* 29: 601–15.

Geschiere, Peter, and Roger Orock. n.d. "Freemasonry, Homophobia and Illicit Enrichment: Postcolonial Imaginaries from Central Africa." Book manuscript.

Gevisser, Mark. 2020. *The Pink Line: Journeys Across the World's Queer Frontiers*. La Vergne: Jonathan Ball Publishers.

Giddens, Anthony. 1992. *The Transformation of Intimacy: Sexuality, Love, and Eroticism in Modern Societies*. Stanford, CA: Stanford University Press.

Githuku, Nicholas K. 2016. *Mau Mau Crucible of War: Statehood, National Identity, and Politics of Postcolonial Kenya*. Lanham, MD: Lexington Books.

Goldstone, Brian, and Juan Obarrio. 2017. "Introduction: Untimely Africa?" In *African Futures*, edited by Brian Goldstone and Juan Obarrio, 1–20. Chicago: University of Chicago Press.

Gramsci, Antonio. 2000. "Philisophie, Common Sense, Language, and Folklore." In *The Gramsci Reader: Selected Writings, 1916–1935*, edited by David Forgacs, 323–62. New York: International Publishers.

Grewal, Inderpal. 2017. *Saving the Security State: Exceptional Citizens in Twenty-First-Century America*. Durham, NC: Duke University Press.

Guss, Jeffrey R. 2010. "The Danger of Desire: Anal Sex and the Homo/Masculine Subject." *Studies in Gender and Sexuality* 11 (3): 124–40.

Gutmann, Matthew C. 2007. *Fixing Men: Sex, Birth Control, and AIDS in Mexico*. Berkeley: University of California Press.

Guyer, Jane I. 2007. "Prophecy and the Near Future: Thoughts on Macroeconomic, Evangelical, and Punctuated Time." *American Ethnologist* 34 (3): 409–21.

Hackman, Melissa. 2018. *Desire Work: Ex-Gay and Pentecostal Masculinity in South Africa*. Durham, NC: Duke University Press.

Halberstam, Judith. 2005. *In a Queer Time and Place: Transgender Bodies, Subcultural Lives*. New York: New York University Press.

Hall, Stuart, et al. 1978. *Policing the Crisis: Mugging, the State, and Law and Order*. London: Macmillan.

Hawkins, Gay. 2001. "Plastic Bags: Living with Rubbish." *International Journal of Cultural Studies* 4 (1): 5–23.

Hemmings, Clare. 2012. "Sexuality, Subjectivity . . . and Political Economy." *Subjectivity* 5 (2): 121–39.

Hendriks, Thomas. 2016. "SIM Cards of Desire: Sexual Versatility and the Male Homoerotic Economy in Urban Congo: SIM Cards of Desire." *American Ethnologist* 43 (2): 230–42.

Herdt, Gilbert. 2009. *Moral Panics, Sex Panics: Fear and the Fight over Sexual Rights*. New York: NYU Press.

Herranen-Tabibi, Annikki. 2022. "Resurgent Ecologies of Care: An Ethnography from Deanuleahki, Sápmi." PhD diss., Harvard University.

Herzfeld, Michael. 1997. *Cultural Intimacy: Social Poetics and the Real Life of States, Societies, and Institutions*. New York: Routledge.

Hjort, Andreas, and P. C. Salzman. 1981. "Ethnic Transformation, Dependency and Change: The Ilgira Samburu of Northern Kenya." In *Change and Development in Nomadic and Pastoral Societies*, edited by J. Galaty, 50–67. Leiden: Brill.

Hoad, Neville Wallace. 2007. *African Intimacies: Race, Homosexuality, and Globalization*. Minneapolis: University of Minnesota Press.

Hodder, Ian. 2012. *Entangled: An Archeology of the Relationship Between Humans and Things*. Oxford: Wiley.

Hodgson, Dorothy Louise. 2001. *Once Intrepid Warriors: Gender, Ethnicity, and the Cultural Politics of Maasai Development*. Bloomington: Indiana University Press.

———. 2005. *The Church of Women: Gendered Encounters between Maasai and Missionaries*. Bloomington: Indiana University Press.

———. 2011. *Being Maasai, Becoming Indigenous: Postcolonial Politics in a Neoliberal World*. Bloomington: Indiana University Press.

———. 2017. *Gender, Justice, and the Problem of Culture: From Customary Law to Human Rights in Tanzania*. Bloomington: Indiana University Press.

REFERENCES

Hodžić, Saida. 2017. *The Twilight of Cutting: African Activism and Life after NGOs.* Oakland: University of California Press.

Hofmann, Corinne. 2005. *The White Masai.* London: Bliss Books.

Holbraad, Martin, and Morten Axel Pedersen. 2017. *The Ontological Turn: An Anthropological Exposition.* Cambridge: Cambridge University Press.

Holtzman, Jon. 2004. "The Local in the Local: Models of Time and Space in Samburu District, Northern Kenya." *Current Anthropology* 45 (1): 61–84.

———. 2006. "The World Is Dead and Cooking's Killed It: Food and the Gender of Memory in Samburu, Northern Kenya." *Food and Foodways* 14 (3–4): 175–200.

Homewood, Nathanael. 2019. "Leaky Anuses, Loose Vaginas, and Large Penises: A Hierarchy of Sexualized Bodies in the Pentecostal Imaginary." In *Routledge Handbook of Queer African Studies*, edited by S. N. Nyeck, 113–28. New York: Routledge.

Honwana, Alcinda M. 2012. *The Time of Youth: Work, Social Change, and Politics in Africa.* West Hartford, CT: Kumarian Press Pub.

Hubert, Henri, and Marcel Mauss. 1964. *Sacrifice: Its Nature and Function.* London: Cohen & West.

Ingold, Tim. 2007. "Materials against Materiality." *Archaeological Dialogues* 14 (1): 1–16.

Inhorn, Marcia C. 2012. *The New Arab Man: Emergent Masculinities, Technologies, and Islam in the Middle East.* Princeton, NJ: Princeton University Press.

Ireland, Patrick R. 2013. "A Macro-Level Analysis of the Scope, Causes, and Consequences of Homophobia in Africa." *African Studies Review* 56 (2): 47–66.

Irvine, Janice M. 2008. "Transient Feelings: Sex Panics and the Politics of Emotions." *GLQ* 14 (1): 1–40.

Ivaska, Andrew. 2011. *Cultured States: Youth, Gender, and Modern Style in 1960s Dar Es Salaam.* Durham, NC: Duke University Press.

Jakobsen, Janet. 2007. "Sex, Secularism, and the 'War on Terror': The Role of Sexuality in Multi-Issue Organizing." In *A Companion to Lesbian, Gay, Bisexual, Transgender, and Queer Studies*, edited by Molly McGarry and George Haggerty, 19–37. London: Wiley-Blackwell.

Jeffrey, Craig. 2010. *Timepass: Youth, Class, and the Politics of Waiting in India.* Stanford, CA: Stanford University Press.

Jones, Jeremy L. 2010. "'Nothing Is Straight in Zimbabwe': The Rise of the Kukiya-Kiya Economy 2000–2008." *Journal of Southern African Studies* 36 (2): 285–99.

Judge, Melanie. 2017. *Blackwashing Homophobia: Violence and the Politics of Sexuality, Gender and Race.* New York: Routledge.

Kangaude, Godfrey Dalitso, and Ann Skelton. 2018. "(De)Criminalizing Adolescent Sex: A Rights-Based Assessment of Age of Consent Laws in Eastern and Southern Africa." *Reproductive Health in Sub-Saharan Africa* (October–December): 1–12.

Kanogo, Tabitha M. 2005. *African Womanhood in Colonial Kenya, 1900–50.* London: James Currey.

Kasfir, Sidney L. 1999. "Samburu Souvenirs: Representations of a Land in Amber." In *Unpacking Culture: Art and Commodity in Colonial and Postcolonial Worlds*, edited by Ruth B. Phillips and Christopher Burghard Steiner, 67–83. Berkeley: University of California Press.

———. 2007. *African Art and the Colonial Encounter: Inventing a Global Commodity.* Bloomington: Indiana University Press.

Kassa, Derese G. 2018. *Refugee Spaces and Urban Citizenship in Nairobi: Africa's Sanctuary City.* New York: Rowman & Littlefield.

Kenyatta, Jomo. 1938. *Facing Mount Kenya: The Tribal Life of the Gikuyu*. London: Secker and Warburg.

Kiama, Wanjira. 1999. "Men Who Have Sex with Men in Kenya." In *AIDS and Men: Taking Risks or Taking Responsibility?*, edited by Martin Foreman, 115–26. London: Panos.

Kibicho, Wanjohi. 2009. *Sex Tourism in Africa: Kenya's Booming Industry*. Farnham: Ashgate.

Kilshaw, Susie. 2009. *Impotent Warriors: Perspectives on Gulf War Syndrome, Vulnerability and Masculinity*. London: Berghahn.

Kintu, Deborah. 2017. *The Ugandan Morality Crusade: The Brutal Campaign Against Homosexuality and Pornography Under Yoweri Museveni*. Jefferson, NC: McFarland.

Kombo, Zeina W. 2016. "Beading: The Undefined Offence in Kenya." MA thesis, University of Nairobi.

Koselleck, Reinhart. 2004. *Futures Past: On the Semantics of Historical Time*. New York: Columbia University Press.

Kratz, Corinne Ann. 1994. *Affecting Performance: Meaning, Movement, and Experience in Okiek Women's Initiation*. Washington, DC: Smithsonian Institution Press.

Lacan, Jacques. 1977. *Écrits: A Selection*. New York: Norton.

———. 1985. *Feminine Sexuality: Jacques Lacan and the École Freudienne*. W. W. Norton & Company.

———. 1988. *The Seminar of Jacques Lacan, Book I: Freud's Papers on Technique, 1953–1954*. New York: W. W. Norton.

———. 1993. *The Psychoses: The Seminar of Jacques Lacan*. New York: Routledge.

———. 2017. *Formations of the Unconscious: The Seminar of Jacques Lacan, Book V*. Cambridge: Polity Press.

Lancaster, Roger N. 2011. *Sex Panic and the Punitive State*. Berkeley: University of California Press.

Larick, Roy. 1987. "The Circulation of Spears among Loikop Cattle Pastoralists of Samburu District, Kenya." *Research in Economic Anthropology* 9: 143–66.

Lavau, Stephanie. 2011. "The Nature/s of Belonging: Performing an Authentic Australian River." *Ethnos* 76 (1): 41–64.

Leinaweaver, Jessaca B. 2008. *The Circulation of Children: Kinship, Adoption, and Morality in Andean Peru*. Durham, NC: Duke University Press.

Lekembe, Simon. 2010. "The Contribution of Wildlife-Based Tourism to Community Development: A Case Study of Communities Adjacent to Samburu National Reserve." BA thesis, Moi University.

Lesorogol, Carolyn K. 2008a. *Contesting the Commons: Privatizing Pastoral Lands in Kenya*. Ann Arbor: University of Michigan Press.

———. 2008b. "Setting Themselves Apart: Education, Capabilities, and Sexuality among Samburu Women in Kenya." *Anthropological Quarterly* 81 (3): 551–77.

Lewis, Desiree. 2011. "Representing African Sexualities." In *African Sexualities: A Reader*, edited by Sylvia Tamale, 199–216. Oxford: Pambazuka.

Lorway, Robert. 2014. *Namibia's Rainbow Project: Gay Rights in an African Nation*. Bloomington: Indiana University Press.

———. 2020. "Experimental Entanglements: Surveillance Science, Sex Worker Activism, and Evidentiary Politics in Kenya." *Medical Anthropology Quarterly* 34 (3): 398–418.

Lpatilan, Lekerimui Josephat. 2014. "Effect of Retrogressive Culture on Girl-Child Education in Primary and Secondary Schools: A Case Study of Samburu East Constituency in Samburu County, Kenya." MA thesis, Mount Kenya University.

REFERENCES

Macharia, Keguro. 2013. "Queer Kenya in Law and Policy." In *Queer African Reader*, edited by S. Ekine and H. Abbas, 273–89. Nairobi: Pambazuka.

———. 2019. *Frottage: Frictions of Intimacy Across the Black Diaspora*. New York: New York University Press.

———. 2020. "belated: interruption." *GLQ* 26 (3): 561–73.

Mack, Mehammed Amadeus. 2017. *Sexagon: Muslims, France, and the Sexualization of National Culture*. New York: Fordham University Press.

Magubane, Zine. 2004. *Bringing the Empire Home: Race, Class, and Gender in Britain and Colonial South Africa*. Chicago: University of Chicago Press.

Maina, Grace Njoki. 2017. "Transformation of Masculinities among the Agikuyu of Mathira, Nyeri County, Kenya, 1952–2014." MA thesis, Kenyatta University.

Mains, Daniel. 2011. *Hope Is Cut: Youth, Unemployment, and the Future in Urban Ethiopia*. Philadelphia: Temple University Press.

Malkki, Liisa H. 2015. *The Need to Help: The Domestic Arts of International Humanitarianism*. Durham, NC: Duke University Press.

Manalansan, Martin F. IV. 2009. "Homophobia at New York Central." In *Homophobias: Lust and Loathing across Time and Space*, edited by David A. B. Murray, 34–47. Durham, NC: Duke University Press.

Manalansan, Martin F., Chantal Nadeau, Richard T. Rodríguez, and Siobhan B. Somerville. 2014. "Queering the Middle: Race, Region, and a Queer Midwest." *GLQ: A Journal of Lesbian and Gay Studies* 20 (1–2): 1–12.

Mannava, Priya, Scott Geibel, Nzioki King'ola, Marleen Temmerman, and Stanley Luchters. 2013. "Male Sex Workers Who Sell Sex to Men Also Engage in Anal Intercourse with Women: Evidence from Mombasa, Kenya." *Plos One* 8 (1): 1–5.

Masquelier, Adeline. 2005. "Dirt, Undress, and Difference: An Introduction." In *Dirt, Undress, and Difference: Critical Perspectives on the Body's Surface*, edited by Adeline Masquelier, 1–33. Bloomington: Indiana University Press.

———. 2019. *Fada: Boredom and Belonging in Niger*. Chicago: University of Chicago Press.

Matory, J. Lorand. 2018. *The Fetish Revisited: Marx, Freud, and the Gods Black People Make*. Durham, NC: Duke University Press.

Mayer, Stefanie, and Birgit Sauer. 2017. "'Gender Ideology' in Austria: Coalitions Around an Empty Signifier." In *Anti-Gender Campaigns in Europe. Mobilizing against Equality*, edited by Roman Kuhar and David Patternote, 23–40. London: Rowman and Littlefield.

Mazzarella, William. 2017. *The Mana of Mass Society*. Chicago: University of Chicago Press.

M'Baye, Babacar. 2013. "The Origins of Senegalese Homophobia: Discourses on Homosexuals and Transgender People in Colonial and Postcolonial Senegal." *African Studies Review* 56 (2): 109–28.

Mbembe, J.-Achille. 2001. *On the Postcolony*. Berkeley: University of California Press.

———. 2020. "The Sexual Potentate: On Sodomy, Fellatio, and Other Postcolonial Privacies." In *Reading in Sexualities from Africa*, edited by Rachel Spronk and Thomas Hendriks, 296–99. Bloomington: Indiana University Press.

McClintock, Anne. 1995. *Imperial Leather: Race, Gender, and Sexuality in the Colonial Contest*. New York: Routledge.

McCurdy, Sheryl. 2006. "Fashioning Sexuality: Desire, Manyema Ethnicity, and the Creation of the 'Kanga,' ca. 1880–1900." *International Journal of African Historical Studies* 39 (3): 441–69.

Meikle, Jeffrey L. 1995. *American Plastic: A Cultural History.* New Brunswick, NJ: Rutgers University Press.

Meiu, George Paul. 2015. "'Beach-Boy Elders' and 'Young Big-Men': Subverting the Temporalities of Ageing in Kenya's Ethno-Erotic Economies." *Ethnos* 80 (4): 472–96.

———. 2016. "Belonging in Ethno-Erotic Economies: Adultery, Alterity, and Ritual in Postcolonial Kenya." *American Ethnologist* 43 (2): 215–29.

———. 2017. *Ethno-Erotic Economies: Sexuality, Money, and Belonging in Kenya.* Chicago: University of Chicago Press.

———. 2019. "Who Are the New Natives? Ethnicity and Emerging Idioms of Belonging in Africa." In *A Companion to the Anthropology of Africa*, edited by Roy Richard Grinker, Stephen C. Lubkemann, Christopher B. Steiner, and Euclides Gonçalves, 145–72. New York: John Wiley & Sons.

———. 2020a. "Panics over Plastics: A Matter of Belonging in Kenya." *American Anthropologist* 122 (2): 222–35.

———. 2020b. "Underlayers of Citizenship: Queer Objects, Intimate Exposures, and the Rescue Rush in Kenya." *Cultural Anthropology* 35 (4): 575–601.

———. 2022. "Queer Futures, National Utopias: Notes on Objects, Intimacy, Time, and the State." In *African Futures*, edited by Clemens Greiner, Michael Bollig, and Steven Van Wolputte, 320–30. Leiden: Brill.

Miller, Daniel. 2005. "Materiality: An Introduction." In *Materiality*, edited by Daniel Miller, 1–50. Durham, NC: Duke University Press.

Mojola, Sanyu A. 2014. *Love, Money, and HIV: Becoming a Modern African Woman in the Age of AIDS.* Berkeley: University of California Press.

Moore, Erin V. 2016. "Postures of Empowerment: Cultivating Aspirant Feminism in a Ugandan NGO." *Ethos* 44 (3): 375–96.

Moore, Henrietta L. 1999. "Gender, Symbolism, and Praxis: Theoretical Approaches." In *Those Who Play with Fire: Gender, Fertility, and Transformation in East and Southern Africa*, edited by Henrietta L. Moore, Todd Sanders, and Bwire Kaare, 3–37. London: Athlone Press.

Morris, Rosalind C. 2008. "Rush/Panic/Rush: Speculations on the Value of Life and Death in South Africa's Age of AIDS." *Public Culture* 20 (2): 199–231.

Morrison, Toni. 1992. "Introduction: Friday on the Potomac." In *Race-ing Justice, En-Gendering Power: Essays on Anita Hill, Clarence Thomas, and the Construction of Social Reality*, edited by Toni Morrison, vii–xxx. New York: Pantheon Books.

Mosse, George L. 1985. *Nationalism and Sexuality: Middle-Class Morality and Sexual Norms in Modern Europe.* Madison: University of Wisconsin Press.

Moussawi, Ghassan. 2020. *Disruptive Situations: Fractal Orientalism and Queer Strategies in Beirut.* Philadelphia: Temple University Press.

Moyer, Eileen, and Emmy Igonya. 2018. "Queering the Evidence: Remaking Homosexuality and HIV Risk to 'End AIDS' in Kenya." *Global Public Health* 13: 1007–19.

Msibi, Thabo. 2011. "The Lies We Have Been Told: On (Homo) Sexuality in Africa." *Africa Today* 58 (1): 55–77.

Mudimbe, V. Y. 1988. *The Invention of Africa: Gnosis, Philosophy, and the Order of Knowledge.* Bloomington: Indiana University Press.

Muhonja, Besi Brillian. 2017. *Womanhood and Girlhood in Twenty-First Century Middle Class Kenya: Disrupting Patri-Centered Frameworks.* Lanham, MD: Lexington Books.

Murray, David A. B. 2009. "Introduction." In *Homophobias: Lust and Loathing across Time and Space*, edited by David A. B. Murray, 1–15. Durham, NC: Duke University Press.

REFERENCES

———. 2012. *Flaming Souls: Homosexuality, Homophobia, and Social Change in Barbados*. Toronto: University of Toronto Press.

Mutongi, Kenda. 2017. *Matatu: A History of Popular Transportation in Nairobi*. Chicago: University of Chicago Press.

Mwangi, Evan. 2014. "Queer Agency in Kenya's Digital Media." *African Studies Review* 57 (2): 93–113.

Mwangi, Meja. 2000. *The Last Plague*. Nairobi: East African Publishers.

Nakamura, Kyoko. 2005. *Adornments of the Samburu in Northern Kenya: A Comprehensive List*. Kyoto: Center for African Area Studies, Kyoto University.

Ndjio, Basile. 2012. "Post-Colonial Histories of Sexuality: The Political Intervention of a Libidinal African Straight." *Africa* 82 (4): 609–31.

———. 2016. "The Nation and Its Undesirable Subjects: Homosexuality, Citizenship and the Gay 'Other' in Cameroon." In *The Culturalization of Citizenship: Belonging and Polarization in a Globalizing World*, edited by Jan Willem Duyvendak, Peter Geschiere, and Evelien Tonkens, 115–36. London: Palgrave Macmillan UK.

Newell, Sasha. 2012. *The Modernity Bluff: Crime, Consumption, and Citizenship in Côte D'Ivoire*. Chicago: University of Chicago Press.

Njoroge, Ruth. 2016. *Body Adornment among the Samburu: A Historical Perspective*. Saarbrücken: Lambert.

Nyamnjoh, Francis B.. 2006. *Insiders and Outsiders: Citizenship and Xenophobia in Contemporary South Africa*. London: Zed Books.

———. 2018. "Citizenship." In *Critical Terms for the Study of Africa*, edited by Desai Gaurav and Adeline M. Masquelier, 56–68. Chicago: University of Chicago Press.

Nyanzi, Stella, Barbara Nyanzi, Bessie Kalina, and Robert Pool. 2004. "Mobility, Sexual Networks and Exchange among Bodabodamen in Southwest Uganda." *Culture, Health & Sexuality* 6 (3): 239–54.

Nyeck, S. N. 2013. "Mobilizing Against the Invisible: Erotic Nationalism, Mass Media, and the 'Paranoid Style' in Cameroon." In *Sexual Diversity in Africa: Politics, Theory, Citizenship*, edited by S. N. Nyeck and Marc Epprecht, 151–69. Montreal: McGill-Queen's University Press.

Nyeck, S. N., ed. 2019. *Routledge Handbook of Queer African Studies*. New York: Routledge.

Nzegwu, Nkiru. 2011. "Osunality (Or African Eroticism)." In *African Sexualities Reader*, edited by Sylvia Tamale, 253–70. Oxford: Pambazuka.

Obudho, Mary Achieng. 2019. "A Postmodern Reading of Bodaboda Riders' Verbal Performance: Constructing Gender and Sexuality through Mbaka in Western Kenya." *Mambo!* 16 (7): 1–7.

Ocobock, Paul. 2017. *An Uncertain Age: The Politics of Manhood in Kenya*. Columbus: Ohio University Press.

Odhiambo, Tom. 2007. "Sexual Anxieties and Rampant Masculinities in Postcolonial Kenyan Literature." *Social Identities* 13 (5): 651–63.

Okech, Awino. 2019. *Widow Inheritance and Contested Citizenship in Kenya: Building Nations*. New York: Routledge.

Ott, Elisabeth. 2004. *Nkanyit und Gewalt: Häusliche Gewalt gegen Frauen in Samburu zwischen Tradition und Willkür*. Berlin: Weissensee Verlag.

Oucho, John O. 2002. *Undercurrents of Ethnic Conflicts in Kenya*. Leiden: Brill.

Ouma, Christopher, and Mphathi Mutloane. 2014. "Performing Queer in Time and Space." In *Reclaiming Afrikan: Queer Perspectives on Sexual and Gender Identities*, edited by Zethu Matebeni, 37–43. Athlone: Modjaj Books.

Oyěwùmí, Oyèrónkẹ́. 1997. *The Invention of Women: Making an African Sense of Western Gender Discourses.* Minneapolis: University of Minnesota Press.

Pandian, Anand. 2016. "Plastic." *Cultural Anthropology Website.* https://culanth.org/fieldsights/plastic (accessed June 12, 2019).

Parsitau, Damaris, and Adriaan van Klinken. 2018. "Pentecostal Intimacies: Women and Intimate Citizenship in the Ministry of Repentance and Holiness in Kenya." *Citizenship Studies* 22 (6): 586–602.

Parsitau, Damaris Seleina. 2021. "Law, Religion, and the Politicization of Sexual Citizenship in Kenya." *Journal of Law and Religion* 36 (1):105–29.

Partridge, Damani J. 2012. *Hypersexuality and Headscarves: Race, Sex, and Citizenship in the New Germany.* Bloomington: Indiana University Press.

Piot, Charles. 2010. *Nostalgia for the Future: West Africa after the Cold War.* Chicago: University of Chicago Press.

Plummer, Ken. 2011. *Intimate Citizenship: Private Decisions and Public Dialogues.* Seattle: University of Washington Press.

Porter, Mary A. 1995. "Talking at the Margins: Kenyan Discourses on Homosexuality." In *Lavender Lexicon: Authenticity, Imagination, and Appropriation in Lesbian and Gay Languages*, edited by W. Leap, 133–53. New York: Gordon and Breach.

Povinelli, Elizabeth A. 2006. *The Empire of Love: Toward a Theory of Intimacy, Genealogy, and Carnality.* Durham, NC: Duke University Press.

Puar, Jasbir K. 2007. *Terrorist Assemblages: Homonationalism in Queer Times.* Durham, NC: Duke University Press.

Rahier, Nick. 2021. "Overheated Stomachs: Notes on Urban Life and Toxicity in Nakuru, Kenya." *Africa* 91 (3): 453–72.

Ralph, Michael. 2008. "Killing Time." *Social Text* 26: 1–29.

Rao, Rahul. 2020. *Out of Time: The Queer Politics of Postcoloniality.* New York: Oxford University Press.

Reid, Graeme. 2013. *How to Be a Real Gay: Gay Identities in Small-Town South Africa.* Scottsville, Pietermaritzburg, South Africa: KwaZulu-Natal Press.

Richards, Audrey. [1956] 1982. *Chisungu: A Girl's Initiation Ceremony among the Bemba of Zambia.* New York: Routledge.

Rigby, Peter. 1992. *Cattle, Capitalism, and Class: Ilparakuyo Maasai Transformations.* Philadelphia: Temple University Press.

Rodriguez, S. M. 2019. *The Economies of Queer Inclusion: Transnational Organizing for LGBTI Rights in Uganda.* Lanham, MD: Lexington Books.

Roitman, Janet. 2018. *Fiscal Disobedience: An Anthropology of Economic Regulation in Central Africa.* Princeton, NJ: Princeton University Press.

Rubin, Gayle. 1984. "Thinking Sex: Notes for a Radical Theory of the Politics of Sexuality." In *Pleasure and Danger: Exploring Female Sexuality*, edited by Carole Vance, 267–317. London: Pandora Press.

Scherz, China. 2014. *Having People, Having Heart: Charity, Sustainable Development, and Problems of Dependence in Central Uganda.* Chicago: University of Chicago Press.

Schwandt, M., C. Morris, A. Ferguson, E. Ngugi, and S. Moses. 2006. "Anal and Dry Sex in Commercial Sex Work, and Relation to Risk for Sexually Transmitted Infections and HIV in Meru, Kenya." *Sexually Transmitted Infections* 82 (5): 392–96.

REFERENCES

Sempele, Lorna. 2017. *The Colourful Bead Necklace of My Mother Tongue*. Nairobi: Empiris.

Shadle, Brett Lindsay. 2006. *"Girl Cases": Marriage and Colonialism in Gusiiland, Kenya, 1890–1970*. Portsmouth, NH: Heinemann.

Shaw, Carolyn Martin. 1995. *Colonial Inscriptions: Race, Sex and Class in Kenya*. Minneapolis: University of Minnesota Press.

Shepherd, Gill. 1987. "Rank, Gender, and Homosexuality: Mombasa as a Key to Understanding Sexual Options." In *The Cultural Construction of Sexuality*, edited by Pat Caplan, 240–70. New York: Tavistock.

Shipley, Jesse Weaver. 2010. "Africa in Theory: A Conversation Between Jean Comaroff and Achille Mbembe." *Anthropological Quarterly* 83 (3): 653–78.

Silberschmidt, Margrethe. 1999. *"Women Forget That Men Are the Masters": Gender Antagonism and Socio-Economic Change in Kisii District, Kenya*. Uppsala: Nordic Africa Institute.

Simpson, Audra. 2014. *Mohawk Interruptus: Political Life Across the Borders of Settler States*. Durham, NC: Duke University Press.

Simpson, George L. 1994. "On the Frontiers of Empire: British Administration in Kenya's Northern Frontier District, 1905–1935." PhD diss., West Virginia University.

Smith, James H. 2008. *Bewitching Development: Witchcraft and the Reinvention of Development in Neoliberal Kenya*. Chicago: University of Chicago Press.

Sommers, Marc. 2001. "Young, Male and Pentecostal: Urban Refugees in Dar Es Salaam, Tanzania." *Journal of Refugee Studies* 14 (4): 347–70.

Spencer, Paul. 1965. *The Samburu: A Study of Gerontocracy*. London: Routledge.

———. 1973. *Nomads in Alliance: Symbiosis and Growth among the Rendille and Samburu of Kenya*. London: Oxford University Press.

Sperling, Valerie. 2015. *Sex, Politics, and Putin: Political Legitimacy in Russia*. Oxford: Oxford University Press.

Sprenger, Guido. 2004. "Encompassment and Its Discontents: The Rmeet and the Lowland Lao." In *Grammars of Identity/Alterity: A Structural Approach*, edited by Gerd Baumann and André Gingrich, 173–91. New York: Berghahn.

Stoler, Ann Laura. 2002. *Carnal Knowledge and Imperial Power: Race and the Intimate in Colonial Rule*. Berkeley: University of California Press.

Stoller, Paul. 1989. *The Taste of Ethnographic Things: The Senses in Anthropology*. Philadelphia: University of Pennsylvania Press.

Spronk, Rachel. 2011. "'Intimacy Is the Name of the Game': Media and the Praxis of Sexual Knowledge in Nairobi." *Anthropologica* 53 (1): 145–58.

———. 2012. *Ambiguous Pleasures: Sexuality and Middle-Class Self-Perceptions in Nairobi*. New York: Berghahn.

Stoll, Florian. 2018. "The City and Its Ways of Life: Local Influences on Middle-Income Milieus in Nairobi." *African Cities and the Development Conundrum* 10: 275–301.

Straight, Bilinda. 2002. "From Samburu Heirloom to New Age Artifact: The Cross-Cultural Consumption of Mporo Marriage Beads." *American Anthropologist* 104: 1–21.

———. 2004. "Cutting Time: Beads, Sex and Song in the Making of Samburu Memory." In *The Qualities of Time: Anthropological Approaches*, edited by Wendy James and David Mills, 267–83. London: Routledge.

———. 2007. *Miracles and Extraordinary Experience in Northern Kenya*. Philadelphia: University of Pennsylvania Press.

———. 2020. "Land Conflict, Murder, and the Rise of 'Timeless Culture' and Girl Blaming (Samburu, Kenya)." *Ateliers d'anthropologie* 47 (January), http://journals.openedition.org.ezp-prod1.hul.harvard.edu/ateliers/12553.

Strathern, Marilyn. 1988. *The Gender of the Gift: Problems with Women and Problems with Society in Melanesia.* Berkeley: University of California Press.

Talle, Aud. 1988. *Women at a Loss: Changes in Maasai Pastoralism and Their Effects on Gender Relations.* Stockholm: Department of Social Anthropology, University of Stockholm.

Tallie, T. J. 2019. *Queering Colonial Natal: Indigeneity and the Violence of Belonging in Southern Africa.* Minneapolis: University of Minnesota Press.

Tamale, Sylvia, ed. 2011. *African Sexualities: A Reader.* Oxford: Pambazuka.

Tambe, Ashwini. 2019. *Defining Girlhood in India: A Transnational History of Sexual Maturity Laws.* Urbana: University of Illinois Press.

Taussig, Michael. 1993. *Mimesis and Alterity.* New York: Routledge.

Thiong'o, Ngũgĩ wa. 2012. *Globalectics: Theory and the Politics of Knowing.* New York: Columbia University Press.

Thomas, Lynn M. 2003. *Politics of the Womb: Women, Reproduction, and the State in Kenya.* Berkeley: University of California Press.

Thompson, Katrina Daly. 2017. *Popobawa: Tanzanian Talk, Global Misreadings.* Bloomington: Indiana University Press.

Thoreson, Ryan Richard. 2014. "Troubling the Waters of a 'Wave of Homophobia': Political Economies of Anti-Queer Animus in Sub-Saharan Africa." *Sexualities* 17 (1–2): 23–42.

Thornton, Brendan Jamal. 2016. *Negotiating Respect: Pentecostalism, Masculinity, and the Politics of Spiritual Authority in the Dominican Republic.* Gainesville: University Press of Florida.

Tonkens, Evelien, and Jan Willem Duyvendak. 2016. "Introduction: The Culturalization of Citizenship." In *The Culturalization of Citizenship: Belonging and Polarization in a Globalizing World*, edited by Evelien Tonkens, Peter Geschiere, and Jan W. Duyvendak, 1–20. London: Palgrave.

Turner, Victor. 1968. *The Drums of Affliction: A Study of Religious Processes Among the Ndembu of Zambia.* London: International African Institute.

Uys, Leana, Maureen Chirwa, Priscilla Dlamini, and Minrie Greeff. 2005. "Eating Plastic, Winning the Lotto, Joining the WWW: Descriptions of HIV/AIDS in Africa." *Journal of the Association of Nurses in AIDS Care* 16 (3): 11–21.

Van Klinken, A. S. 2013. *Transforming Masculinities in African Christianity: Gender Controversies in Times of AIDS.* Aldershot: Ashgate.

———. 2019. *Kenyan, Christian, Queer: Religion, LGBT Activism, and Arts of Resistance in Africa.* University Park: Pennsylvania State University Press.

Vance, Carole S. 2012. "Innocence and Experience: Melodramatic Narratives of Sex Trafficking and Their Consequences for Law and Policy." *History of the Present* 2 (2): 200–218.

Verdery, Katherine. 2018. *My Life as a Spy: Investigations in a Secret Police File.* Durham, NC: Duke University Press.

Wa-Mũngai, Mbũgua. 2013. *Nairobi's "Matatu" Men: Portrait of a Subculture.* Nairobi: Twaweza Communications.

Wangila, Mary Nyangweso. 2007. *Female Circumcision: The Interplay of Religion, Culture and Gender in Kenya.* New York: Orbis Books.

Wanyoike, Pauline Nasesia. 2011. "The Perceptions of Rural Samburu Women in Kenya with Regard to HIV/AIDS: Towards Developing a Communication Strategy." PhD diss., University of South Africa.

Warah, Rasna. 2019. "Why I'm No Longer Talking to Kikuyus About Tribe." *The Elephant* (blog), July 20. https://www.theelephant.info/op-eds/2019/07/20/why-im-no-longer-talking-to-kikuyus-about-tribe/ (accessed December 20, 2022).

Warnier, Jean-Pierre. 1993. *L'espirit d'entreprise au Cameroon*. Paris: Karthala.

Waweru, Peter. 2012. *Continuity and Change in Samburu Pastoralism*. Saarbrücken: Lambert.

Weber, Cynthia. 2016. *Queer International Relations: Sovereignty, Sexuality, and the Will to Knowledge*. Oxford: Oxford University Press.

Weiss, Brad. 1996. *The Making and Unmaking of the Haya Lived World: Consumption, Commoditization, and Everyday Practice*. Durham, NC: Duke University Press.

———. 2004. "Introduction. Contesting Futures: Past and Present." In *Producing African Futures: Ritual and Reproduction in a Neoliberal Age*, edited by Brad Weiss, 1–19. Leiden: Brill.

Weiss, Margot. 2022. "Queer Theory from Elsewhere and the Im/Proper Objects of Queer Anthropology." *Feminist Anthropology* (Early View).

Weitzberg, Keren. 2017. *We Do Not Have Borders: Greater Somalia and the Predicaments of Belonging in Kenya*. Athens: Ohio University Press.

Wentzell, Emily A. 2013. *Maturing Masculinities: Aging, Chronic Illness, and Viagra in Mexico*. Durham, NC: Duke University Press.

Wiegman, Robyn, and Elizabeth A. Wilson. 2015. "Introduction: Antinormativity's Queer Conventions." *differences* 26 (1): 1–25.

White, Luise. 1990. "Separating the Men from Boys: Constructions of Gender, Sexuality, and Terrorism in Central Kenya, 1939–1959." *International Journal of African Historical Studies* 23 (1): 1–25.

Wijngaarden, Vanessa. 2018. "Maasai Beadwork Has Always Been Modern: An Exploration of Modernity through Artifacts." *Cultural Dynamics* 30 (4): 235–52.

Wyrod, Robert. 2016. *AIDS and Masculinity in the African City: Privilege, Inequality, and Modern Manhood*. Berkeley: University of California Press.

Zhang, Everett. 2015. *The Impotence Epidemic: Men's Medicine and Sexual Desire in Contemporary China*. Durham, NC: Duke University Press.

Zupančič, Alenka. 2017. *What Is Sex?* Cambridge, MA: MIT University Press.

Index

abortion, 11, 91, 97
Adorno, Theodor W., 15
adult diapers, 35–36, 142–49, 151–62. *See also* anal sex
aesthetics of vulgarity, 161
Africa's Last Taboo (Barnwell and Samura), 27
Ahmed, Sara, 13, 158, 201n5
AIDS, 40, 49, 51, 68, 130. *See also* HIV
alcoholism, 70–72
Alexander, M. Jacqui, 10, 64
Al-Shabaab, 118, 175–76
Amadiume, Ifi, 76
Amar, Paul, 10, 46, 133
Amuyunzu-Nyamongo, Mary, 67–68
anal sex, 15–18, 35, 37, 74, 142–45, 147–52, 158–60. *See also* adult diapers
Angelides, Steven, 93, 110
anthropology, 26, 30–31, 92, 120, 162, 185. *See also* scholarship
anti-homosexuality: as African, 24, 26, 143; campaigns, 8; demonstrations, 19, 21–22, 84; discussion of, 25–26; and gender nonconformity, 3; around globe, 7–8, 22; imaginaries, 159–60, 163, 169, 193, 197; politics of, 9, 25–27, 163; rhetoric, 18, 22, 142–43, 161, 175. *See also* Christianity; foreignness; globalization; law; marriage; protest; rescue campaigns; violence
Appadurai, Arjun, 183
Archambault, Julie Soleil, 153
"aspirant feminists," 115. *See also* feminism
autochthony, 4, 7, 10, 33, 94, 119–22, 127, 139
Axel, Brian, 165

Bachmann, Jan, 174–75
Bahati, David, 22
Barnwell, Robin, 27

Barthes, Roland, 121, 140–41
"Beading" (Kombo), 98
bead necklaces, 35, 87–107, 109–11, 113–16, 196–97. *See also* "boy with beads"; "girls of the beads"; plastic
Bedford, Kate, 45
belonging: and class, 84, 104, 136; ethnic, 5, 95, 100, 104–5, 107, 113, 115–16, 134, 137–38; and intimate rescue, 47, 57; and language, 80; and materiality, 35, 119–22, 127–28, 131, 138–40; national, 18, 33, 40, 57, 87, 94, 134, 138. *See also* citizenship; kinship
Benjamin, Walter, 19
Berlant, Lauren, 8, 11, 40
Bersani, Leo, 142
Blunt, Robert, 146
bodaboda, 19, 22, 32, 35, 59–60, 76–81, 85–86, 178–80, 184
Boellstorff, Tom, 161
boma, 109–10. *See also* kinship
Bompani, Barbara, 53–54
bondage, 89, 94, 97, 106, 114–15
Bonhomme, Julien, 68, 183–84
Borofsky, Robert, 207n8
Bosia, Michael J., 9, 163
"boy with beads," 2, 5–7, 32, 36, 185–89, 197. *See also* "girls of the beads"
Brickell, Chris, 201n5
bridewealth, 101, 182
Broch-Due, Vigdis, 25
Bryant, Anita, 176
Bryce, Jane, 74

calabashes, 129–30, 136
Campbell, Jan, 69
Česnulytė, Eglė, 49

INDEX

Chai, Lawrence, 21–22, 32
children, 41–43, 50, 88–99, 107, 110, 113. *See also* bead necklaces; "girls of the beads"; kidnapping; ombani na ngweko; sex education
Children Act, 110
Chimbalanga, Tiwonge, 163
Chisungu (Richards), 13–14
Christianity, 4, 20–21, 33–34, 48–50, 59–63, 100, 143, 170–73, 176
citizenship: *anti-*, 161; culturalization of, 5, 10; and ethnicity, 94; exceptional, 33, 36, 47, 52–53, 57, 61–63, 93, 138, 145–46, 158, 172–73, 182, 196; heteropatriarchal, 118; heterosexual, 158; intimate, 8–12, 15, 19, 28, 33–36, 39–40, 46, 87, 115–16, 144, 158, 161–62, 178, 191, 193, 197; and power, 9–10; regional, 69; technologies of, 18, 36, 144–45, 154, 157, 162, 164–65, 172, 177, 194. *See also* subject of intimate rescue
Cohen, Stanley, 39
Collard, Judith, 201n5
colonialism, 46, 52–56, 64, 67–71, 94, 100–101, 107–8, 113, 136–37
Colorful Bead Necklace of My Mother Tongue, The (Sempele), 95
Comaroff, Jean, 121
Comaroff, John, 121
community-based organizations (CBOs), 82–83, 149
community of affliction, 53, 58, 66, 119–20, 122, 130, 133–34, 143–46, 161, 194
confessional narratives, 63, 172, 176
conservativism, 3, 126, 143, 160, 168
constitutive resonance, 122, 140, 144
culturalization of citizenship, 10
culturalization of sexuality, 4, 10
curses, 93–94, 107, 110–12

Davidson, Guy, 201n5
Davis, Heather, 120–21, 139–40
Death, Carl, 121
"desire for desire of the state," 18–19
Developing Partnerships (Bedford), 45
Diaper Mentality (art exhibit), 144–45, 154–57, 194
diapers. *See* adult diapers
disambiguation, 183
disavowal, 183
displacement, 183
Donham, Donald L., 12–13
Dorman, Sara, 10
Douglas, Mary, 131
Duale, Aden, 173
Dumont, Louis, 107, 204n11
Durkheim, Émile, 1
Duyvendak, Jan Willem, 10

Edelman, Lee, 43, 50
Edgerton, Robert B., 186

ekidet dolls, 16
emasculation, 65, 71, 75, 79, 129. *See also* masculinity
empowerment, 1, 45, 72, 87–89, 93, 98, 102, 109, 111–15. *See also* humanitarianism
encompassment, 35, 87, 91, 94, 105–7, 109–11, 113–17, 204n11
engagement rings, 23–24
entrepreneurship, 30, 47, 124–26, 136, 138–39
environmentalism, 134
eroticism, 13, 118, 157, 177
ethnicity, 4–5, 7, 9, 55, 69–71, 74–76, 95, 101, 109, 134, 138–39, 196
ethnographic detours, 34, 36, 117–18, 164, 192–93
ethnography, 8–9, 12–15, 18, 26–27, 30–34, 163–64, 192–93

Facing Mt. Kenya (Kenyatta), 108
faith-based organizations (FBOs), 48
Fanon, Frantz, 44
Farris, Sara R., 92–93, 113–14
Fear of Child Sexuality, The (Angelides), 93
female genital mutilation (FGM), 11, 98, 111–12, 114. *See also* initiation
femininity, 1, 6–7, 12, 95–97, 115
feminism, 63–64, 69, 82, 84, 89, 92, 98, 110, 113–15. *See also* "aspirant feminists"; women
femonationalism, 92, 114
Ferguson, James, 110
Ferme, Mariane C., 153
fetishism, 13, 64, 192
fistula, 147–48
"Forecasters' Road Map of the 1980's," 28–29
foreignness, 3, 6–7, 9–10, 18, 117–22, 127–29, 132–34, 142–43
fractal Orientalism, 56
Francis, Paul, 67–68
Freud, Sigmund, 17–18, 34, 163, 192
future-making, 28–32, 47, 131–33, 180, 184

Gado, 156
Gatwiri, Kathomi, 147–48
gayism: as business, 23; and Christianity, 117; as contagious, 6, 11, 21, 50, 74, 133, 161, 169, 172–73, 178, 180, 189, 207nn5–6, 207n11; discourses, 160–61; institutionalization of, 182; and materiality, 169; perceptions of, 160; as pollutant, 18, 133–34, 164; protests against, 19–21; and recruitment, 176; and schools, 4, 7; and terrorist body, 165, 170–71, 173–77, 197; and transformation, 170. *See also* homosexual body
gender binaries, 72–76
gender leaking, 35, 64, 72–76, 86, 117, 160, 189, 195–97
gender roles, 3, 10, 45, 61–63, 166–68, 183
Geschiere, Peter, 176

Giddens, Anthony, 118, 140
girl-child, 113–14
"girls of the beads," 1–2, 4, 6–8, 89–104, 111, 113–14, 197. *See also* bead necklaces; "boy with beads"
globalization, 5, 7, 10, 23, 36, 46, 94, 133
Glyons, Jason, 40
grammars, 39–40, 44, 47, 50, 122, 157, 164, 177, 194
Gramsci, Antonio, 39–40
Grewal, Inderpal, 33, 47, 62
Gupta, Akhil, 110
Gutmann, Matthew, 66
Guyer, Jane, 30–31

Hackman, Melissa, 172
Hall, Stuart, 39
Hammett, Daniel, 10
Hemmings, Clare, 47
Hendriks, Thomas, 180
heteronormativity, 4–6, 13, 17–18, 24, 80, 101–2, 133–34. *See also* morality
heteropatriarchy, 64, 69, 74, 84–85, 107, 109, 118, 158, 167–68, 179, 182, 185
HIV, 19–22, 37–38, 42, 49, 54–55, 68, 83, 130, 149–50. *See also* AIDS
Hodgson, Dorothy, 93
Hodžić, Saida, 114–15
homophobia. *See* anti-homosexuality
homosexual body: ambiguity of, 165–69, 172–73, 175–78, 182–83, 192; descriptions of, 164–65; discussion of, 188–89; and logics of rescue, 39, 51; objectification of, 178, 180, 182–84, 189; outrage against, 5, 8, 27, 36, 86, 117, 144, 159, 162, 191; and queer objects, 6, 8, 24, 31, 116, 140, 145, 158, 162, 164, 171, 173, 191–94, 201n5; as sacrifice, 184, 190; violent imaginaries of, 143, 163, 165, 175. *See also* gayism
Howarth, David, 40
Hubert, Henri, 184
humanitarianism, 32–33, 38–39, 42–50, 57, 92–94, 98–104, 113–15, 138. *See also* empowerment
humanitarian subject, 46–47
human-security regime, 46, 133–34. *See also* morality
Hussein, Ali, 21–22
hypervisibilization, 10–11

Ilgira, 127–28
imagined community, 53
impotence, 66, 70–71, 74
incest, 103, 109
indigenous people. *See* bead necklaces; bridewealth; curses; "girls of the beads"; kinship; polygamy; rescue campaigns
inflationary discourse, 142–43, 158, 177
informal economy, 9

initiation, 2–4, 105, 111–12, 185, 187–89. *See also* female genital mutilation (FGM); morans; ritual
Inspire and Transpire Youth Organization, 172
International Monetary Fund (IMF), 45–46
intersex, 187–88
intimacy: and belonging, 18; and colonization, 10; cultural, 9, 32–33; and ethnicity, 4; and exposure, 36; familial, 41–42; and male-power, 64; moral, 164; and political imaginaries, 8, 12; and reform, 45; regulation of, 11; traditional, 4. *See also* subject of intimate rescue
intimate citizenship. *See* citizenship: intimate
intimate disorganization, 52
intimate exposures, 144–46, 151, 157, 162, 171
intimate governance, 46
intimate politics, 43
intimate rescue, 37, 39–54, 57–58. *See also* rescue campaigns
intimate scenes, 40, 50, 52
"In Time and Space" (Musangi), 166
Islam, 170–71

Jones, Jeremy, 31

Kairu, Pauline, 118
Kakai, Grace, 23
Karanja, Henry, 169–72, 184
Kasfir, Sidney L., 204n10
Kenya Films and Classification Board, 142
Kenya Medical Research Institute (KEMRI), 19–23, 28, 37–38, 177–78, 181–82
Kenyatta, Jomo, 108–9
Kenyatta, Uhuru, 70–71, 156, 194
kidnapping, 41–42, 99–100, 104. *See also* children
kinship, 104–7, 109, 111–13, 115, 119, 123, 127–29, 137. *See also* boma
Kombo, Zeina W., 98
kuharibika, 147
Kulea, Josephine, 97, 99

Lacan, Jacques, 17–18, 34, 44, 52, 63, 69, 114, 192, 197
land alienation, 112–13, 119, 188
language, 3, 17, 25, 48, 113
Last Plague, The (Mwangi), 51–53
latukuny, 129
law, 5, 20, 22–23, 98, 110, 126, 132, 143, 175
lchatat, 95–96
lesbianism, 4, 6, 11, 196
Lesorogol, Carolyn, 95
Lesuuda, Naisula, 5
liberalism, 24–25, 28, 143, 160, 173, 191, 193
lkereti, 1, 112
lkunono, 127–30
logics, 39–40, 46–48, 50, 62, 113, 117, 119, 147, 164, 169, 178

lorora, 105
Lorway, Robert, 18, 50

Macharia, Keguro, 52, 108–9
Mack, Mehammed, 75–76
maendeleo, 151
Maina, Grace Njoki, 71–73
"Making of a Casino Nation, The" (Ngotho), 29–30
Malawi, 22
male-power, 35, 60–71, 74–82, 85, 117, 168, 194–95
Malinowski, Bronislaw, 108
Malkki, Liisa H., 38–39, 46–47
Manalansan, Martin, 25, 85
margarine, 65
marriage, 21–24, 27–28, 98, 108, 171
Marxian thought, 15, 17, 23
masculinity, 2–4, 62, 66–73, 76–86, 196. *See also* emasculation; middle-ground vitality
Masquelier, Adeline, 134
materialization, 122, 127
Mauss, Marcel, 184
Mazzarella, William, 122, 140
Mbembe, Achille, 59, 74, 161, 168
mbusa, 13–15, 182
McKenzie, David, 97, 99
Michael, Said, 80
middle-ground vitality, 82–85. *See also* masculinity
Miller, Daniel, 122
Moi, Daniel Arap, 146
moneymaking schemes, 152–53, 159
Moore, Henrietta L., 14, 115
morality, 5–6, 19, 21, 32–35, 46, 54–58, 132, 152–53. *See also* heteronormativity; human-security regime
morans, 3, 6, 35, 55–56, 87–88, 91, 96, 98, 100–103, 105, 114, 128. *See also* initiation
Morris, Rosalind C., 142–43
Morrison, Toni, 37, 44–45
Moussawi, Ghassan, 56
Mugambi, Joyce, 61–62
Munyaka, Maureen Muia, 169
Murray, David A., 11, 25
Musangi, Neo, 166–69, 193
Museveni, Yoweri, 22
Muthai, Mark, 132
Muthai, Martin, 65
Mutloane, Mpathi, 166–67
Mutua, Ezekiel, 133, 142–43, 145, 159
Mutunga, Willy, 175
Mwangi, Boniface, 144, 154–57
Mwangi, Evan, 22
Mwangi, Meja, 51–53
Mwanza, Eddy, 5
Mwirichia, Kawira, 193

naarida, 95
nacimbusa, 15
Nadeau, Chantal, 85
National Environment Management Authority (NEMA), 118
National Gender and Equality Commission (NGEC), 98
nationalism, 4–5, 11, 46, 71, 108–9
national resources, 126–27
Nderitu, Tabitha, 87
Ndjio, Basile, 4
neoliberalism, 33, 43, 151
Ngotho, Kamau, 29–30
Ngwiri, Magesha, 65–66
Njuguna, Kimani wa, 65
Nkai, 130–31
Nkanatha, Joshua, 142–43, 145, 159
nkang, 95, 104
nkorno, 102–3, 111, 113
nkyama dorop, 103–4
nostalgia, 104, 131
Nugent, Paul, 10
Nyamnjoh, Francis B., 145, 162
Nyanzi, Stella, 78
Nzegwu, Nkiru, 160

Obama, Barack, 173–75
object-cause of desire, 18
objectification, discussion of, 13–18, 92, 113–14, 120
Ocobock, Paul, 67
Odhiambo, Tom, 67
"Of Bodaboda Sex Predators on High School Girls," 80
ombani na ngweko, 108–9
ontological negativity, 17, 140
"Operation Gays Out," 22
Orientalism, fractal, 56
Orock, Rogers, 176
other scenes, 17–18, 34, 163–64, 192
Ouma, Christopher, 166–67
Owuor, David, 173
Oyěwùmí, Oyèrónkẹ́ẹ́, 76

Pala, Oyunga, 157
Pandian, Anand, 120
panics, 5–6, 10–11, 35–36, 39, 110, 120–21, 132–33, 142–43, 173–75, 178
Parsitau, Damaris S., 175
Pentecostals. *See* Christianity
performative contradictions, 114
peripheral capitalism, 126
phallus, 59, 63–64, 69–71, 74–75, 78, 81, 84–86, 160, 168, 196
"pink line," 24–25
plastic, 7–8, 13, 18, 35, 94, 117–41, 171–73, 194, 196–97

INDEX

plastic boys, 119–28, 134–40
Plastic Boys' Self-Help Group, 138
plastic hair, 128–29
plastic morans, 128
plastic rice, 35, 115, 120–21, 132–33
plastic sexuality, 140
Plummer, Ken, 11
point de capiton, 114
political economy of homophobia, 26, 193
politics of passing, 120–21
politics of pretense, 153
polygamy, 101, 104–6
Porter, Mary, 184
poverty, 23, 27–28, 45, 56–57, 123, 125. *See also* wealth
prostitution. *See* sex work
protest, 19–24, 27–28, 30, 33, 71–75, 177–84, 203n11
public space, 157, 161, 163–65, 168, 175

queer customary, 101, 115
queer moments, 31
queer theory, 160
queer timing, 140
quilting point, 114

racism, 26, 46, 92–93, 108. *See also* xenophobia
radicalization, 9
Rao, Rahul, 27, 193
real abstract formation, 165, 168–69
reform. *See* humanitarianism; law; rescue campaigns
rescue campaigns, 19, 22, 31–48, 60–63, 68–74, 79–83, 89–91, 97–100, 150–51, 157–58, 179–80. *See also* intimate rescue; young men
Richards, Audrey, 13–14, 182
Rigby, Paul, 126
ritual, 110–11, 113, 131, 170–72, 187–89. *See also* initiation
Rodríguez, Richard T., 85
Rooney, Monique, 201n5
rush, 76–78

Samburu Girls Foundation (SGF), 98
Samburu Women for Education and Environment Development Organization (SWEEDO), 88–91
"Samburu Women See Red in Their Stunning Beads" (Nderitu), 87
Samburu Women Trust (SWT), 98
Samura, Sorious, 27
scholarship, 5–6, 26, 113, 162, 173, 205n6. *See also* anthropology; ethnography
schools, 4, 155–56, 207n5
"security feminists," 62
"security mom," 47
Sempele, Lorna, 95
senkera, 92, 102–3

sensitization, 28, 38, 98, 193
serrerr, 186
sex, as signifier, 17
sex education, 11, 20, 82–83, 108, 110, 149, 204n13. *See also* children
Sexual Offences Act, 110
sex work, 40–42, 44, 48–50, 59–60, 80, 146–49, 153–54, 157. *See also* women
Shabaab, Al-, 118, 175–76
Shared Moments with Justus, 169
Silberschmidt, Margrethe, 68
Smith, James, 43
snakes, as symbolic, 171–73, 184
social media, 1–2, 4–5, 7, 75, 83, 157, 166, 169, 172, 185
Somerville, Siobhan B., 85
somi, 100, 204n10
Sonko, Mike, 156, 194
"sovereign child," 43
spectral sexuality, 11
Sprenger, Guido, 87, 107
stereotyping, 5, 27, 55–57, 92, 184
Stoller, Paul, 34
Straight, Bilinda, 96, 99, 129, 131
Strathern, Marilyn, 107
subject of intimate rescue, 34–35, 40, 194
sunkulaate, 185–89

tactics of hypervisibilization, 10–11
Tallie, T. J., 100–101
target functions, 177
Taussig, Michael, 15
technologies of talk, 114
temporality, 168
Thiong'o, Ngũgĩ wa, 117
Tonkens, Evelien, 10
tourism, 88–89, 147
transgenderism, 3, 169
tribalism, 25, 137–38
"Tribe Where Same-Sex Marriage Is Allowed in Kenya" (Mwanza), 5
Turner, Victor, 53

Uganda, 7–8, 22
unconscious, 17–18, 34, 164

Valois, Caroline, 53–54
Vance, Carole, 99
Verdery, Katherine, 177
villages, 4
violence, 20, 23–28, 32, 79–80, 99–100, 104, 144, 157, 159–62, 178–79, 183
vulgarity, aesthetics of, 161

Warah, Rasna, 75
Warnier, Jean-Pierre, 197

wealth, 9, 23, 30, 43, 49, 81–82, 135–36, 148, 169–71, 176. *See also* poverty
weddings. *See* marriage
Weiss, Brad, 53, 129, 163
Weiss, Margot, 201n8
Weiss, Meredith L., 9
welfare, 20, 23, 45
Wijngaarden, Vanessa, 94
women, 35, 38–43, 61–62, 68–76, 79–81, 92, 130–31. *See also* empowerment; femininity; feminism; "girls of the beads"; lesbianism; protest; sex work

"women of the beads," 95
World Bank, 45–46
World Future Society, 28–29

xenophobia, 121. *See also* racism

young men, 9, 59–67, 69–82, 125–26, 202n20, 203n9. *See also* morans

Zhang, Everett, 66
Zupančič, Alenka, 17

Printed and bound by CPI Group (UK) Ltd, Croydon, CR0 4YY
24/04/2024

14488191-0003